SAILORS OF STONEHENGE

*The Celestial & Atlantic Origin of Civilization
(Revised Edition)*

Manuel Vega

Published by CS (2012). Revised Edition (2013)
Officially registered as intellectual property
(Registro de la Propiedad Intelectual, Madrid, code 16/2012/8817)
Sailors of Stonehenge is also available in Spanish (*Marineros de piedra*),
under the author's full name: José Manuel Gómez Vega
Both books can be obtained from Amazon

*"Imagination is more important than knowledge:
Knowledge is limited; imagination encircles the world."*

— Albert Einstein

CONTENTS

PREFACE, 3
   Technical Note, 5
   About the Author, 6
   Acknowledgments, 7
1. INTRODUCTION, 9
   Megalith Builders, 11
   The Sky, 14
   Megalithic Art, 16
2. CARNAC, 21
   The Royal Mausoleum, 23
   Celestial Royal Periods, 25
3. AVEBURY, 29
   The Sky over Avebury, 33
   The Ceremony to Renew the Monarchy, 35
   Summary, 39
4. STONEHENGE, 43
   Change of Venue and Solstice, 44
   The Celestial Mirror, 46
   The Crowning, 51
   The Transportation of the Stones, 51
   The Attendants to the Ceremony, 54
   Summary, 57
5. THE ORKNEY ISLANDS, 61
   Crossroads, 63
   Hyperborea, 65
   Summary, 73
6. NEWGRANGE, 77
   Hierosgamos, 77
   Spiritual Technology, 81
   The Royal Necropolis, 86
   Summary, 92

7. JASON & THE ARGONAUTS, 95
   The Expeditions, 96
   The Myth, 101
   The Dark River, 105
   The Circumnavigation, 111
   Summary, 114
8. ALMENDRES, 117
   The Iberian Connection, 117
   The Cromlech, 121
   The Victory of the Sun, 124
   The Pyrenees and the Golden Fleece, 126
   Summary, 129
9. THE IBERIAN ZODIAC, 131
   The Axis mundi or Pillar, 133
   Ancient Astronomical Lore, 136
   The Knights of the Round Table, a Chimera?, 139
   The Cosmology of Stonehenge, 144
10. THE GREAT CELESTIAL MIRROR, 155
    The Guanches, 156
    Argo Navis, 159
    The Milky Way, 161
    Sirius, 163
11. THE ARCHANGEL ORION, 167
    Megalithic Lines, 169
    The Celestial Beasts, 172
    The Unicorn, 177
    The Tower of Hercules, 181
12. ATLANTIS, 189
    Minoans, Iberians, Celts and Tartessians, 195
    Chronology, 197
    Corollary, 198

APPENDIX: BRIGHTEST STARS, 201
LIST OF FIGURES, 203
INDEX, 209
TIMELINE, 222

PREFACE

In my academic years as a researcher in chemistry, the most rewarding moments always came after having to face the most disturbing results, those that did not fit into the preconceived scheme and, in some cases, were even obtained from experiments designed to prove the opposite. The repetition of the experiment assuming an error of procedure only served to confirm the unwelcome result. The situation caused a nagging discomfort which lasted until a convincing explanation that incorporated the new evidence was found. The solution only came after painfully relinquishing some of the fondest working hypotheses in use up to that moment. From a wider and higher perspective there were not conflicting results, only initially valid interpretations within limited frames of reference. This anecdote—not original at all among researchers in any field—is applicable, more than anywhere else, to prehistory.

I entered into the subject of this book with the archaeological and the astronomic expertise of an amateur, ignorant about the ideas that I found out only later are so dominant regarding the prehistoric people who inhabited Western Europe during the Neolithic Age, known as "Megalith Builders" because they used big (mega) stones (lith) in some of their constructions. After several years of studying this subject I arrived at the conclusion that, if we really want to have a coherent view of our prehistoric ancestors, we need to relinquish some preconceived ideas, no matter how useful they were up until now. We must raise our eyes to the sky while keeping our feet on the ground, because the landscape our megalithic ancestors interacted with was the land below, the seas around and the sky above, without sharp demarcations between them.

It is impossible to be objective in writing about history—much less about pre-history—when instead of written documents we have rock carvings, when the archaeological remains have been ravaged by the passing of millennia and the artifacts retrieved mostly from tombs. The academic interpretations equate the lack of archaeological remains to non-existence, from where only very limited hypotheses can arise. Restricting judgment to the physical evidence can render interpretation as removed from reality as giving free rein to the imagination, both are equally off the mark—archaeologists tend to err on the former, and what they disparagingly call "pseudoscientific works" on the latter. I state in advance that this is not a scientific work nor intended to be; it has a more overarching purpose than being a research into prehistory. I try to vindicate the wholesome use of our imagination (the analogical mind that establishes analogies) against the exclusivism of the analytical or scientific one, as a valid tool to derive a knowledge that can give us a more complete picture of our field of study.

In the course of this book we will discover that the Megalith Builders were neither tribal people dressed in furs who lived in scattered chiefdoms where aggression and superstition ruled supreme, nor did they constitute a paradisaical society. We will see that they could have had customs closer to our understanding of what a classical culture is, organized in societies expanding over large territories and able to navigate long distances. But, overall, they could have reached a deep understanding of the cycles of life and death, of the interconnection between the Earth below, the sky above and the humans in between.

Anachronism is one of the main arguments used against the suggestions of possible links between modern-day traditions and prehistoric times, but this accusation only holds because of the partial data we have at our disposition. If we had all the information, we might see that the origins of many traditions and local names are much older than we currently regard them. Somehow they have survived from generation to generation, changing details but retaining their essence. This book is based on the assumption that much of the knowledge of the Megalith Builders' culture may not be properly represented in the archaeological record, but it may have survived and reached us encapsulated in myths, as well as in all kinds of cultural, political and religious manifestations of modern society. We could say that this book is going to interpret the results of a very special archaeological excavation, one that does not dig in the soil but in the prehistoric strata where the memories of our megalithic ancestors remain stored: in our collective unconscious.

I hope the readers who open this book will equally open their minds to see our prehistoric ancestors under a new light that reveals them as tremendously curious people, and adventurous travelers whose main legacy is not so much the big stones of their monuments but the foundation of our civilization.

May this work benefit everyone.

Manuel Vega
Madrid & Berkeley, Spring 2013

Technical Note

This revised edition of *Sailors of Stonehenge* is delivered only eight months after the first one. The main reason was to fully proofread the text. Capitalizing on that editorial intervention, I decided to introduce several modifications that I hope will make for a more fluid reading experience. For example, the footnotes were moved to the end of each chapter, the quality of the paper and the font were improved, and the number of pages was increased considerably to accommodate larger figures and photos.

The acronyms BC and AD are used to indicate dates "before and after Common Age" respectively. Square brackets and bold font may be inserted in the quotations from other authors containing a clarification or to signal breaks. Non accurate values may be preceded by the abbreviation *ca.* (from Latin *circa*, meaning *approximately*). The sky illustrations were created with the program Cartes du Ciel V3.0, with dates in the Julian calendar. The images of the constellations were taken from two stellar atlases of the 17th century: *Uranographia* by Johannes Hevelius, and *Uranometria* by Johann Bayer. Many of the geographical maps were obtained from Google Earth. The pictures were taken by me or from Wikimedia Commons under its policy of fair-use contents. The credit to the authors requiring identification is given at the end of the book (my apologies if I have inadvertently omitted anyone to whom acknowledgement is due). The references are inserted as notes at the end of each chapter. The access date of those available online is June 21st 2012.

About the Author

Manuel Vega was born in 1967 in Astorga (León, Spain).

In 1990, he graduated in Chemistry from the University of Alcalá de Henares (Madrid).

In 1996, he was awarded a Ph.D. in Chemistry from the University of Oviedo (Asturias).

In 1997, he moved to the Lawrence Berkeley National Laboratory (California, USA) as a Postdoctoral Fellow, to investigate new biomaterials.

In 1999, he moved to Japan, where he worked as Associate Researcher at Nagoya University (School of Engineering), in the field of nanomaterials.

In 2002, he gave away all his belongings and began to travel by bicycle all over Japan—he even completed the Shikoku pilgrimage of the 88 temples. He also travelled in India, Nepal and the Himalayas (Sikkim).

After one year living as a nomad, he decided to settle down and joined a Buddhist monastery (City of Ten Thousand Buddhas, north of San Francisco, California). He was a trainee there for one year, and a novice for another four at monasteries in Canada and Berkeley (Institute of the World Religions).

In 2008, he did not take the next step into full ordination and returned to lay life.

He has co-authored tens of papers and patents in the fields of bio- and environmental-technologies, written extensively about the interface of science and spirituality, and has been the recipient of several literary awards in Spanish.

Manuel Vega writes the blog
circleofmeditation.wordpress.com

Acknowledgments

My parents in Spain and Alice in America are the pillars who provided me with the unconditional support necessary to pursue the dream of writing this book.

Alex and Javi were very sympathetic, always ready to listen patiently to their brother's "esoteric journey" while hiking in the mountains or taking Ananda out for a walk.

Steven, Lucía and Kristen have contributed in different forms and phases to the deliverance of the book.

I met Artur and Luis in Japan a long time ago, and soon we developed an affinity that went beyond our common Iberian roots. These friends confirmed the well deserved fame of Portuguese hospitality during my trips to visit the most important megalithic monuments of Portugal and England. Besides, they were the first reviewers of the original manuscript, and their priceless suggestions contributed decisively to its improved final form.

Anna was the catalyst I needed to finally publish the book. She is even shooting a movie based on it, in Greece!

My gratitude goes to all the Goodreads readers who were willing to provide me with priceless editorial feedback and insightful reviews, especially to Ellie.

I must single out one person: Gill, for her wonderful contribution to this Revised Edition. I am truly indebted to this Welsh—or should I say *Cymraes*—bodhisattva... *diolch yn fawr!*

The Guadarrama Range in Madrid where I let my sight rest for long periods, the Strawberry Creek that flows through the campus of Berkeley University in California, and Lucy, the cat who sat on my lap during my writing hours in Madrid (as right now), have witnessed most of the insights and reflections contained in the book, so it would not be fair to close these acknowledgments without expressing my most sincere gratitude to these most natural friends.

1
INTRODUCTION

A starry night can be one of the most arresting spectacles of nature. The sense of awe and wonder brought by this vision had more impact for our ancestors, when the light pollution of cities and towns did not diminish the night-sky intensity, and the glaring artificial stimuli did not divert their attention. The curiosity of our ancestors would move them to pose questions about the cycles of the sky. Generation after generation of constantly inquiring about them, they would gradually develop a cosmology to explain the creation of the world and the purpose of living in it. Much of this knowledge has reached us in the myths of the different parts of the world, mostly hidden in allegories, metaphors and a symbolic language not accessible to literal or historical exegesis, approaches that cannot penetrate the surface of the texts.

During the last three centuries, science has provided a cosmology without any religious or spiritual ideas associated with it. The resulting universe contains billions of galaxies each one containing billions of stars scattered in an unimaginable vast expanse of space, all of it originated 13.7 billions of years ago after a huge explosion—Big Bang—out of "nothingness." As amazing as this view may be, its spiritual impact on a modern person is negligible compared to the impact that ancient cosmologies had on our ancestors, for whom the landscape they walked upon extended into a familiar skyscape populated by spiritual beings, giants, monsters and gods interfering directly in lives, all of them intrinsically connected through religious beliefs to the cycles of life and death. Accordingly, the stars were grouped into constellations represented by figures that conveyed the meaning and function associated with them.

For our ancestors, the Earth was at the center of a celestial sphere that moved around with the stars fixed in it, among which some "wanderers" (planets) had more freedom of movement. In fact, this was the model accepted until the 16th century AD, when Copernicus placed the Sun in the center, and the planets—Earth included—became merely bodies orbiting around it.

The luminaries (Sun, Moon and five visible planets: Mercury, Venus, Mars, Jupiter and Saturn) move apparently along a pathway called the Ecliptic at the center of a band of the celestial sphere called the Zodiac, each one at its own pace—from the month it takes the Moon to complete a cycle, up to the thirty years of Saturn. Based on the annual revolution of the Sun around the Zodiac, this is divided into four seasons separated by two solstices and two equinoxes. Midwinter (winter solstice) happens on the longest night of the year, and midsummer (summer solstice) on the longest day. Equinoxes occur when the days and nights are of equal duration.

A practical way to determine the solstices would be to watch the horizon from where the Sun rises and sets, since the northernmost point would signal midsummer and the southernmost midwinter (in the northern hemisphere). Associated with these simple observations would come more advanced ones, related to the cycles of the Moon and the planets. Ancient people would select the location from which to watch the sky based on the visibility of some conspicuous features on the horizon that served as references, which could be refined by nearer artificial ones created with poles or rocks. The observatory would progressively become more complex and important in function due to the calendrical purposes that served to regulate the affairs of a society equally developing in complexity. Agriculture would bring proto-urban settlements linked by similar beliefs, architecture, art and festivals, all of them rooted in the celestial cosmology developed during many generations, over centuries, even millennia.[1]

Fig. 1: Old picture of Stonehenge (ca. 1850).

The Megalith Builders

The theory of astronomer Gerald Hawkins, considering Stonehenge as a prehistoric astronomical observatory (Fig. 1),[2] arouse a lot of media interest, yet it was the detailed and rigorous research of Alexander Thom that brought initial credibility to the theories that speculated about astronomical orientations of prehistoric megalithic constructions.[3] Thom was an Emeritus Professor of Engineering at Oxford University who meticulously measured hundreds of megalithic structures in the British Isles and France. Based on the vast amount of collected data, he concluded that a common unit of space was in use at these sites, which he called the Megalithic Yard (ca. 2.72 ft / 0.83 m). This finding is still very controversial, because a common unit of measurement over large territories and at such a remote period (Neolithic) would prove that the Megalith Builders were much more developed, mobile and interconnected than currently assumed.[4]

During the past four decades, archeoastronomy has established itself as a respectable field of knowledge, in part due to the critical self-evaluation that overcame the shortcomings of its pioneering works. Through serious statistical studies, it has been confirmed—without any reasonable doubt—that a great portion of the megalithic constructions were intentionally built according to celestial orientations. However, this emphasis on statistics is in itself a limited methodology that fails to provide answers for the most unique megalithic monuments, such as Stonehenge, Avebury, the Alignments of Carnac, Maeshowe or Newgrange—constructions that will be studied later in more detail.

Who were these Megalith Builders? Archaeologist Colin Renfrew, in his review of a collective volume dedicated to the topic, expressed the state of the art:[5]

*"**The central mystery remains.** Why was it in western and northwestern Europe, and only in those regions, that the phenomenon of megalithic burial developed and prospered so mightily? The few cases documented for such practices elsewhere in the world only serve to emphasize the far grander scale of the European manifestation. And I am still intrigued by the problem of origins [...] It is now at least 40 years since the impact of radiocarbon dating, especially in Brittany, brought about a revolution in our understanding of the European megaliths, clearly implying their independence from architectural traditions in the east Mediterranean. That point now seems universally accepted. But beyond that the situation seems as confused as it was 40 years ago [...] The pieces of the jigsaw (if one may use that rather misleading analogy) are being meticulously dusted off and fitted together. **Yet the big picture remains obstinately obscure.**"*

Archaeologists agree about the independent origin of European megalithism,[6] but neither about the origin nor the kind of relationship—if any—existent among the various megalithic areas (Fig. 2). The typical "diffusionist-inventionist" controversy is very present in this case. Diffusionists emphasize the role of diffusion, i.e. the spread of cultural elements from one area or group of people to others by contact, rather than independent invention or discovery.

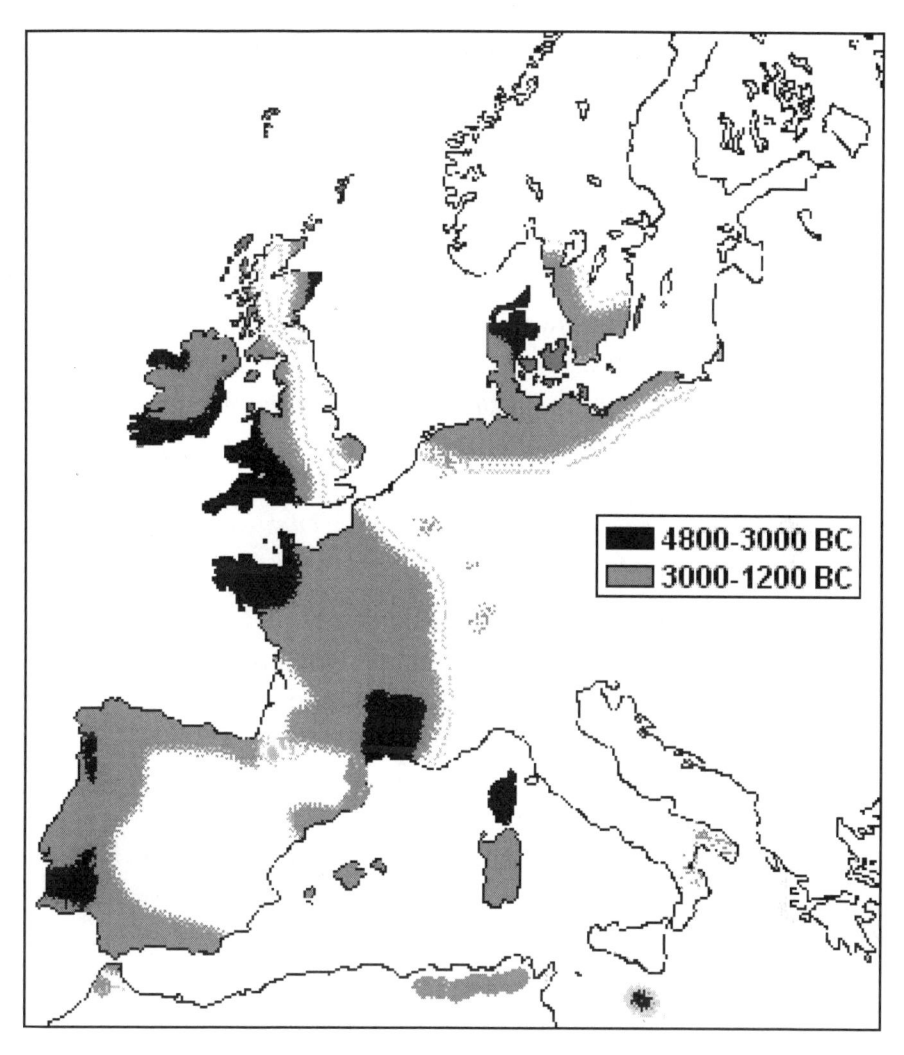

Fig. 2: Principal areas of megalithism in Western Europe.

The discussion becomes very subtle in megalithism because it is not clear where the borderlines—and of what kind—lay among the European Neolithic inhabitants, and to what extent these people were able to travel and interact with each other. A series of articles from Euan Mackie versus the responses from Clive Ruggles and Gordon Barclay reflects the polarity of opinions within academia about this topic:[7]

*"We [Ruggles & Barclay] fully accept that the existence of many lower-precision astronomical alignments that were confirmed in the 1984 survey served as a remarkable confirmation of Thom's ideas that astronomical alignments were incorporated in many Neolithic monuments. Indeed, Ruggles himself has said this and given due credit to Thom on many occasions. What is in dispute is the interpretation of such alignments in terms of a consistent tradition carried across Neolithic Britain by a theocratic elite [...] Our arguments were against 'theocratic elites' and MacKie's clearly stated belief in a 'complex, **highly stratified hierarchical organization with advanced political structure and many specialized groups, almost a proto-urban society in fact**' (a view which goes far beyond the idea of a chiefdom as we might consider it in the Neolithic), not against the idea of a later Neolithic in which hierarchies were more pronounced."*

There was another reply and counter-reply between the same authors,[8] only to emphasize the divergent points of view that, based on the interpretation of the physical archaeological remains, can be held within academia about the degree of social development that was present in Europe during the Neolithic Age.

This book will align with MacKie's side, and will go much further. We will start by proposing as a working hypothesis that the builders of one of the most extraordinary megalithic monuments, the Alignments of Carnac, could belong to a solar culture organized in a dozen or so kingdoms ruled by kings for a limited period of time according to a celestial cycle.[9] The importance that they conferred on the sky to regulate their society politically and religiously will become gradually more evident as the investigation advances and other great megalithic complexes are also studied.

The Sky

Not all cultures have grouped the stars in the same way. The pattern of constellations used nowadays is derived from Classical Greece, which in turn derived it from the Babylonians. In the early first millennium BC, this Mesopotamian civilization already divided the Zodiac into 12 constellations represented by the figures (mostly animals) we are familiar with (Fig. 3).[10]

Fig. 3: Zodiac with the classical twelve constellations or signs. (Equinoxes and solstices for the megalithic epoch.)

However, whether the Babylonians created this representational system of the firmament or derived it from earlier sources remains controversial. The astronomer Hugh Thurston states that the constellations had to have been fashioned earlier, and he presents three arguments to sustain his proposition.[11] The first, the empty southern part of the sky which does not contain any of the traditional 48 constellations was not visible to people living at latitudes above 36º around 2900 BC. The second, the representations are tipped at an angle in respect to the actual cardinal directions that would fit better for 2900 BC. And the third, the classical Greek poet Aratus mentions risings and settings of stars that had to be observed from latitudes of 36 ± 2º about 2600 ± 400 years BC.[12] Based on these points, Thurston proposes that the creators of the traditional constellations could be from Mesopotamia, because the inhabitants of this part of the world were already very active in the fourth millennium BC at latitudes of about 36º (north of Egypt, south of Greece). However, Thurston forgets to mention another possible candidate that would also fit the conditions: the Western European Megalith Builders, because they were also very active during the fourth millennium BC (and even earlier), the southern extreme of the Iberian Peninsula at the Strait of Gibraltar being situated at exactly 36º of latitude.

The possibility that the Megalith Builders were actually the creators of the classical constellations was reinforced as the investigation progressed, to the point of becoming one of its pillars. Consequently, to use the traditional representations of the sky in the following discussion is not anachronistic but will help to reveal the rationale behind them.

Since we are going to encounter many "anachronisms" in the course of the book, perhaps it would be convenient to introduce here a brief reflection about this issue. Basically, an anachronism is an inconsistency in the chronological arrangement, misplacing objects or events out of their natural time of occurrence. However, some seeming anachronisms could be more a reflection of our ignorance about history than genuine chronological anomalies. The mainstream current understanding of history, as a linear development from a primitive status up to the present times, is prone to judge as "anachronism" any artifact that may contradict this conception, thus potentially underestimating the creativity and degree of development that could be reached in ancient cultures.

Megalithic Art

The Megalith Builders did not leave written records, but carvings and a few paintings that have resisted erosion and human onslaught during their millennia of existence—very likely a residual amount from the original stock—known collectively as "megalithic art" (Fig. 4).

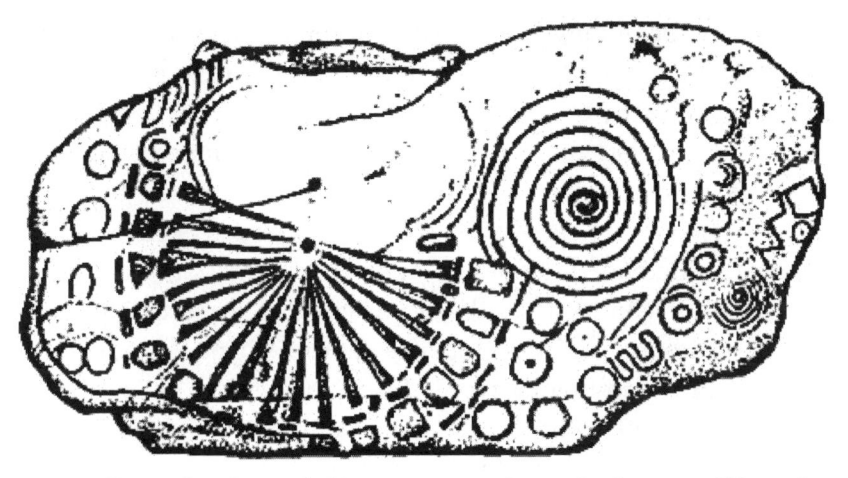

Fig. 4: Example of megalithic art engraved on a kerbstone of Knowth, a passage mound in Ireland.

Although a great effort was made by archaeologist during the past century to catalogue and describe this art, its interpretation remains as a persistent intractable challenge. The two main approaches—ethnographic analogies, and attempting to decipher an inherent order from which to deduce meaning—have rendered very dissimilar results, and no explanation of its possible meaning has won general acceptance. One of the main difficulties of this art is its schematism: spirals, labyrinths, arcs, serpentiforms or wavy lines, dot-in-circles, zigzags (chevrons), U motifs, lozenges, radials or star shapes, parallel lines and all kinds of geometric figures such as circles, triangles, squares, trapezoids, etc., sometimes repeated and interwoven, which make it really difficult to elucidate what they could represent and the message they conveyed. Archaeologist Elisabeth Shee-Twohig said about the megalithic art:[13]

"Motifs became increasingly stylized and symbols whose meaning had been self-evident became accessible only to the initiated. All of the evidence suggests an increasing restriction of participation in ritual and access to ritual knowledge."

Megalithic art is therefore so schematic that we are not going to find naturalistic representations of the constellations or any other element of the Megalith Builders' cosmology, because the artists—

most likely belonging to an elite of priests-astronomers—could have eventually omitted them in their own artistic expressions. However, in their wish to share their knowledge with the rest of the society, or to plan the unfolding of some ceremonies opened to larger audiences, or even to transmit it to other cultures, they would have devised a representational system imbued with mnemonic stories that facilitated the assimilation of information otherwise too abstract. So it would be in those posterior cultures that preserved this oral tradition and developed a more realistic art where these images, motifs and themes would begin to develop. Throughout the book we are going to present several examples of how these images appeared in Greek mythology.

The existence of early contacts between Neolithic and even Mesolithic European inhabitants separated by relatively long distances is seriously considered by some archeologists who have noticed clear similarities among the different expressions of European megalithic art, as indicated in the following quotation from Manuel Calado:[14]

*"It is difficult to interpret the analogies between Tagus-Sado [Iberian rivers] and Brittany [French peninsula] in terms of autonomous foci in the 'invention' of the megalithic phenomenon. There were, of course, different developments, but **it is necessary to accept direct contacts**, sometimes of a special nature, between the Mesolithic populations and in paths to the Neolithic way of life, in the two areas, **between the sixth and the fifth millennia BC** [...] allowing for new bridges between Brittany and Portugal, including Galicia [Spain] and, less directly and just a little later, Ireland. In this framework, **the connection by sea** between areas as distant as Brittany and Tagus-Sado **appears the most plausible."***

The initial working hypothesis of an organized confederation of kingdoms extending all over Western Europe, self-regulated politically and religiously according to the cycles of the sky, is going to be elaborated, refined and corrected by studying their largest monuments until a much clearer and coherent vision about the Megalith Builders will be finally presented.

Endnotes

[1] The Stone Age is usually divided into three broad categories: The Paleolithic which lasted until the ice from the last glaciations retreated, the Mesolithic until the developing of farming techniques, and the Neolithic until metalworking commenced. However, these events began at different times in different parts of the globe and, in many cases, their distinctions—in particular between the Neolithic and the later periods—are not clear cut.

[2] *Stonehenge Decoded*, by Gerald Hawkins; Doubleday & Company, Inc. (1965)

[3] *Megalithic Sites in Britain*, by Alexander Thom; Oxford University Press (1967) (this is just one of his earliest publications)

[4] Thom himself considered quite meaningful the exact coincidence between the Megalithic Yard and the *vara*, the pre-metric unit in Spain.

[5] *Megaliths: Perspective improves; central mystery remains*, by Colin Renfrew; Antiquity, Vol. 74:285, pp. 726-8 (2000)

[6] The earliest megalithic constructions in Western Europe predate those in the east Mediterranean. One exception is Göbekli Tepe, a unique archaeological site in SE Turkey that has megalithic constructions that reach back into the Mesolithic Age. (The temples are round with dry-stone walls divided by monolithic T-shaped pillars up to 10 ft / 3 m tall.)

[7] *Cosmology, calendars and society in Neolithic Orkney: a rejoinder to Euan MacKie*, by Gordon J. Barclay & Clive Ruggles; Antiquity, Vol. 74:283, pp. 62-74 (2000). *Maeshowe and the winter solstice: ceremonial aspects of the Orkney Grooved Ware culture*, by Euan W. MacKie; Antiquity, Vol. 71:272, pp. 338-60 (1997)

[8] *The structure and skills of British Neolithic Society: a brief response to Clive Ruggles & Gordon Barclay*, by Euan W. MacKie; Antiquity, Vol. 76:293, pp. 666-8 (2002). *Will the data drive the model? A further response to Euan MacKie*, by Gordon J. Barclay & Clive Ruggles; Antiquity, Vol. 76:293, pp. 668-71 (2002)

[9] The use of the terms king and kingdom—even monarchy—is deliberate, not an exaggeration, as we will see.

[10] The word *Zodiac* derives from the Greek *zoon-diakos* which means *wheel of animals*: Aries (goat or ram), Taurus (bull), Gemini (twins), Cancer (crab), Leo (lion), Virgo (virgin), Libra (scales), Scorpio (scorpion), Sagittarius (archer centaur), Capricorn (hybrid of goat and fish), Aquarius (water-bearer) and Pisces (two fishes).

[11] *Early Astronomy*, by Hugh Thurston; New York Springer-Verlag, pp. 135-7 (1994)

[12] The Earth, besides moving around the Sun and rotating around its axis, also wobbles, i.e. the North Pole does not always aim towards the same point in the sky (Celestial Pole) but toward the points of a circle. This cyclical movement provokes an equivalent shift in the points of the Ecliptic where the Sun is situated when days and nights are of equal duration (equinoxes) or their difference is maximum (solstices). It takes about 26,000 years for the Celestial Pole to return to the same point—or for the equinoxes and solstices to come back to the same points of the Ecliptic. This cycle is known as *Platonic* or *Great Year*, and the phenomenon is dubbed as *precession of the equinoxes* because the Sun at the equinoxes and solstices moves over the Ecliptic (ca. 1º every 72 years) in counter direction to its annual movement around the Zodiac. The periods in which the Sun at the Spring equinox retrogrades over a constellation are commonly called Ages, and they last a bit more than two millennia (26,000/12). An effect of the precession of the equinoxes is that the declination of the stars (height above the horizon) changes along the centuries, and some stars that in the past were visible from certain latitudes become invisible later in time, and vice versa.

[13] *The megalithic art of Western Europe*, by Elisabeth Shee-Twohig; Oxford University Press, Clarendon Press, Oxford (1981)

[14] *Standing Stones and Natural Outcrops*, by Manuel Calado (2005); available online at: crookscape.org/textjan2005/text_eng.html

2
CARNAC

THE European megalithic phenomenon lasted approximately three millennia (ca. 4600-1600 BC), Brittany (NW peninsula of France) and Alentejo (central Portugal) being the regions where the oldest constructions can be found.

The Alignments of Carnac are located in Brittany, and they constitute the grandest and most spectacular of the megalithic monuments. This unique construction contains just on its own more than 3,000 menhirs (standing stones) of local granite aligned in rows along a stretch of approximately 2.5 miles (4 km), divided into three main modules: Le Ménec, Kermario and Kerlescan, and a comparatively much smaller and degraded one known as Petit-Ménec.[1]

Many hypotheses have been put forward, some quite bizarre, to explain the purpose of these alignments. For example, an antiquarian proposed that it could be the fossil of a great snake, others suggested that it could be a Roman camp, or an avenue towards nonextant temples, or even a huge earthquake detector. A local legend says that the stones were Roman soldiers petrified by God to protect St Cornelius, the local patron. Alexander Thom advocated—as he did with many other megalithic constructions—that it could be an ancient astronomic observatory.

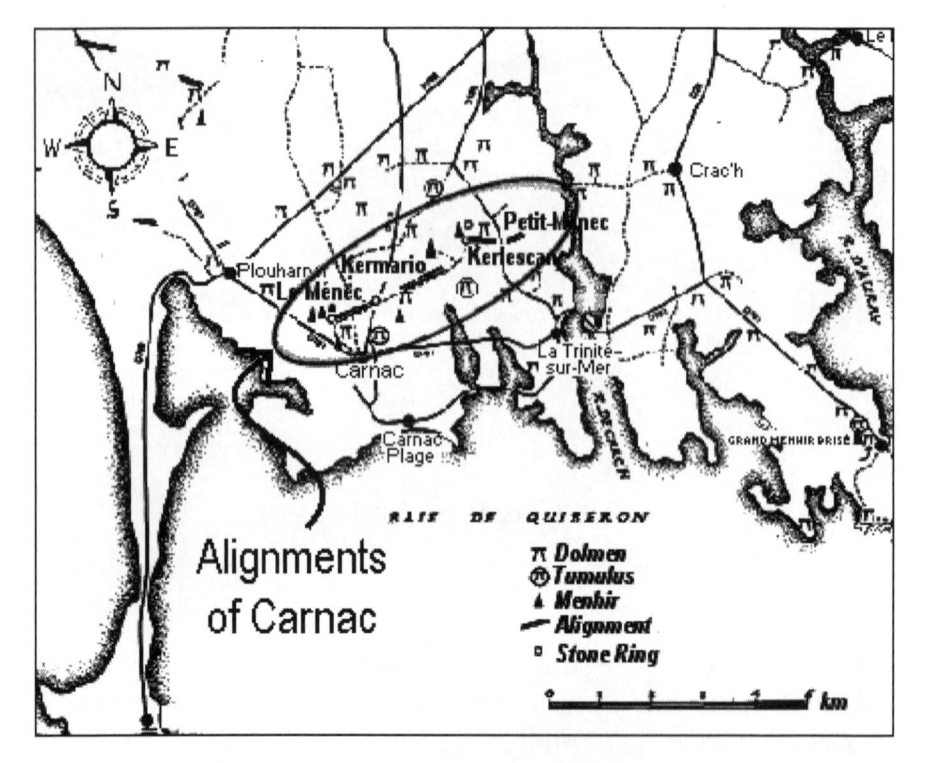

Fig. 5: Map of south Brittany (Quiberon Bay) where the Alignments of Carnac are located.

However, the most widely accepted hypothesis is that it served as a great necropolis; indeed, the name *Kermario* derives from the Breton language *House or Village of the Dead*, and in the vicinity of the alignments there are several burial mounds with a more evident funerary function, such as Saint-Michel tumulus, one of the oldest (Fig. 5 & Fig. 6).

Such a huge megalithic monument must have required an equally huge amount of manual labor to build it. Astronomer Peter Lancaster Brown provides an insightful reflection on this topic:[2]

"Archaeology is now faced with finding a Megalithic society to suit its monuments. *What kind of social organization was necessary for such a society to function? Although not all prehistoric societies with celestial-inspired calendars developed for agrarian purposes were hierarchical, some evidence for British hierarchical societies is certainly*

Fig. 6: Saint-Michel tumulus, next to the Alignments of Carnac. (Christianized with a chapel on top.)

found in the archeological record. It would be interesting indeed if native British Megalithic societies were one day proven to have been egalitarian, but the well-documented evidence from Egypt, Babylonia and the later neo-Megalithic societies of Middle and South America shows these to have been strongly hierarchical. Studies utilizing the comparative method might indeed be fruitful. If the astronomical achievement is proved valid, there is a need to establish that an elitist intellectual astronomer-cum-priest class (provided by the Lockyer-Thom-Hoyle model) could, or would, be supported by its peasant farmers. Back in history elitist astronomer-priest classes are certainly well documented in Egypt, Babylonia and the Americas [...] **There is no valid reason why the British Megalithic culture was not also evolved and then maintained by astro-engineers of similar caliber."**

The Royal Mausoleum

Based on the mainstream hypothesis—that Carnac was a necropolis—and on the fact that the use of large amounts of manual labor is a typical characteristic of hierarchical societies, it can be speculated that the rocks had a representative function.

Fig. 7: Module of Kermario.

The unfortunate incident of the disappearance of some stones impedes precision, but it could still be interesting to make a rough calculation, at least with the three main modules.[3] Le Ménec is the most western one, with 1,100 menhirs in 11 rows that would, therefore, represent 100 leaders of a confederation of 11 chiefdoms. Kermario has 982 menhirs in 10 rows, indicating again another 100 leaders of a confederation of 10 chiefdoms, and Kerlescan has about 550 menhirs in 13 rows, and would represent half the number of the two previous modules (50 leaders). The height of the menhirs decreases from west to east in each of the modules (Fig. 7), which could be explained assuming that the time direction moved also from west to east, because it seems more reasonable to expect that the previous leaders were more revered. If this is so, Le Ménec would be the representational mausoleum of the first 100 leaders, Kermario of the next 100, and Kerlescan of the last 50 (of each chiefdom). At this point in the history of the confederation, the mausoleum would be continued in a much reduced scale until its complete cessation, corresponding this terminal phase to the module of Le Petit-Ménec.

In conclusion, we could round up this calculation to indicate a confederation of a dozen or so chiefdoms, that lasted for the tenure of 250 successive leaders.

There is not a clear date of construction of this monument, which given the huge amount of labor and corresponding extent of time that it would have required is not surprising, though it is estimated that its main phase of construction took place during the final centuries of the fourth millennium BC. Therefore, we could propose that this was about the time its builders decided to immortalize in stone their records, a work that they would continue in the following centuries, at the same time that they added stones representing the successive leaders of their present epoch.

If we now consider the 3,000 years of the megalithic phenomenon in Western Europe as the time span this confederation was effective, we would conclude that each leader would have ruled an average of 12 years (3,000/250). Obviously, if we were to choose a different time span, the result would be different. For instance, if we assume a longer span, stretching from 4800 to 1200 BC—as proposed by some authors—we would obtain an average of 14.5 years per leader (3,600/250). The main point of this calculation is not to be precise, but to show that its outcome is a reasonable one.

Celestial Royal Periods

The different cycles of the sky would permit control of the duration of a royal tenure. For example—to continue with the previous calculation—if the 12 years of mandate calculated were actually not the average but the exact time of a ruling tenure, then the arrival of Jupiter over a specific star of the Ecliptic (path of the Sun and planets) would be the most natural way to signal the monarchical renewal, because that is its period of revolution around the Zodiac.

Bones from the Neolithic period strongly suggest that the lifespan was much shorter than in more recent epochs, averaging approximately 30 to 40 years. Therefore, three revolutions of Jupiter around the Zodiac would make up a regular lifetime of 36 years (Fig. 8).

At the apex of the megalithic epoch (fourth and third millennia BC), the Sun in midsummer (longest days) transited the region of the sky where the brightest star directly over the Ecliptic is located: Regulus (from the Latin ruler). Both the names and locations of Leo and Regulus are so fitting for the purpose of marking the arrivals of a luminary that signaled the monarchical renewal of a solar culture that, under this apparent anachronism—the names of this constellation and star were supposedly given much later—could be hidden a clue to something more solid than mere speculation.[4]

Fig. 8: Jupiter transiting over Leo.

Consequently, we can propose as a working hypothesis that the builders of the Alignments of Carnac belonged to a solar culture that was organized as a "confederation" of a dozen or so kingdoms, each one hierarchically organized with a king at the top ruling during a fixed period determined by a cycle of the sky.

There are many examples in anthropology specifying cultures that had fixed royal tenures, as James Frazer compiled them in his encyclopedic book *The Golden Bough*, the following being just one instance:[5]

> "The festival at which the king of Calicut [SW coast of India] staked his crown and his life on the issue of battle was known as the 'Great Sacrifice.' [...] As the date of the festival was determined by the position of Jupiter in the sky, and the interval between two festivals was twelve years, roughly Jupiter's period of revolution, we may conjecture that the splendid planet was supposed to be in a special sense the king's star and to rule his destiny, **the period of its revolution in heaven corresponding to the period of his reign on Earth.**"

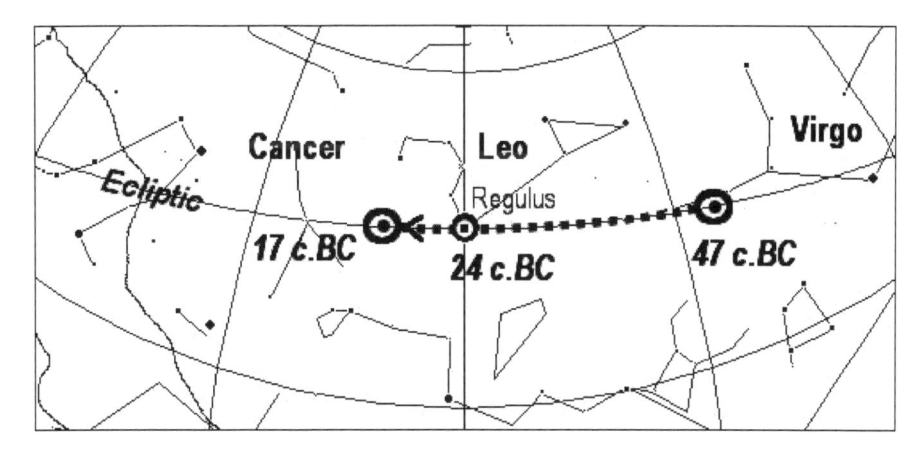

Fig. 9: Retrograding of the Sun in midsummer during the 3,000 years of megalithism (47th to 17th c. BC).

The relation between midsummer and Regulus during the approximately three millennia of megalithism in Western Europe could provide some clues about the renewal of the proposed "monarchy." Due to the precession of the equinoxes, the Sun in midsummer retrograded during those millennia along the whole constellation of Leo (from Virgo towards Cancer), moving over Regulus during the 24th century BC (Fig. 9).[6] Given that Regulus and midsummer were key elements of our working hypothesis, the astronomical event in which the Sun in midsummer transited over Regulus should have been noteworthy for the Megalith Builders. Although no clear effect of this date can be detected on Carnac, there are a couple of extraordinary megalithic complexes in the neighboring island of Great Britain for which this date was quite meaningful: Avebury and Stonehenge.

The 24th century BC was about the time the most monumental phase of construction was in progress at Stonehenge, resulting in the architectural masterpiece we still admire today, but this was also the time the activity diminished at a neighboring megalithic complex known as Avebury (ca. 17 miles / 28 km north of Stonehenge). In view of that, the relationship between all these sites, dates and events deserves further investigation.

Endnotes

[1] In some cases the rows are not alike, although it cannot be ascertained if that was part of its original design or a consequence of the disappearance, modification or destruction of some of their rocks along its extended history.

[2] *Megaliths, Myths and Men: An Introduction to Astro-Archaeology*, by Peter Lancaster Brown; Courier Dover Publications, pp. 257-8 (2000)

[3] We must have in mind that this is just an estimation due to the loss of some stones, and also because not all of them belong to the rows; at the modules' edges there were stones forming rings or short lines, signaling their beginnings and ends.

[4] This must be about the time when it was decided that the stars of this part of the sky were represented by a lion (Leo), since the symbolic relationship between the Sun in midsummer and a lion is more than evident. The European Lion inhabited the southern regions of Europe—principally the Iberian Peninsula and the Balkan Mountains—until historical times, when it became extinct due to hunting, among other factors, an activity very popular among the Romans.

[5] *The Golden Bough*, by James Frazer, chapter 24, section 3. Available online (1922 edition) at: en.wikisource.org/wiki/The_Golden_Bough

[6] The precession of the equinoxes and solstices retrogrades so slowly (ca. 1º every 72 years) that it is more practical to indicate the transit of the solstice over a star in the scale of centuries.

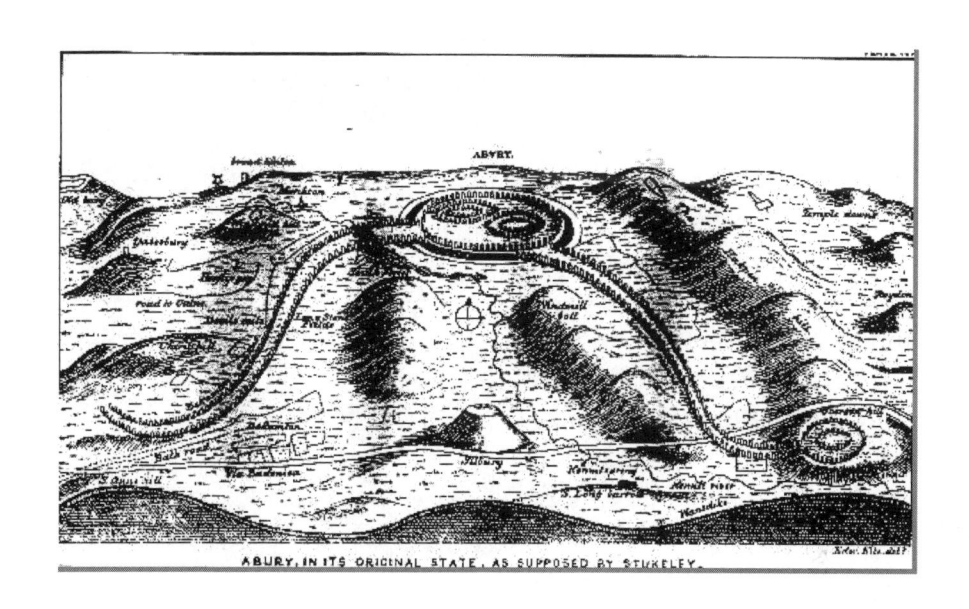

ABURY, IN ITS ORIGINAL STATE, AS SUPPOSED BY STUKELEY.

3
AVEBURY

THE third millennium BC witnessed some very significant events in the two most important megalithic monuments of Great Britain, the large island located just across the English Channel from Brittany (Fig. 10). In the 24th century BC, activity had declined significantly in Avebury whereas it increased in Stonehenge.

Like Carnac, Avebury is a huge megalithic complex. It comprises several stone circles, avenues, enclosures, mounds and long barrows, its principal element being a large henge (ca. 460 yd / 400 m in diameter), a type of megalithic construction consisting of a stone ring surrounded by a ditch and a bank (Fig. 11). The first signs of activity at this megalithic complex can be traced back to the first half of the fourth millennium BC, but it was not until the end of this millennium that construction began on a larger scale, about the same time as happened in Carnac.

The megalithic complex at Avebury has suffered severe damage, mostly from the 14th century AD onwards due to farming and religious zealotry, although reports from antiquarians and archaeological research have helped to virtually reconstruct it (Fig. 12).[1]

Inside the henge there were two additional stone rings; the north one containing three large stones (two extant) at its center known as The Cove, and the south one containing a tall monolith called The Obelisk.

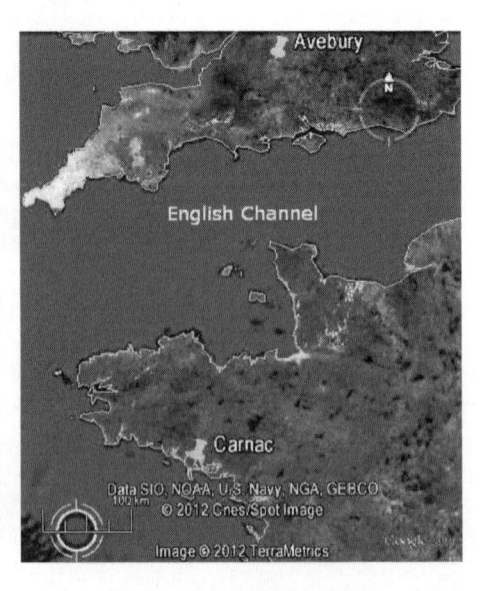

Fig. 10: English Channel, separating the Peninsula of Brittany (Carnac) from the island of Great Britain (Avebury).

Fig. 11: Aerial view of Avebury's henge.

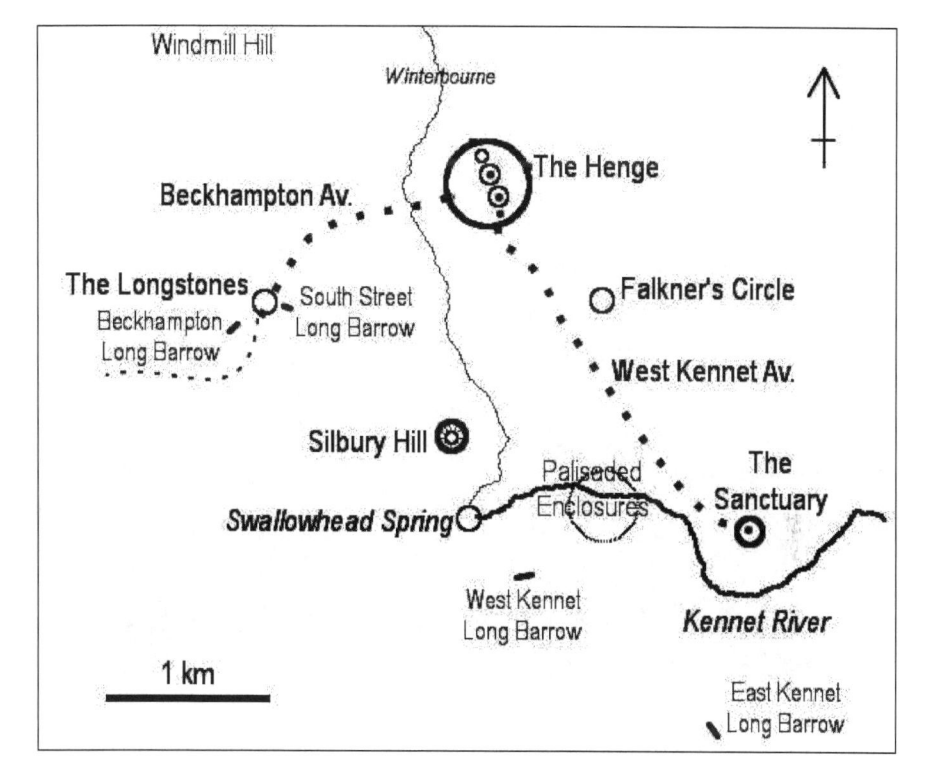

Fig. 12: Plan of Avebury's megalithic complex.

The henge had four opposing entrances, the south one connected with an avenue, the West Kennet Avenue, formed by paired standing stones that ended—or started depending at which point one begins—on top of a hill (Overton Hill), at a wooden circle called The Sanctuary.

A stone ring known as Falkner's Circle lay on the margin of the avenue, between the henge and The Sanctuary. A similar avenue, the Beckhampton Avenue, led out from the western entrance of the henge towards a structure similar to The Cove, of which a pair of stones, called The Longstones (or Adam and Eve), are extant. Whether this avenue ended at this point or continued farther westwards is uncertain.

A huge man-made mound, the largest in Europe (pre-modern times), known as Silbury Hill, is the other great element of the complex. It has a conical shape with a base diameter of 548 ft (167 m)

Fig. 13: Silbury Hill (ca. 131 ft / 40 m high).

and an imposing height of 131 ft (40 m) ending in a platform that was reached by a spiraling ramp around the mound (Fig. 13). Silbury Hill was erected near the source of the Kennet River, known as Swallowhead Spring. The wide ditch that surrounds the mound could have been flooded, which would have turned it into an artificial islet.

Scattered in the landscape there are some burial mounds, among which the long barrows deserve a special mention on account of their dimensions and antiquity. The West Kennet and East Kennet Long Barrows are located in the southern part of the complex, whereas the Beckhampton and South Street Long Barrows lie in the western part, next to The Longstones. These long barrows are the oldest structures of the complex, along with a settlement on high grounds at the NW called Windmill Hill.

Both avenues were among the last elements to be implemented, and Silbury Hill was even enlarged when the activity in the rest of

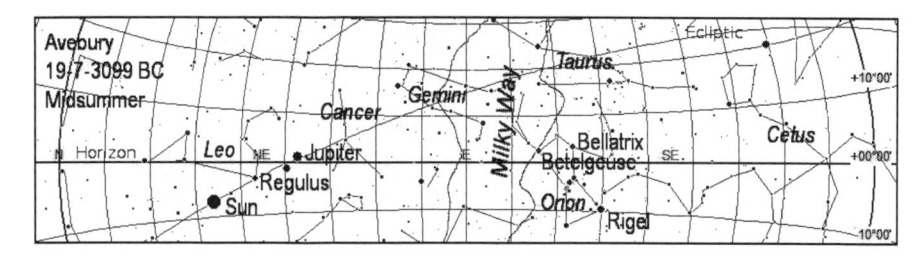

Fig. 14: Eastern horizon of Avebury at midsummer dawn.

the complex had almost ceased. Some remains of Palisaded Enclosures were found in the low grounds between The Sanctuary and Silbury Hill, also of a late execution.

As mentioned, the activity at the complex decreased to a large extent around the middle of the third millennium, when the West Kennet Long Barrow passage was filled with soil containing abundant shards, charcoal, bones and beads, apparently by the Beaker People.[2]

The function of this huge megalithic complex remains a mystery, although archaeologists speculate that it could have been the venue for the performance of a special ceremony, probably related to fertility and/or death—terms systematically used whenever the purpose is unknown. Subsequently we are going to propose a relatively simple hypothesis that accurately depicts the ceremonial use of Avebury.

The Sky over Avebury

Avebury's eastern horizon (stars grouped in traditional constellations) during the dawning of midsummer as they would have appeared at the end of the fourth millennium BC—at the apex of its activity—can be seen in Fig. 14.

In midsummer, Regulus (Leo's brightest star) was too close to the Sun and remained invisible, so it would have been necessary to wait another 18 days for its heliacal rising.[3]

Another group of very bright stars was rising, about the same time as Leo, from the SE: Orion. The stars in the upper part of this constellation (Betelgeuse and Bellatrix) were rising heliacally in midsummer, but it would be necessary to wait about 24 more days

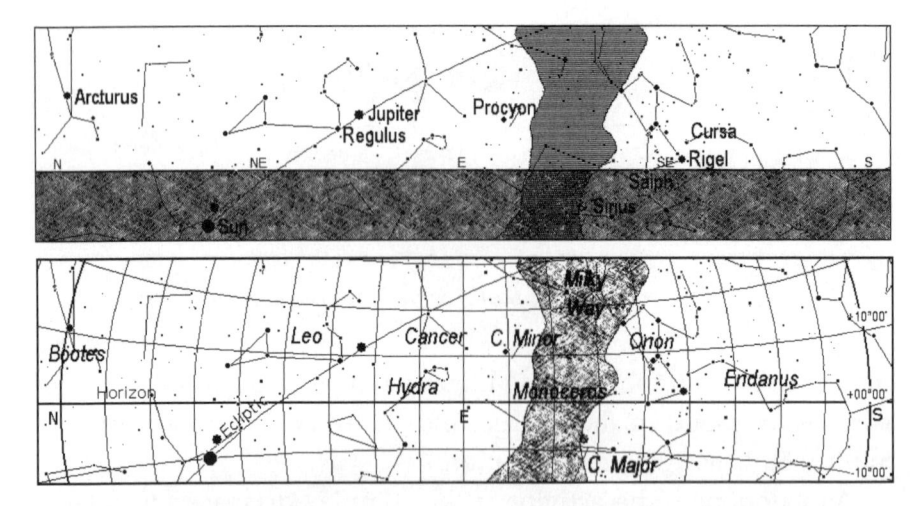

Fig. 15: Heliacal rising of Rigel from Avebury. (Top map with the stars' names, and lower with the constellations' and grid. August 13, 3099 BC.)

to witness the heliacal rising of Orion's brightest star, Rigel—a few days after Regulus. The firmament visible directly above Avebury's eastern horizon before midsummer sunrise contained, therefore, two main constellations: Leo and Orion, so it could be interesting to visualize them when they were seen just above the horizon, during the heliacal rising of Rigel (Fig. 15).

Leo and Orion were almost fully visible within approximately 20º, rising from the NE and SE respectively. They were separated by the Milky Way, which was rising perpendicularly to the horizon, crossed by the Monoceros constellation.

Cancer, the top of Hydra and Canis Minor constellations were also visible between Leo and the Milky Way, whereas Canis Major was at lower declinations and remained invisible, on Orion's side of the Milky Way.

The Eridanus constellation was rising heliacally from the southern horizon. On the opposite side from Eridanus, the circumpolar constellation of Boötes could be seen the closest it could get to the northern horizon. Boötes contains the star Arcturus, the brightest of the northern hemisphere, a very conspicuous star that, at that moment, was visible 10º above the horizon, signaling with precision the direction north.[4]

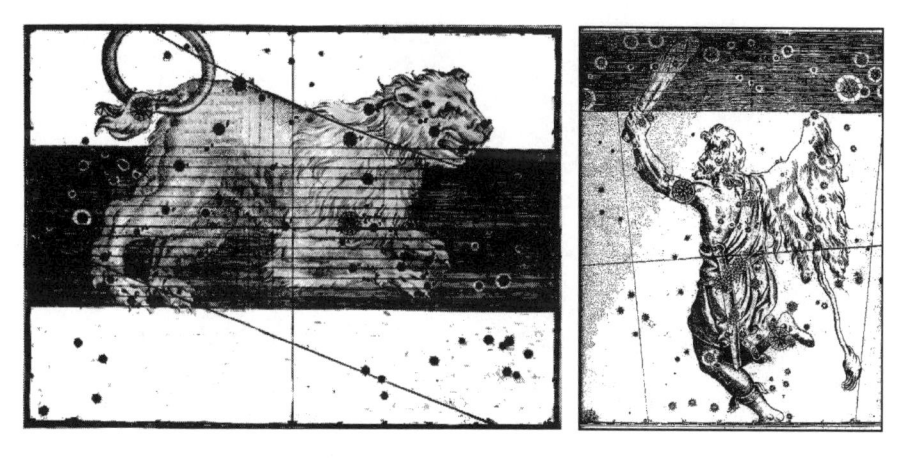

Fig. 16: Leo and Orion (J. Bayer). (Orion holds a lion skin.)

The Ceremony to Renew the Monarchy

In order to discern any possible correlation between this celestial scene and Avebury's design it is necessary to figure out the symbolism associated with each one of these constellations by the Megalith Builders. To this end we have a substantial line of investigation to pursue, since we are presupposing that it could be related to the renewal of their monarchy. The two obvious set of characters would be the kings and the princes. In a solar culture, the constellation visited by the Sun in midsummer, Leo, would be related to the kings; whereas Orion would be the logical counterpart related to the princes. Orion is classically represented as a hunter, symbolically very fitting to the prince's mission as a "lion's hunter" (Fig. 16).

Accordingly, Avebury could have been designed as a schematic representation of the celestial scene visible during Rigel's heliacal rising, functioning as a scenario where kings and princes enacted the drama they interpreted was being played out in the sky.

In Fig. 17, the main constellations visible directly over Avebury's eastern horizon are encircled and numbered from south to north. Orion (1) would appear as if "walking" over the line of the horizon, tilted from Eridanus (0) towards the Milky Way (2). Eridanus is represented classically as a celestial river, so the Kennet River could play its role in the complex.

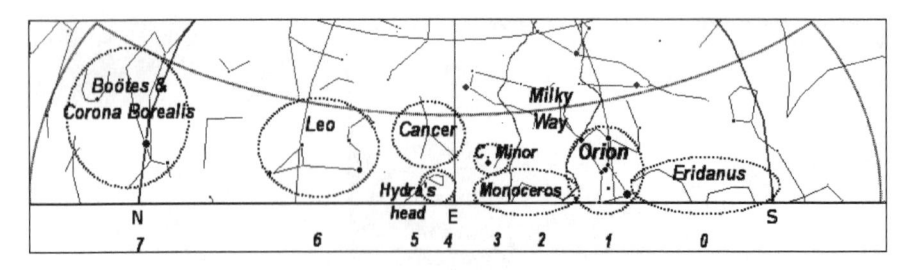

Fig. 17: Principal constellations visible directly over Avebury's S-N horizon, during Rigel's heliacal rising. (August 13, 3099 BC.)

Silbury Hill was erected next to Swallowhead Spring, the source of the Kennet River, so this imposing tumulus could stand for Rigel, Orion's brightest star, located in the sky next to the extreme of Eridanus (star Cursa, of second magnitude).

The princes would have arrived in Avebury by boat, rowing up the Kennet River. After disembarking, they would climb to the top of Silbury Hill where they would embrace Orion in a propitious ritual. Before dawn, the princes would head towards The Sanctuary, where, from its advantageous viewpoint, they would await the heliacal rising of Rigel.[5] Then, they would descend along the West Kennet Avenue towards the south entrance of the henge, in conformity with the side from where Orion would approach Leo if it were to move over the horizon.

The great ditch of the henge could be filled with water, dyed white with the chalk of the local soil, representing the Milky Way that appears in the sky rising perpendicularly from the horizon and separating Orion and Leo. In between Orion and the Milky Way lies Monoceros (2). The Falkner's stone ring built next to West Kennet Avenue, in the path of the princes towards the henge (Milky Way), could, therefore, be related to Monoceros.

The south entrance of the henge is flanked by two particularly large stones (Fig. 18), and on both sides of the corresponding section of the Milky Way there are two equally exceptional bright stars: Sirius and Procyon, in Canis Major and Minor constellations (3), so the logical inference would be that this pair of stones represented this pair of stars.[6]

Fig. 18: South entrance, flanked by two large stones across the ditch.

In the sky, if Orion could cross the "star-gate" formed by Sirius and Procyon, he would first have to face Hydra. Similarly, the princes, right after entering the henge by its south entrance, would encounter a sizeable rock perforated with a hole, known as the Ringstone (Fig. 19), which would fit perfectly with the location and shape of Hydra's head (4).

The remaining pair of stone rings inside the henge would have to represent Cancer (5) and Leo (6). The kings would stay inside the northern circle that corresponded to Leo, at whose center was The Cove (Fig. 20). This element was made up with the biggest stones and the earliest to be erected, marking the focal point of the monument and of the celestial drama that was played out in it. The princes killed the kings at this spot. (The rationale behind this *Rex Nemorensis* practice will be explained later.)

Finally, if circumpolar Boötes and Corona Borealis (7) played a role in the ceremony, as their situation insinuates, then, one should expect an additional third ring in the northernmost part of the henge. A piece of information that is not commonly mentioned confirmed this inference. There was, indeed, a third inner circle, discovered in 1930 by Alexander Keiller, exactly where it was expected.

Fig. 19: Ringstone (Crowstone, Scotland), similar to the non-extant of Avebury.

All this information can now be presented over the same plan of Avebury that appeared as Fig. 12 on page 31, correlating its elements to each of the mentioned constellations and stars (Fig. 21).

Besides, from a wider perspective, we could also identify the domains of each of the characters that participated in the ceremony; for instance, the surroundings of the Kennet River would be preferentially related to the princes, particularly Silbury Hill (Rigel-Orion) and The Sanctuary. Given that West Kennet Avenue was for the princes to parade at the commencement of the ceremony, it could be inferred that the other avenue, Beckhampton Avenue—related to the west direction—would be associated with the kings, with The Longstones playing an equivalent role to The Sanctuary with the princes.

Later in the book, we will talk about the priests and their relation to the north direction, based on what we may now advance that the

Fig. 20: The Cove, in the northern inner circle.

old settlement at Windmill Hill (NW of the henge) could be related to this elite, the celebrants of the ceremony. We will also explain that there was an essential feminine component at play during the ceremony, so the Palisaded Enclosures, built in the valley between The Sanctuary and Silbury Hill, would be the topographical counterpart and, accordingly, the most suitable area to establish a feminine domain for the princesses, complementing the masculine domain of the princes on the proximate hills.

Summary

In this chapter we have proposed that the Megalith Builders erected the complex of Avebury as the venue where they renewed their monarchy. They designed a ceremony that echoed a celestial scene seen over the horizon during the heliacal rising of Rigel (the brightest star of Orion), which took place a few days after midsummer. The major constellations visible in that region of the sky, Leo and Orion, were associated with the kings and the princes respectively. The princes arrived at Avebury by boat, rowing upon the Kennet River up to its source. Then, they climbed to the top of Silbury Hill, the artificial hill they built as a reflection of the star

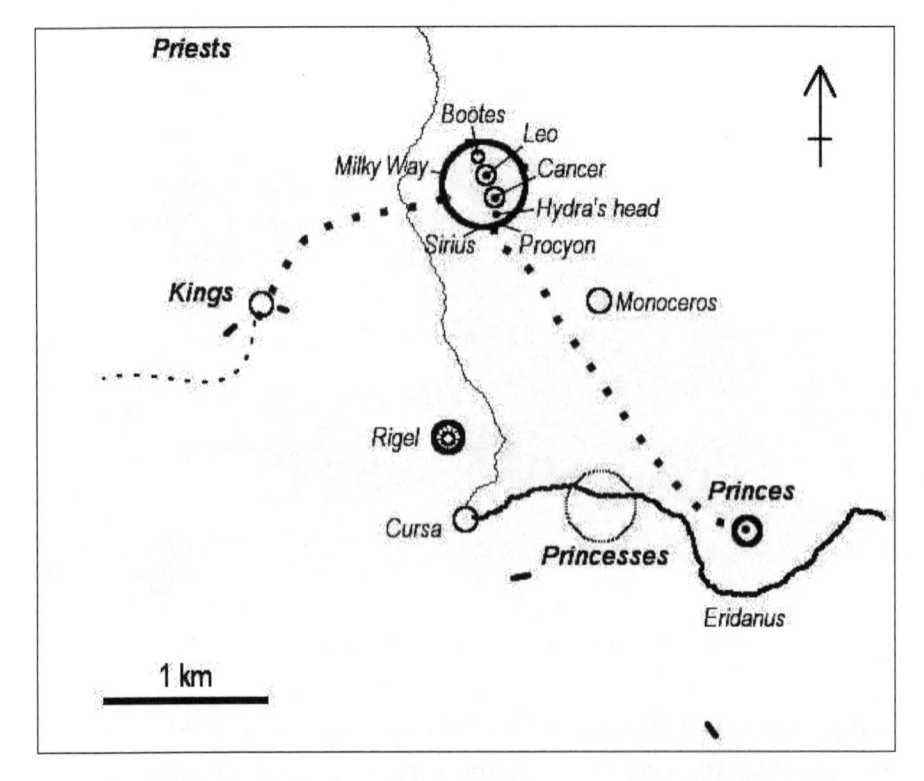

Fig. 21: Plan of Avebury indicating the constellations, stars and characters involved in the ceremony of monarchical renewal.

Rigel on Earth, where they ritualized the incarnation of Orion in themselves.

The kings departed from the Longstones and arrived at the henge parading along Beckhampton Avenue, whereas the princes departed from The Sanctuary and paraded along West Kennet Avenue. The princes sacrificed the kings (their parents) at the center of the inner ring of stones located to the north of the henge (reflection of Leo), in The Cove, thus becoming the new kings of the confederation.

The reason for this "tragedy" will be explained in the following chapters, along with all the details of this crucial ceremony, but first we have to study some other megalithic monuments.

Endnotes

[1] The antiquarians John Aubrey and William Stukeley left behind very valuable reports about Avebury in the late 17th and early 18th century. Alexander Keiller was a businessman and archaeologist who in the 30s dedicated part of his wealth and time to restore the complex.

[2] The Beaker People are the ultimate cultural expression of the Megalith Builders, during the Bronze Age (late third and early second millennia BC), named after the inverted bell-shaped ceramics they spread all over Europe.

[3] The heliacal rising of a star occurs when it first becomes visible above the horizon just before sunrise, after a period in which its proximity (terrestrial perspective) to the Sun impeded its visibility; in other words, the Sun has to be well below the horizon for the star to be visible in the morning twilight. The star's altitude at heliacal events is quite dependent upon the astronomical extinction coefficient (weather conditions), so there may be a variation of some days between its heliacal rising dates.

[4] The brightness of the stars is commonly measured with a parameter called "visual apparent magnitude" (m). Lower values of m indicate higher brightness. Those stars visible with the naked eye have values of m from the first negative magnitude (brightest) to sixth magnitude (weakest but still visible). The brightest stars (m < 1.5) are listed in an appendix on page 201.

[5] Rigel would rise after Regulus, but the time-gap would be reduced gradually from less than one hour to zero around the year 2000 BC.

[6] If this huge rock represented Sirius, then, in theory, it should be located outside the ditch (Milky Way), however, the appearance of it functioning as a star-gate in the company of Procyon would be lost, and so the builders could have decided to put them together to create a more imposing gate. This hypothesis would provide an explanation for the exceptionally big pairs of rocks that were erected at the four entrances of the henge—the Swindon Stone, extant at the north entrance being another good example—since they would represent pairs of stars particularly bright at the four quarters of the Milky Way. For example, if the south entrance represented Sirius & Procyon, the north entrance could represent Vega & Altair, the west Capella & Aldebaran, and the east Rigil Kent & Agena. (The brightness of these stars can be checked in the appendix on page 201.)

4

STONEHENGE

STONEHENGE is without doubt the most famous megalithic monument in the world. It is located on the southern plains of Great Britain, and it began in the early third millennium BC as a circular ditch of ca. 360 ft (110 m) of diameter. Its entrance is oriented to the NE, with a standing stone (the Heelstone) located outside.[1] By the 24th century BC, it also had—among other features—a tall bank along the inner side of the ditch, a concentric ring (108 ft / 33 m in diameter) of 30 standing stones with 30 lintels above (Sarsen Circle), and five huge trilithons inside arranged in the shape of a horseshoe.[2] Another ring and horseshoe of stones called "Bluestones" were also erected later inside the Sarsen Circle. At its center there was a unique stone known as the Altar Stone (Fig. 22). Four "Stationed Stones" were placed next to the inner bank in a rectangle over a ring of 56 holes known as Aubrey Holes. Two rings of holes (Y & Z) were also dug around the Sarsen Circle (Fig. 23).

Fig. 22: Artistic recreation of the Sarsen Circle and its inner elements.

Change of Venue and Solstice

The shift of activity that apparently took place from Avebury to Stonehenge around the 24th century BC could be connected to the transit of the Sun in midsummer over Regulus. The Megalith Builders would observe how, generation after generation, the Sun in midsummer got closer and closer to Regulus, which implied that the day of the celebration of their monarchical renewal ceremony during the heliacal rising of Rigel, a few days after the heliacal rising of Regulus, had to happen each time later after midsummer.[3] The occasion when the Sun in midsummer transited directly over Regulus could be anticipated and seen as a propitious signal to reform the ceremony to stop the slowly but surely drift of its date from midsummer.

We may propose that, facing this problem, the Megalith Builders could have decided to move the ceremony from Avebury to Stonehenge during the 24th century BC. The fact that Stonehenge is located at about the same latitude and longitude as Avebury indicates that the Megalith Builders did not look for a geodesic or geographical adjustment, but one of a different nature. The solution to their problem could be very simple yet revolutionary: to move the ceremony from midsummer to midwinter. This solution is not as contradictory as it may seem at first, certainly not for a people who at

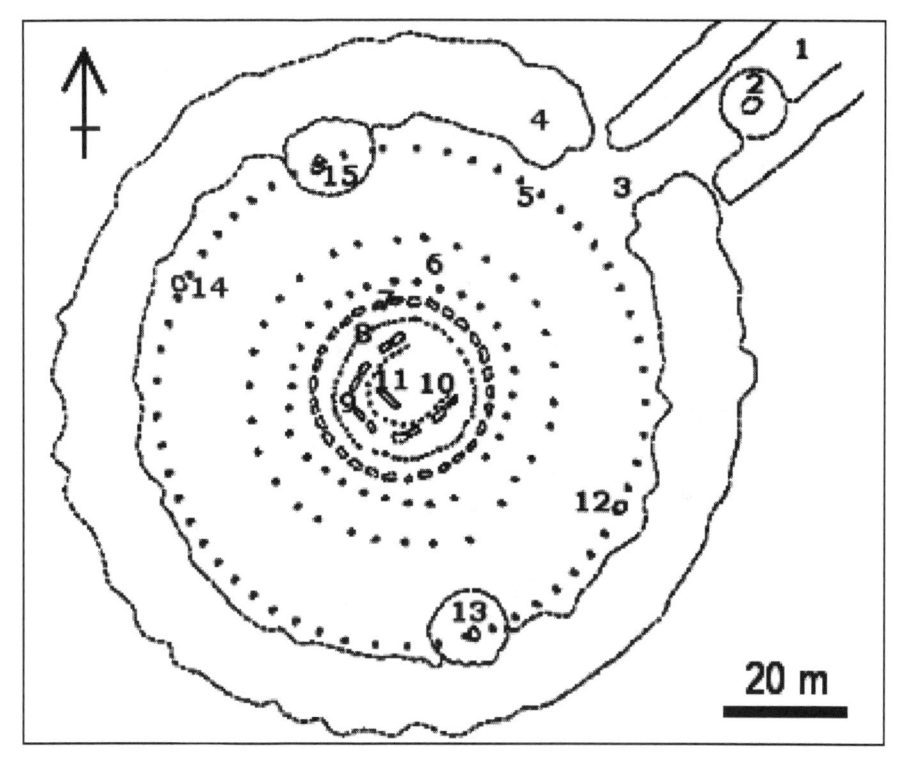

Fig. 23: Plan of Stonehenge: 1) Avenue delineated by parallel ditches and banks, 2) Heelstone, 3) Entrance, with the Slaughter Stone inside, 4) Ditch with banks on both sides, the inner taller, 5) Aubrey Holes, 6) Y & Z Holes, 7) Sarsen Circle, 8) Bluestone Circle, 9) Five trilithons, 10) Bluestone Horseshoe, 11) Altar Stone, 12-15) Stationed Stones.

that point of their history had to know quite well the celestial cycles. In winter, the sunsets occur exactly on the opposite side of the horizon from where the sunrises occur in summer. Therefore, in the 24th century BC, the Sun in midwinter was setting on the opposite side of the horizon from where Regulus was rising. As a result, Leo and the neighboring constellations would keep on elevating over the horizon as it got darker.[4]

But why change the venue they had been using for the last seven centuries? The key difference introduced by changing the ceremony from sunrise to sunset is the visible window-time of the chosen stars. In the former case (sunrise-Avebury), the stars of the selected scene were seen as a snapshot fading away in the dawn, whereas in

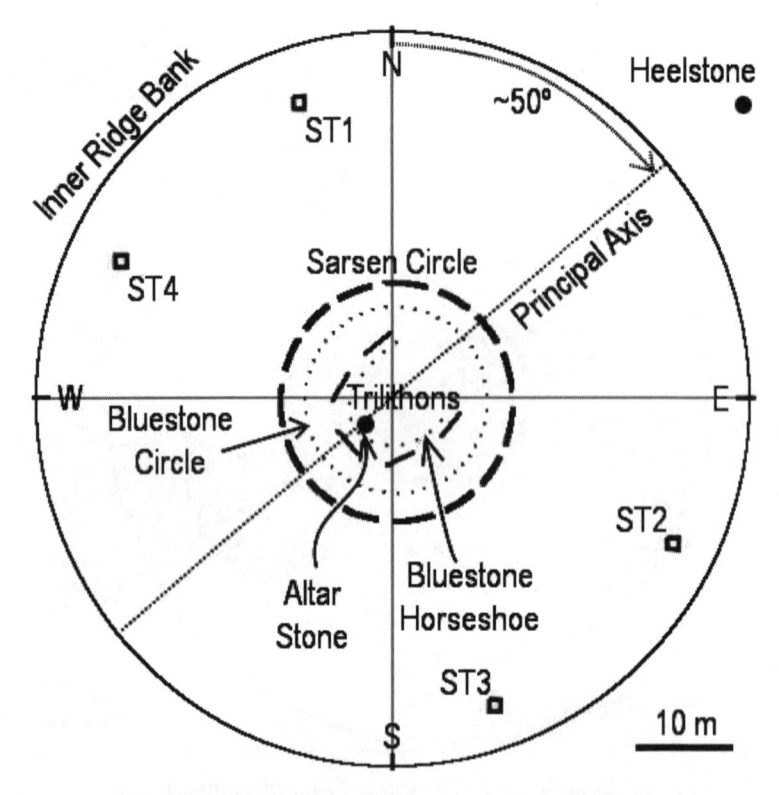

Fig. 24: Schematic plan of Stonehenge.

the latter (sunset-Stonehenge) they would be seen traversing the sky's dome at night. Thus, the reformed ceremony could be based not only on one celestial scene, as in the case of Avebury, but on several. Besides the rising, the culmination and setting of those stars could also be interpreted symbolically.[5]

The inadequacy of Avebury's design to accommodate the necessary shift from a static to a dynamic scenario could be the insurmountable motive behind its abandonment.

The Celestial Mirror

If Stonehenge was planned to be inaugurated during the 24th century BC to replace Avebury, its construction had to begin in anticipation of this, perhaps several generations in advance, by remodeling a center that previously had a different purpose. The presence of a bank inside the ditch is a very unusual feature among

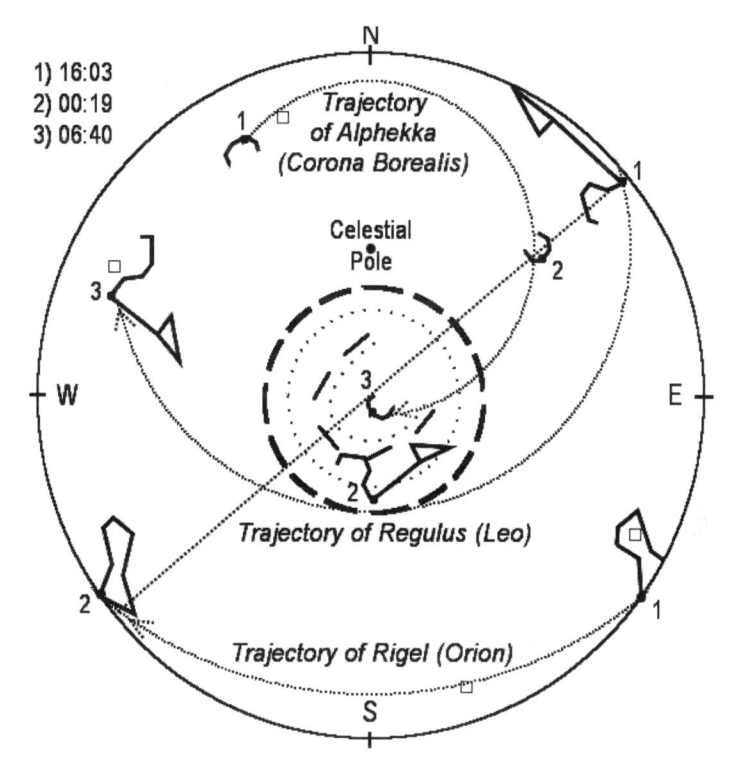

Fig. 25: Trajectories of Regulus, Rigel and Alphekka over Stonehenge in midwinter. (January 8, 2303 BC.) Three times: 1) Regulus rising, 2) Regulus culmination, and 3) Regulus extinction (Alphekka culmination).

megalithic constructions. This inner bank—originally much taller than at present due to weathering—would create a 360º artificial horizon that, from inside, would permit an observer to contemplate the sky's dome as if leaning upon the ridge, with the geometric center of the enclosure just below the zenith. A more schematic plan of Stonehenge is shown in Fig. 24, establishing the ridge of the inner bank as the border of a sort of mirror of the sky.

The projection of Regulus and Rigel's trajectories over Stonehenge during the night that preceded midwinter in a year of the 24th century BC can be seen in Fig. 25.[6] (This figure also includes the trajectory of Alphekka, the brightest star of Corona Borealis,[7] because, as we will see, it also played a decisive role.)

Regulus rose at 16:03, at the same time that the Sun was setting on the opposite side of the horizon, delineating the principal axis of the enclosure (azimuth ca. 50º).[8] The celestial scene visible over the eastern horizon of Stonehenge would gradually become more precise as it got darker, and it was identical to that described from Avebury (Fig. 15, p. 34), when Leo and Orion rose simultaneously, though now this scene did not shape the whole ceremony but only the start. Regulus reached its culmination after midnight (00:19), when Leo reflected on the Sarsen Circle. At that moment, the Corona Borealis was moving over the entrance and Orion began to set on the opposite side. Regulus began to set just before sunrise, at the same time as Alphekka had reached the zenith (06:40).

Since the rising and culmination of Regulus would point out the highlights related to the kings (incarnations of Leo), these events must be investigated in more detail (Fig. 26).

While Regulus culminated, Draco (the Dragon constellation) reflected along the north direction, with the Ecliptic Pole directly above the Celestial Pole (star Thuban during the megalithic epoch), on the north axis.[9] The upper extreme of the Milky Way was also setting on the north, with Cygnus (the Swan constellation) and its brightest star Deneb just below the horizon.[10] Thus, Ursa Major (the Great Bear constellation), Draco and Cygnus were at that time of the ceremony perfectly aligned along the north direction. This particular stellar arrangement could reveal an insight into the after-death beliefs of the Megalith Builders, delineating a celestial route. We propose that the kings were sacrificed at this moment, when Regulus culminated over the Sarsen Circle. The details behind this practice will be described in the following chapters.

The next two key moments of the ceremony are shown in Fig. 27, the first when the Galactic Equator coincided with the line of the horizon, and the second when Alphekka reached its culmination (Regulus extinction). About three hours after Regulus culminated, the Milky Way would completely encircle the henge, and so this whitish celestial band could also be represented, as in Avebury, by the ditch filled with water naturally colored white. The Crux showed up for a moment, skimming over the southern horizon.

STONEHENGE • 49

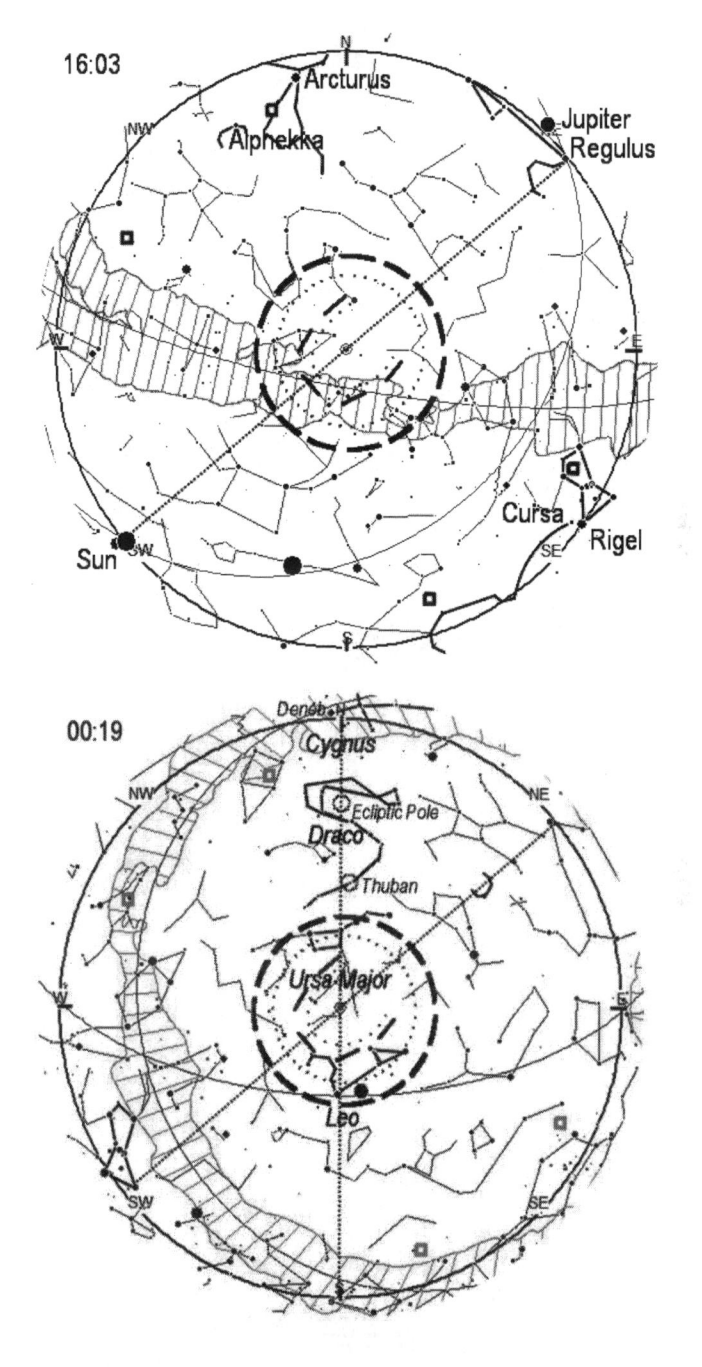

Fig. 26: Projections of the celestial dome on Stonehenge in midwinter, when Regulus was rising (16:03) and culminating (00:19). (January 8 and 9, 2303 BC.)

50 • SAILORS OF STONEHENGE

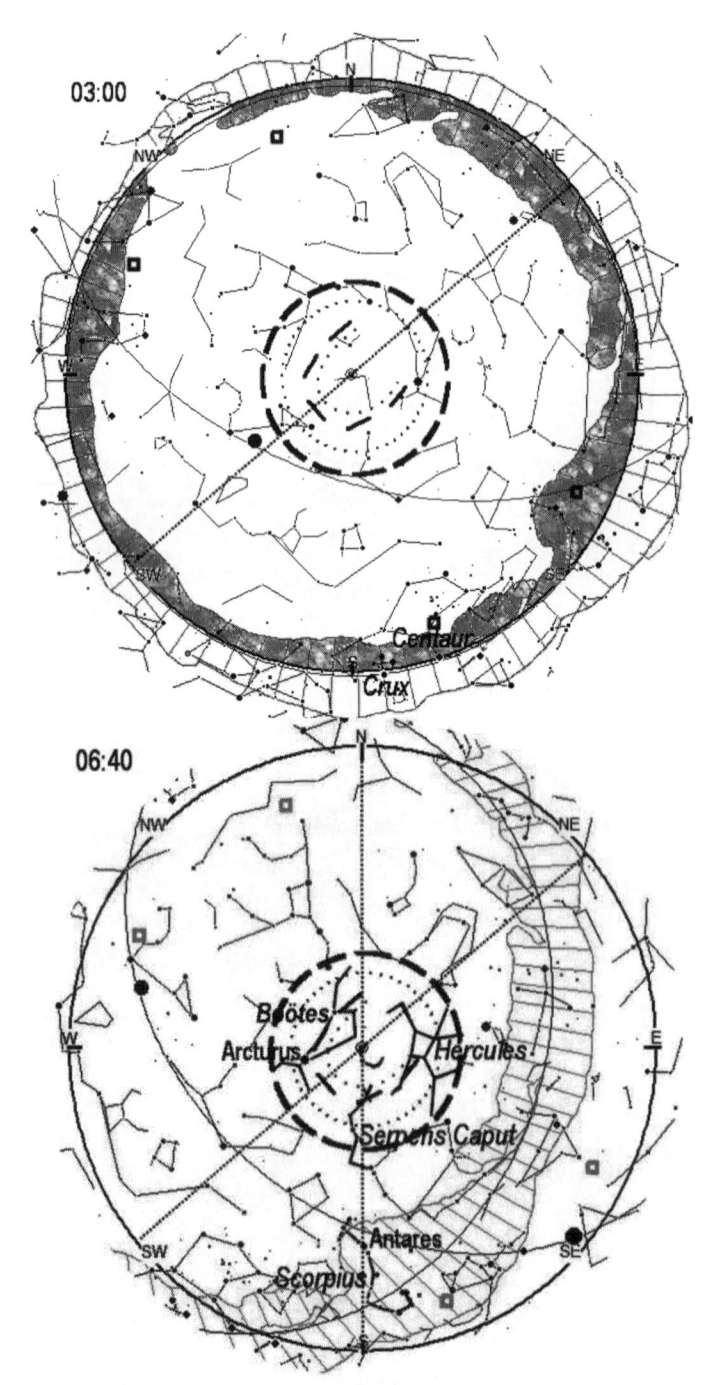

Fig. 27: Projections of the celestial dome on Stonehenge in midwinter, when the Milky Way encircled the site (03:00), and Alphekka culminated (Regulus was getting extinct) (06:40). (January 9, 2303 BC.)

If the visibility of this constellation was important, then the latitude of Stonehenge was right at the upper limit. As a matter of fact, this was the only latitude from where it was possible to see the Milky Way around the horizon, a factor that very likely was taken into consideration at the time of choosing its location.

The Crowning

The Corona Borealis kept on moving towards the zenith, reaching its culmination (86º of star Alphekka) at 6:40, approximately one hour and a half before sunrise. The horseshoe shape of this constellation modeled from above that of the Bluestone and trilithons horseshoes within the Sarsen Circle, with their open sides towards the entrance, thus explaining these features of the monument. This had to be the right time to literally crown the princes, when the Corona Borealis was shining directly from the zenith just before sunrise.

Moreover, the Serpens Caput and Scorpio constellations were aligned along the south direction, with Scorpio's brightest star, Antares, exactly on this meridian.[11] Hercules and Boötes reflected within the Sarsen Circle, the latter containing the star Arcturus, the brightest of the northern hemisphere, so these circumpolar constellations would be intimately associated with the crowning ritual.

Assuming that the ceremony was discontinued around the 17th century BC, when the activity at Stonehenge declined considerably, this monument would have been the venue for renewing the monarchy for approximately seven centuries.[12]

Leo represented as a lion and embodied by the kings, Orion as a hunter of lions embodied by the princes, and Corona Borealis as a "northern crown" functioning as a royal motif, are excellent examples that support the hypothesis that the Megalith Builders were the authors of the traditional system of constellations (Fig. 28).[13]

The Transportation of the Stones

Making use of the information gathered up to this point, we may now recapitulate and think about the function of some minor features of Avebury and Stonehenge not discussed yet. Eridanus is the constellation seen over the horizon towards the south of Orion, and

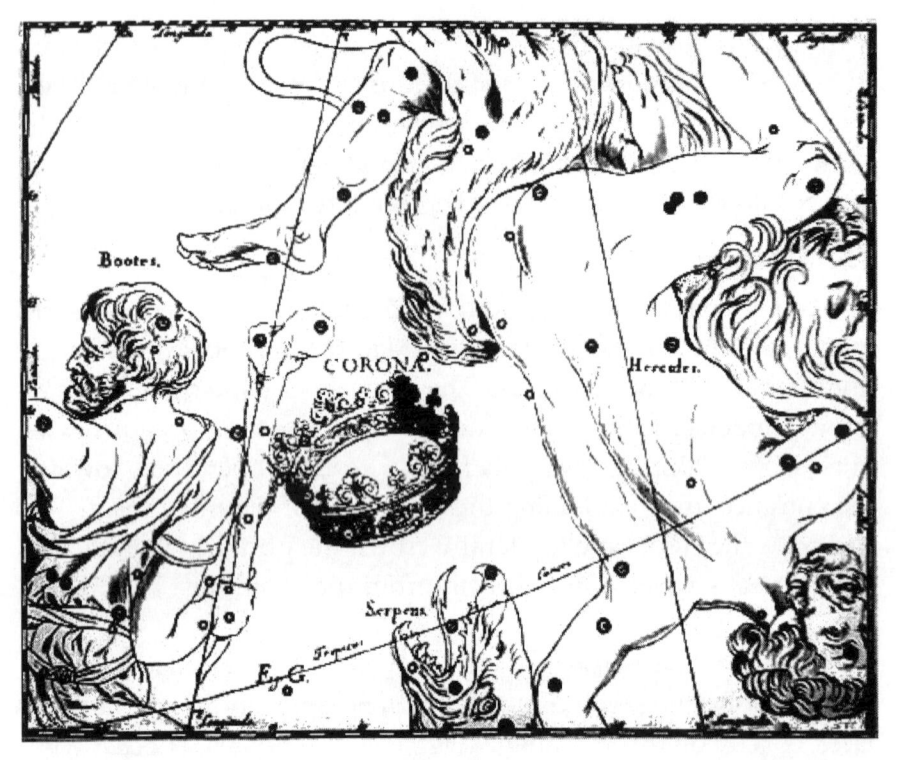

Fig. 28: The Corona Borealis, between Boötes, Serpens Caput and Hercules (inverted and holding a lion skin) (J. Hevelius).

it is represented by a river, so the location of Avebury could be selected based on the presence of an actual river that could reflect Eridanus and, as already discussed, that river could be the Kennet.

The Bluestones placed inside the Sarsen Circle of Stonehenge were collected in Wales, specifically in the Preseli Hills, more than 130 miles (250 km) away from Stonehenge, a fact that has puzzled archaeologists, but for which we can now provide a compelling reason. The circumpolar constellations Boötes and Corona Borealis were seen on the opposite side of the horizon from Eridanus. Given that the course of the Kennet River that represented Eridanus flows towards the east, the logical direction from which to bring the stones to represent Boötes and the Corona Borealis would be the west. The Preseli Hills are in Wales, in the far west, at a distance that suggests an equally large extension for the reflection of Eridanus. The Kennet is a tributary of the Thames, a river that also

Fig. 29: Panel at the entrance to Stonehenge.

flows eastwards and which could also be considered part of the reflection of Eridanus.

Most likely, the Bluestones were transported by boat on the Bristol-Avon River—or even the Salisbury-Avon—up to the point where navigability was not possible any further. For the length of the remaining stretch to their final destination, the stones would have to be transported on terra firma. The current idea about this process depicts the Megalith Builders as people dressed in furs, dragging the stones on logs with the help of very rudimentary tools—as in the panel that welcomes the visitors to Stonehenge (Fig. 29). But, is it too unrealistic to contemplate the possibility that they devised a simpler method to move the stones? For example, any method that would allow rolling them would be much less demanding; perhaps by wrapping them, or by inserting them in rings of stone, or wood, copper or, much better, bronze,[14] with the gaps filled with wood. Animal traction should not be discounted either.

Fig. 30: Midwinter sunset seen from the entrance to Stonehenge.

The Attendants to the Ceremony

In the proximity of Stonehenge's inner bank there were four stones (two still extant) known as "Stationed Stones." The northern and southern ones (ST1 & ST3 in the blueprint of Fig. 24 on page 46) were over mounds.[15] During the sunset, at the commencement of the ceremony, ST1 reflected the region where Boötes and the Corona Borealis were above them in the sky (the stone was equidistant from Alphekka and Arcturus), ST3 corresponded to Eridanus (where it went below the horizon), and ST2 to Orion. The stationed stones could serve, therefore, as pointers to the correct unfolding of the ceremony. The ring of Aubrey Holes concentric to the inner bank and connecting the stationed stones could have contained poles—even people—to accurately determine the position of the stars at each moment.[16]

At Stonehenge, the ceremony had to begin exactly at sunset, when the kings (Regulus rising), walking along the avenue, reached the entrance coming from the NE, illuminated frontally by the last solar rays filtered through the stones (Fig. 30).

The princes would have arrived earlier, and they would stay at ST3 (Eridanus). Once the kings arrived at the henge, the princes

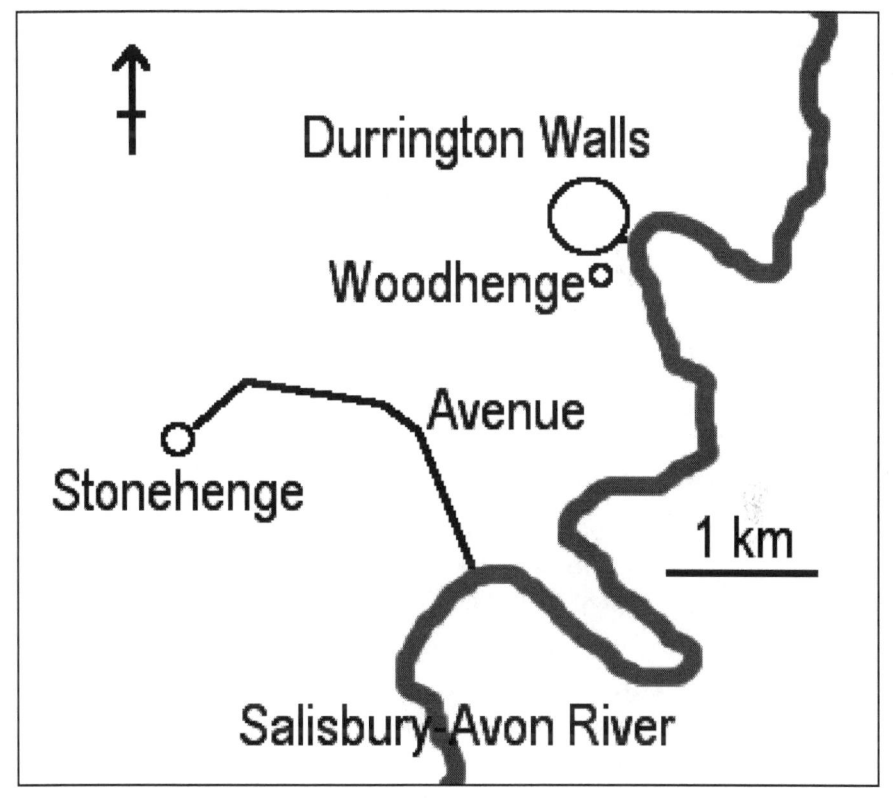

Fig. 31: Map of Stonehenge's neighboring elements.

would move from ST3 to ST2, representing the movement of the lion hunters (Orion) arriving from the celestial river (Eridanus).

Given the key roles played by circumpolar Boötes and the Corona Borealis, the celebrant priests might be stationed on ST1. As for ST4, it is located where Regulus reflected at the conclusion of the ceremony (Fig. 25, p. 47), with a function probably related to this circumstance.

The people gathered for the monarchical renewal ceremony would mostly live in provisional shelters dismantled at its conclusion, next to a good source of water. The locations of the living quarters at Avebury were already suggested for each of the different participants. At Stonehenge, these quarters could be at Woodhenge and Durrington Walls, large henge-type structures built by the Salisbury-Avon River (Fig. 31). This river was connect-

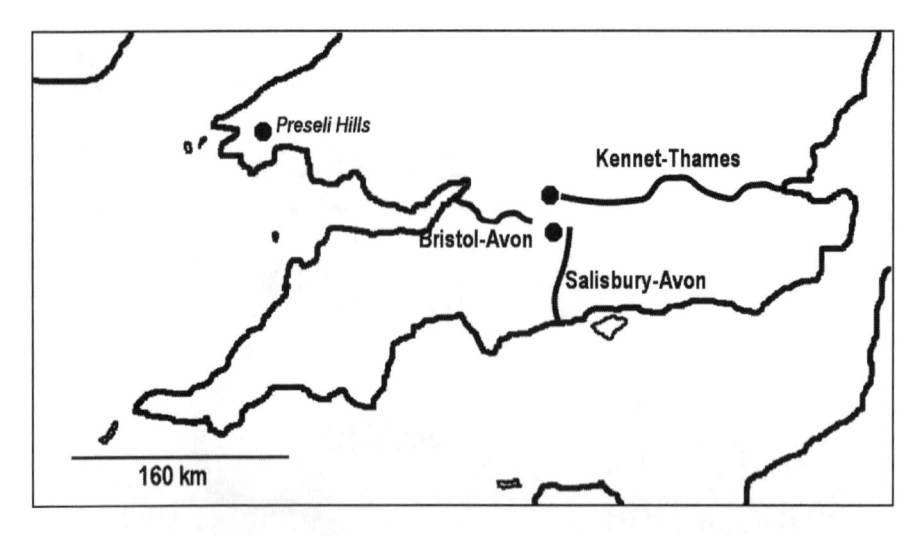

Fig. 32: Confluence of rivers in the area of Avebury and Stonehenge. (The Preseli Hills in Wales are in the opposite direction from the Kennet-Thames Rivers.)

ed to Stonehenge by an avenue of a couple of miles (ca. 3 km) in length, obviously for the exclusive use of the royalty and the clergy.

Archaeologist Mike Parker Pearson has recently proposed that Durrington Walls may have been a domain of the living while Stonehenge would be of the dead,[17] a hypothesis which would coincide with that proposed here, since Durrington Walls and Woodhenge would house the residential area during the celebration of the renewal of the monarchy, whereas Stonehenge would be the site where the regicides took place.

The kings and princes would gather for this ceremony at Stonehenge (formerly Avebury) arriving from different directions; the princes would come from the east navigating on the Thames and Kennet Rivers, whereas the kings would come from the west along the Bristol-Avon River (Fig. 32).

Once the ceremony was over, the new kings would proceed southwards on the Salisbury-Avon River into the English Channel, and from there to Carnac in Brittany to erect the stones in memory of their fathers, the late kings.

During the long periods of inactivity at these monuments, locals could perform cremations and burials on their grounds which would account for some of the remains found in them.[18]

Summary

In this chapter we have proposed that, in the 24th century BC, the ceremonial center where the Megalith Builders renewed their monarchy was transferred from Avebury to Stonehenge, and from summer to winter in order to gain visibility over the celestial scene that served as a model for the ceremony. Due to the precession of the equinoxes, the date of the ceremony had moved too far away from the summer solstice.

The inadequacy of Avebury's design to accommodate the necessary shift from a static to a dynamic scenario led to its replacement by Stonehenge.

The ceremony at Stonehenge began on the night of the winter solstice. The kings were killed by the princes inside the Sarsen Circle when Leo culminated in the sky and Orion began to set over the horizon. The princes were literally crowned when the Corona Borealis shone from the zenith. The ceremony concluded at sunrise, when the princes were invested as the new kings.

Participants arrived by boat; the princes coming from the east going up the Thames & Kennet Rivers, and the kings from the west rowing up the Bristol-Avon River.

Endnotes

[1] Some authors suggest it could already be a henge (containing some stones inside).

[2] Lintels are stones put horizontally over the tops of adjacent standing stones. Trilithons are groups of three stones: two standing stones linked with a lintel on top.

[3] As noted in Chapter 2, early in the megalithic epoch, the Sun in midsummer was located beyond Regulus (towards Virgo), although this stretch (between the Sun's position in the summer solstice and Regulus) was progressively reduced over the coming centuries until it disappeared by the 24th century BC, when the solstitial Sun transited just above Regulus. In later centuries the Sun in midsummer would shine even before Regulus (towards Cancer).

[4] In addition to the practical reason of gaining visibility over the celestial scene upon which they modeled their monarchical renewal ceremony, there is also a symbolic reason: their kings would be regenerated like the Sun is in the sky (in midwinter the sunrises move again northwards over the horizon, and the days get longer).

[5] The culmination of a star occurs when it reaches its highest height over the horizon, while crossing the local north to south meridian.

[6] Times in Universal Time (UT), as directly provided by the software (Cartes du Ciel V3.0). This particular year of the 24th century BC was chosen because the Sun in midsummer transited over Regulus (and Jupiter over Leo).

[7] Alphekka is a second magnitude star (m = 2.24).

[8] Azimuth defined as the angle east of north. The azimuth of Stonehenge's entrance would be ca. 50º. While this monument was active—from approximately the 24th to the 17th centuries BC—Regulus kept on rising from the same azimuth (ca. 48-49º). A typical starlight extinction altitude for Regulus is 2.4º—from the downs of England under favorable conditions—so this star would become visible when its azimuth was over 53º, after crossing hidden from the eye in the dusk directly above the avenue. Although invisible, the Megalith Builders would know perfectly well that Regulus would already be crossing over the entrance while the Sun was setting on the diametrically opposed side of the horizon. The entrance would be, therefore, designed to be oriented towards the rising of Regulus during midwinter, and

not as popularly believed towards the midsummer sunrise. Nevertheless, the monument could be originally oriented towards midsummer sunrise before being remodeled for its new purpose, which could explain the presence from earlier times of the Heelstone in front of the entrance.

[9] This detail suggests the Megalith Builders already knew that the real unmovable point in the sky was not the Celestial Pole but the Ecliptic Pole, around which the Celestial moves, causing the precession of the equinoxes, in a 26,000 years cycle.

[10] Deneb is a first magnitude star (m = 1.25; ranking 20).

[11] Antares is a first magnitude star (m = 1.06; ranking 16).

[12] Due to the precession of the equinoxes, the conditions would have shifted slowly from the original ones; for example, Rigel ended up rising ahead of Regulus, Alphekka's culmination decreased to 82º, and Crux became invisible, deviations from the original conditions that might have contributed to its ending.

[13] Hercules (Greek Heracles) is the greatest of the Greco-Roman heroes, so it might be surprising that it is associated with a group of stars not that bright—third magnitude and higher. However, its importance is not based on its brightness but on its situation, between the Corona Borealis and Draco. This is another good example of the ultimate origin of classical cosmology, derived from the Megalith Builders, for whom the Hercules constellation would be represented as a mighty hero—dressed in a lion skin—equivalent to an immortal Orion. Boötes constellation, and especially its brightest star Arcturus, could be seen as the dwelling of an immortal (circumpolar) celestial king who, from the zenith, imposed the crown upon the heads of the princes. This celestial royal figure brings to mind inevitably the medieval legend of King Arthur, the quintessential archetype of the wise king, not only because his name is remarkably similar to that of the star, but also because his allegedly geographical area of influence was Britain and Brittany.

[14] Copper was among the first metals humans worked for purposes other than ornamentation, yet it was its alloy with tin that resulted in a new material, bronze, with much better mechanical properties. Archeologists have found bronzes in Iran and Mesopotamia dating from as early as the fourth millennium BC, and by the end of the following millennium it was already well known all over Europe. The most im-

portant mines of tin were in Cornwall, the SW peninsula of Great Britain. Consequently, the possibility that the builders of Stonehenge had access to bronze is more than plausible. There are Assyrian and Egyptian panels depicting large crowds pulling huge statues; however, it is not the same to transport a sculpture as a cylindrical stone, and it is not clear that the European demography could cater for such mobilizations of people.

[15] For clarity, the Stationed Stones are named ST1 thru ST4, rather than using the notation of specialized texts (i.e. stones 91 thru 94).

[16] Historian John North argued in favor of astronomical reasons for the design of the megalithic monuments. In the case of the Aubrey Holes, he suggested they could have held posts used for the observation of the sky in conjunction with the surrounding bank (*Stonehenge: A New Interpretation of Prehistoric Man and Cosmos*, The Free Press Ed., p. 329, 1996).

[17] *Stonehenge*, by Mike Parker Pearson; Simon & Schuster Ed. (2012)

[18] In the British Islands there are thousands of stone rings—obviously not as monumental as the ones we have mentioned—where the locals would reunite to enact celestial dramas at key moments of the year.

5

THE ORKNEY ISLANDS

THE Orkney Islands are a Scottish archipelago uniquely rich in Neolithic sites. The "Heart of Neolithic Orkney" is a group of megalithic monuments on the Mainland Island consisting of Maeshowe (a chambered cairn), Skara Brae (one of the best preserved Neolithic villages), the Standing Stones of Stenness (Fig. 33) and the Ring of Brodgar (photo above).[1] The latest is among the northernmost examples of henges in Britain, comparable in size with Avebury and Stonehenge.

The high concentration of Neolithic sites at this location of this northern island is quite remarkable. The people who built Maeshowe and lived in houses like those of Skara Brae, surrounded by such ritual landscape, were contemporaneous with those who built Avebury, Carnac and Newgrange.

62 • SAILORS OF STONEHENGE

*Fig. 33: Above, Ring of Stennes.
Center, a house of Skara Brae.
Below, interior of Maeshowe.*

This chronological coincidence, and the geodesic fact that the Orkney Islands are the northernmost land on the same meridian as Carnac (ca. 3.2° W),[2] may reveal a connection among all these sites.

The hypothesis of MacKie proposing the existence of a theocratic elite with capacity of movement over large territories in Neolithic Britain radiating from the Orkneys in the north (ref. 7, p. 19), would fit within a scheme in which these islands were chosen by the Megalith Builders to construct the headquarters of their priests. But, why build it in such a remote northern archipelago?

Crossroads

There are reasons, both symbolic and astronomical, that could provide answers to this question. "To guide from above" has an evident associated symbolism, especially in a culture deeply interested in the sky. During the monarchical renewal ceremony, the priests would "descend" from the north to celebrate it, while the princes would arrive from the east and the kings from the west. At its conclusion, the priests would go back to the north, while the new kings would go down southward, to the mausoleum at Carnac.

Therefore, Avebury and Stonehenge were at the center of a very important crossroads (Fig. 34).

In addition to this intuitive symbolism, there is an astronomical meaning that was very likely also taken into consideration. A culture that had studied the cycles of the sky for many generations, and was able to travel considerable distances, would have noticed that Thuban, the polar star, increased its altitude over the horizon as they moved to higher latitudes. From this observation and others equally simple, they could figure out that there had to be a terrestrial pole, the "highest" and "loftiest" point of a spherical Earth, directly below the celestial pole.

The Megalith Builders would explore the northern seas, discovering that the northernmost land above Carnac was the Orkney Isles, about a third of the way from the top of the Earth (59° of latitude). That would be the location where they would establish the counter pole of their royal mausoleum, inhabited by priests supported by farmers from outside.

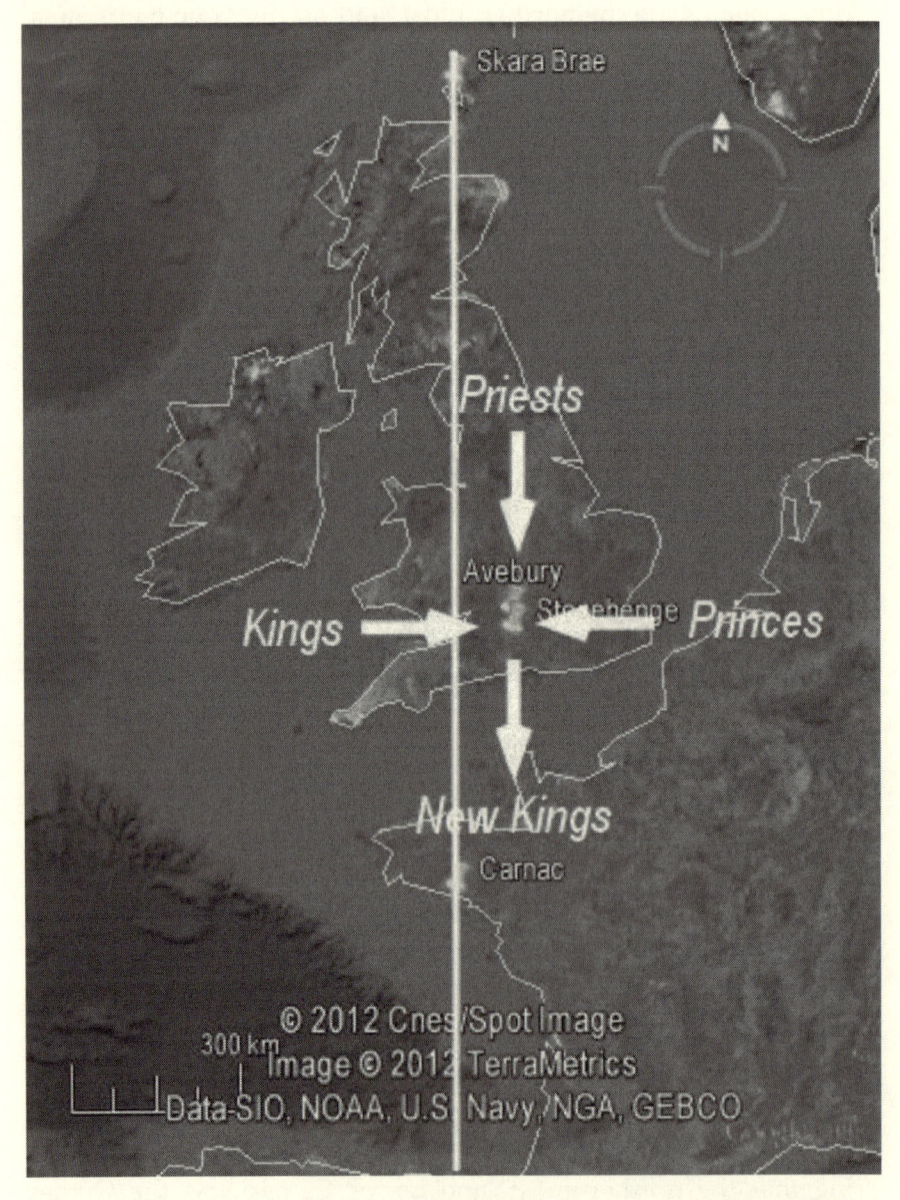

Fig. 34: The movements of the main characters who participated in the ceremony to renew the Megalith Builders' monarchy. (Carnac and the Orkney Islands lie on the same meridian.)

Hyperborea

There are few anthropological phenomena more open to diverse interpretations than myths. Some would disregard them as remnants of superstitious beliefs and obsolete religious rites, some as mere rules for proper socialization or entertainment, some as psychological insights of our ancestors into the unconscious. Yet others would perceive them as traumatic pre-historical events such as cataclysms or conflagrations narrated in metaphorical language. Probably, there should not be a single interpretation of myths, as there is not a single type of myth. Myths may be so appealing and have lasted millennia precisely for this characteristic, their ability to release the wisdom they contain in different layers according to the capacity of each interpreter. For Classical Greece, the megalithic culture was as remote in the past as Classical Greece is from us. As a result, their knowledge of the Megalith Builders would already be shrouded in myth, even more since this information would have come to them fundamentally through an oral tradition.

Thule and Hyperborea were two of the *terrae incognitae* for the Greeks and Romans in their limited knowledge of the geography of the world (Fig. 35), where supposedly people lived to a great age and enjoyed great happiness. The Greek explorer Pytheas was the first one to mention Thule in his now lost work *On the Ocean* (fourth century BC), where he claimed that Thule was a six-day sail north of the land of the Celts and there were no nights around midsummer. Thule often appears in classical European literature and maps as an island in the far north. There is more information about Hyperborea, Diodorus Siculus being the author who provided more details about this mythical land and its inhabitants:[3]

"Of those who have written about the ancient myths, Hecataeus and certain others say that in the regions **beyond the land of the Celts there lies in the ocean an island no smaller than Sicily**. *This island, the account continues, is situated in the north and is inhabited by the Hyperboreans, who are called by that name because their home is beyond the point whence the north wind (Boreas) blows; and the island is both fertile and productive of every crop, and since it has an unusually temperate climate it produces two harvests each year."*

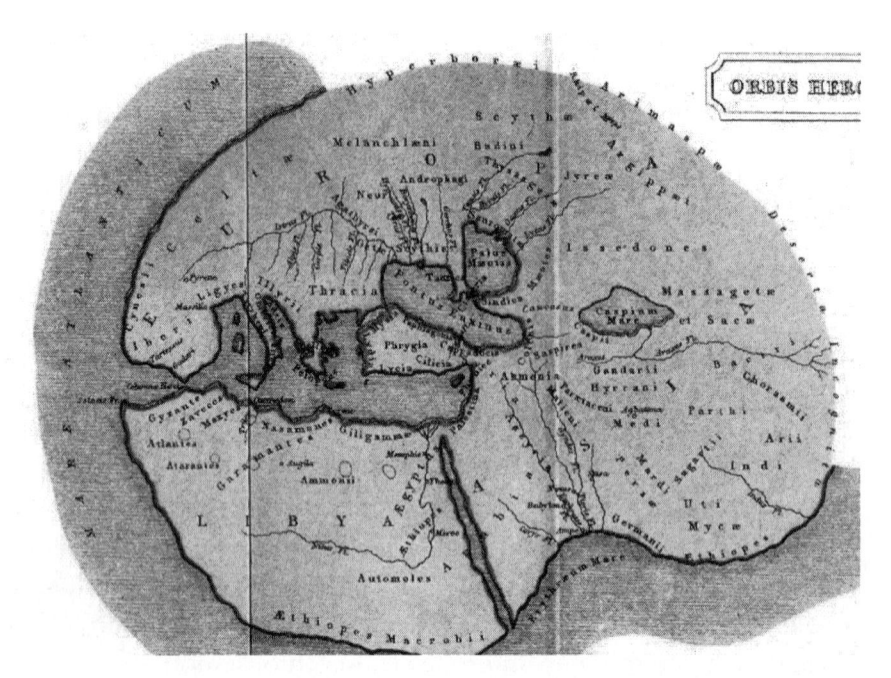

Fig. 35: World map according to Herodotus. (Hyperborea is on the top. By S. Butler, 1907.)

An island, not smaller than Sicily and located beyond the land of the Celts, could certainly be a fitting description of Great Britain. The British archipelago had a warmer climate during the megalithic epoch than at present, so it would be perfectly apt for productive farming practices.

Diodorus continues his description of Hyperborea:

"Moreover, the following legend is told concerning it: Leto was born on this island, and for that reason Apollo is honored among them above all other gods (Fig. 36),[4] and the inhabitants are looked upon as priests of Apollo, after a manner, since daily they praise this god continuously in song, and honor him exceedingly. And **there is also on the island both a magnificent sacred precinct of Apollo and a notable temple which is adorned with many votive offerings and is spherical in shape.** *Furthermore, a city is there which is sacred to this god, and the majority of its inhabitants are players on the cithara; and these continually play on this instrument in the temple and sing hymns of praise to the god, glorifying his deeds."*

*Fig. 36: Apollo with the solar halo of Helios.
(Roman mosaic at El Djem, Tunisia, second c. AD.)*

The description of a notable spherical temple dedicated to a solar god could fit with any of the main stone rings in Great Britain, such as Stonehenge, Avebury or the Ring of Brodgar. The sacred city whose inhabitants are considered as priests of a solar god would match better with the proposed headquarters of the priests at Skara Brae, in the Orkney Islands.

Diodorus continues as follows:

*"They say also that the Moon, as viewed from this island, appears to be but a little distance from the Earth and to have upon it prominences, like those of the Earth, which are visible to the eye. The account is also given that **the god visits the island every nineteen years, the period in which the return of the stars to the same place in the heavens is accomplished**; and for this reason the nineteen-year period is called by the Greeks the year of Meton."*[5]

68 • SAILORS OF STONEHENGE

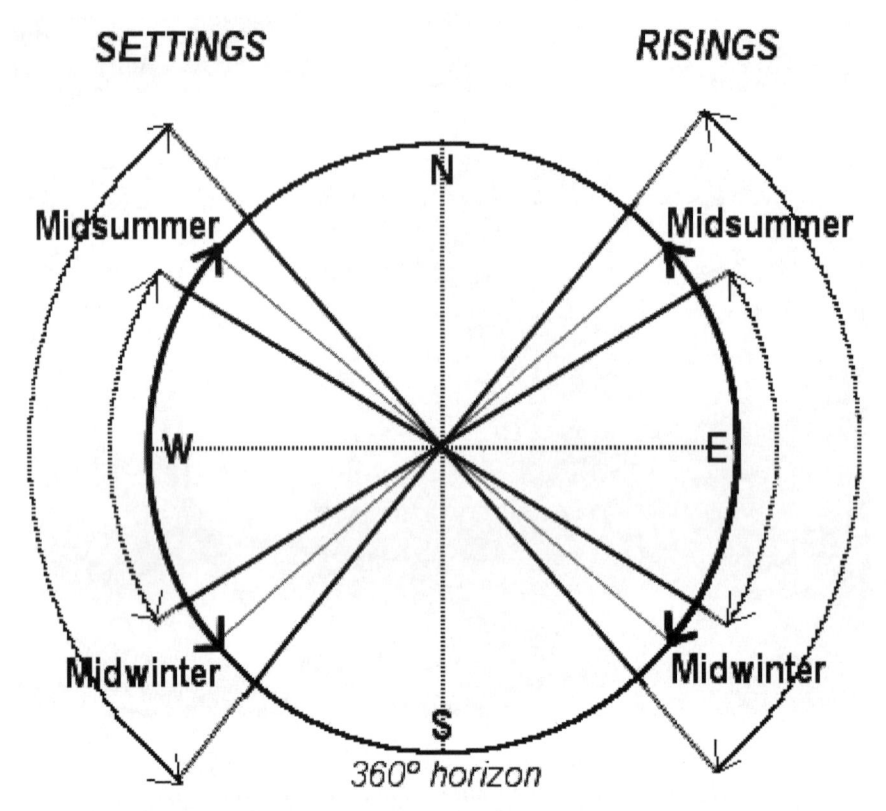

Fig. 37: Ranges of risings and settings over the horizon, covered by the Sun between solstices (range on the circle), and by the Moon between lunastices (major and minor ranges, outside the circle). (The values are for Stonehenge's latitude.)

The daily sunrisings (or sunsettings) move back and forth over the line of the horizon in a cycle of one year, always sweeping the same section of the horizon between the points that signal midsummer and midwinter.

In contrast, the risings (or settings) of the Moon cover different ranges from one cycle to the next, following a second cycle with a periodicity of 19 years, known as "Metonic." Due to this Metonic Cycle, the Moon can be seen rising (or setting) further north and south than the solar extremes, the difference being maximum during the "lunar major standstills." This phenomenon, referred to as "lunastice," is illustrated in Fig. 37.[6]

Fig. 38: Above, Recumbent Stone Circle of Easter Aquhorthies, with its recumbent stone flanked by a pair of standing stones. Below, Callanish Stones (Isle of Lewis).

A special type of stone rings, known as "recumbent stone circles," mostly present in the NE regions of Scotland, have a stone not standing but laid on its side, forming an artificial horizon that allows the contemplation of the full Moon at a lunastice skimming over its surface. Another example of a lunar observatory in Scotland could be at Callanish (Fig. 38), a group of standing stones on the Isle of Lewis where, during the lunastices, the full Moon near midsummer reaches only 3.5° above the horizon and is viewed between the stones of this monument. During the megalithic epoch, the remarkable event of a circumpolar full Moon (never setting in midwinter

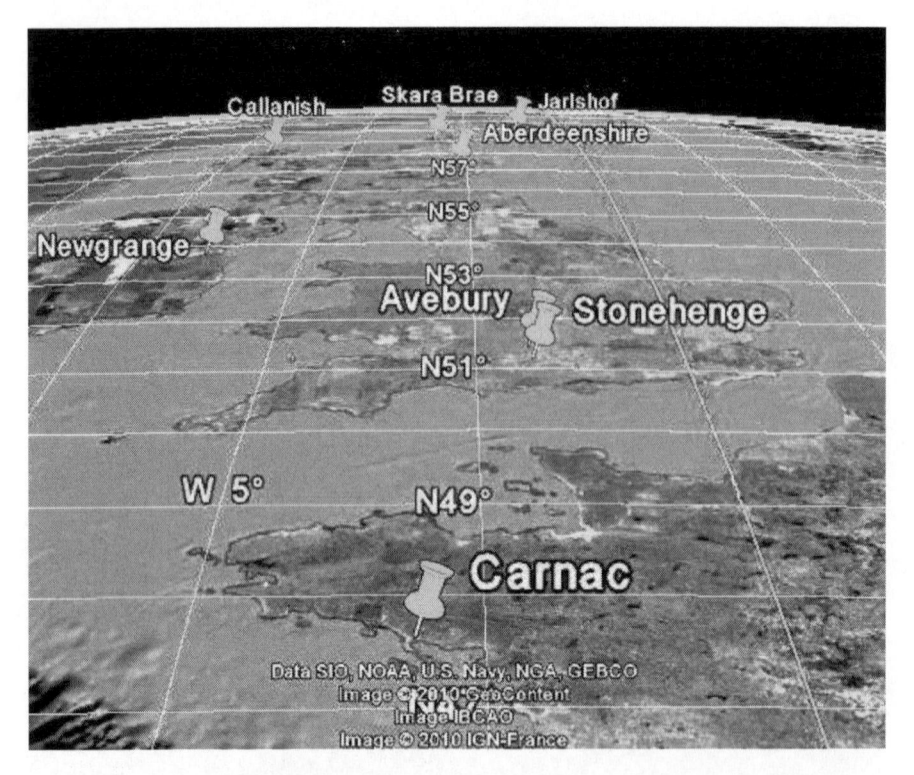

Fig. 39: The Scottish megalithic sites, located "above."

and never rising in midsummer) could be watched from the Shetland Islands.[7] At this remote archipelago there is also evidence of Neolithic activity as far back as the middle of the third millennium BC. In fact, structures similar to Skara Brae have been found in Jarlshof (in Shetland's Mainland Island).

This special connection between the Moon and the megalithic monuments located in the northernmost regions of Britain, together with the information presented about Hyperborea, could hint that this territory (mostly Scotland) was the source of the myth of Hyperborea—*"where the Moon appears to be but a little distance from the Earth."*

Probably, the priests would rule the religious affairs of the Hyperboreans or Megalith Builders "from above" (Fig. 39), according to a celestial calendar derived mainly from the cycles of the Sun and the Moon.[8]

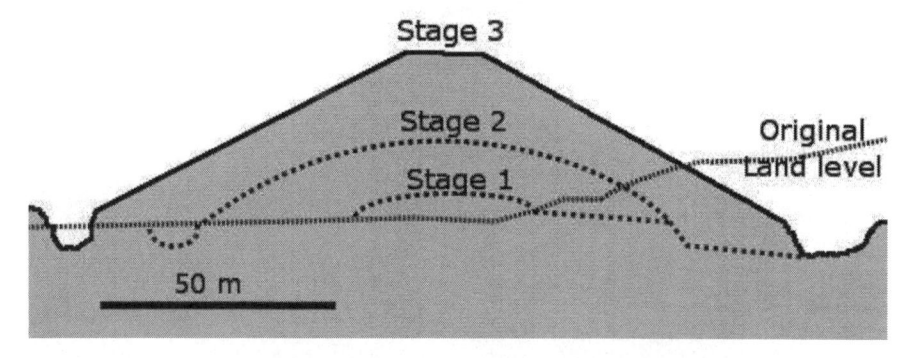

Fig. 40: Phases of construction of Silbury Hill, between the 28th and 24th centuries BC.

Diodorus wrote, *"The god visits the island every nineteen years, the period in which the return of the stars to the same place in the heavens is accomplished."*

We are considering as a working hypothesis that the Megalith Builders observed a celestial cycle to renew their monarchy, and tentatively proposed that it could be the arrival of Jupiter over Regulus every 12 years. However, if the Megalith Builders are connected with the myth of the Hyperboreans, then the previous quotation would suggest that the celestial cycle that they observed was not the revolution of Jupiter but the Metonic Cycle, when the Sun, the phase of the Moon, Earth and the stellar background are back in nearly the same relative orientations.[9]

Since we are proposing that the princes arrived at Avebury and Stonehenge to incarnate Orion during the monarchical renewal ceremony, this constellation could be perceived by the Megalith Builders as a "celestial god" who incarnated in the princes (at this island and during the lunastices).

After Avebury was replaced by Stonehenge, Silbury Hill would still continue to be visited by the princes immediately before the ceremony to embody Orion at that sacred place. This would explain why this hill was remodeled to its fullest expression whilst the rest of the complex had been already abandoned (Fig. 40).

*Fig. 41: Alignments of Carnac.
Each stone represented a king ruling during a Metonic Cycle.*

We may even speculate on the possibility that some of the stones used to remodel Stonehenge were already taken directly from Avebury at that early time by the same megalithic constructors.

If the Hyperborean myth is related to the Megalith Builders, then we should reconsider our working hypothesis and establish the royal term as nineteen years. Maintaining the same line of argument that considered Carnac as the royal representational mausoleum of 250 successive kings, the proposed duration of the royal tenure would increase the total extent of the Megalith Builders' confederation from 3,000 (250 x 12) to 4,750 (250 x 19) years (Fig. 41).[10]

Diodorus gives another important clue about the Hyperboreans:

"And the kings of this city and the supervisors of the sacred precinct are called Boreadae, since they are descendants of Boreas, and **the succession to these positions is always kept in their family.**"

The succession in the Megalith Builders' royalty (and clergy) would be hereditary. Two Metonic Cycles would be necessary for a typical lifespan of 38 years. At the end of the first cycle, when the princes were 19, they should be crowned as kings, as well as get married to engender a descendant to replace them at the end of their mandate, 19 years later.[11]

Accepting a royal term of nineteen years does not invalidate the previous discussion about the design and purpose of Avebury and Stonehenge; it simply implies that it was the Moon instead of Jupiter the luminary that regulated the royal tenure. The celestial scene starring Leo and Orion would remain as the template upon which to model the ceremony.

The incorporation of the Metonic Cycle into the ceremony meant that the Megalith Builders managed to combine the brightest luminaries in the sky at their maximum elongations (lunastices and solstices), the Moon indicating a larger cycle of 19 years and the Sun a shorter annual one. Basically, the priests would have to observe three celestial events related to the ceremony: the lunastice to determine the year, the solstice to determine the day, and the heliacal rising of Rigel to determine the hour.

Summary

In this chapter we have proposed that the Megalith Builders chose the Orkney Islands to build a sacred city inhabited by an elite of priest-astronomers.

This archipelago was privileged because it was at the same meridian as Carnac and "above" the rest of the megalithic territories of Western Europe.

The myth of Hyperborea could be related to the Megalith Builders and the British Isles.

The Metonic Cycle of approximately nineteen years between lunastices determined the duration of the royal terms.

Endnotes

[1] Additionally, a recent archaeological site called Ness of Brodgar has been excavated between the Rings of Brodgar and Stenness, which has provided evidence of housing, decorated stone slabs, a massive stone wall with foundations, and a large building dubbed as "the cathedral."

[2] Latitude can be easily estimated by measuring the altitude over the horizon of the Celestial Pole (star Thuban in the megalithic epoch), and longitude by watching the movements of the Moon in relation to the rest of the luminaries. These observations are also relatively simple, especially on firm land; the main objection is that, to use this method, the Megalith Builders should have kept a sort of "almanac" with astronomic information. Could this be a clue to interpret some of their megalithic art? *"Bishop Browne, who in 1919 studied these markings [carvings on stone circles in Scotland], discovered that many of them were accurately arranged to form patterns of various constellations of the heavenly bodies. But in every case the image was reversed as if the stars were reflected in a mirror."* Quoted from *The New View over Atlantis*, by John Michell, Thames & Hudson Ed., p. 33 (1983)

[3] Book II-47, by Diodorus Siculus (first c. BC), in *The Library of History of Diodorus Siculus*, published in Vol. II of the Loeb Classical Library (1935 edition); available online at: penelope.uchicago.edu

[4] In Greek mythology, Leto was the mother of the solar God Apollo. Helios and Apollo were originally different gods—sometimes Helios was considered a titan— though over time they became the same God Sol (the Sun-God of the Romans).

[5] Meton was an Athenian astronomer of the fifth century BC, credited with the discovery of a lunar cycle of ca. 19 years.

[6] The Moon moves around the Earth in a plane tilted 5.1º relative to the plane of the Ecliptic, which causes it to be able to rise and set further north than the Sun in midsummer and further south than the sun in midwinter. Once every 18.61 years, when the Moon rises and sets at its extremes, it experiences a major lunar standstill or lunastice for about one year. The suitability of calling this phenomenon "luna-stice" is based on its equivalence to "sol-stice" (from Latin *sun-stop*), in reference to the Sun rising and setting for three days over the same points of the horizon at the extremes of its range before reversing its movement. (9.3 years after a major lunar standstill, there is a "lunar minor standstill," which would qualify also as a lunastice; however,

unless otherwise indicated, that term will refer only to the major lunar standstill.) At a lunastice, the Moon covers the maximum range of the horizon in one single cycle, i.e. its risings (and settings) sweep the largest possible section of the horizon. It takes approximately one month to go back and forth one full cycle, so the Moon passes in only two weeks from transiting very high in the sky to do it very low. The elongation (the range or section of the horizon covered) grows with the latitude, so the higher the latitude the more conspicuous this phenomenon is, especially when the Moon is full. For example, at the equator (0º of latitude) the Moon rises during a lunastice 5.1º further north than the Sun, but in the Orkney Islands (59º of latitude) that difference extends up to 16.2º. The full Moon can occur only when it is at the opposite side of the Sun, so, given that in summer the sun sets on the NW, the full Moon must rise from the SE. This implies that the full Moon close to both solstices rises the furthest south in midsummer, and the furthest north in midwinter. One of the peculiarities of Stonehenge's latitude is that the axes of the lunastices are perpendicular to the axes of the solstices, possibly another factor that the Megalith Builders took into consideration when choosing its location.

[7] The Earth's axial tilt has decreased by about half a degree (from 24.1º to 23.5º) since the megalithic epoch, which affects the accuracy with which some celestial phenomena can be seen at present compared to the past.

[8] The Thornborough Henges are located in North Yorkshire, England, and they are considered the most important megalithic complex between Stonehenge and the Orkney Islands. Their main element consists of three huge connected henges, aligned as if mirroring the three stars of Orion's Belt. Due to its location, dimensions and layout, this monument was most likely also related to the royalty and clergy of the Megalith Builders.

[9] It takes a Metonic Cycle (19 years, or 235 lunations, or 6939 days) for the Moon to return with the same phase to the same spot in the sky. (To be precise, 19 tropical years are briefer than 235 synodic months by about 2 hours, so the Metonic Cycle's error is one full day every 219 years.)

[10] At Carnac, the modules of Le Ménec and Kermario, representing each 100 kings in each row, would correspond to 1,900 instead of 1,200 years, while Kerlescan, representing the last 50 kings, would serve for 950 instead of 600 years. Assuming the 12th century BC as

the end of the confederation, then its origin would go back into the early sixth millennium BC (1200 + 4750 = 5950 BC), at the onset of the Neolithic.

[11] In the case of Jupiter functioning as the celestial marker, the princes should have a descendant at the young age of 12 to replace them 24 years later. Although biologically possible, it seems less reasonable than at the more developed age of 19.

6
NEWGRANGE

IN this chapter we are going to deal with one of the most spectacular megalithic monument: Newgrange, in Ireland (photo above). But first we must investigate more deeply the ceremony of monarchical renewal to reveal the religious substrate that underlined the political one aforementioned.

Hierosgamos

When the function of Avebury's complex was first described, it was proposed that the two inner circles within the henge represented Leo and Cancer, and that the regicides took place at the north one (Leo). However, the south one representing Cancer was not explained. Leo is the solar zodiacal sign because it was visited by the Sun in midsummer, whereas the previous one, Cancer, is traditionally considered its counterpart, the lunar sign (Fig. 42).

Fig. 42: Traditional representations of the Sun and the Moon. A king holds a shining mirror (Sun) in front of a lion (Leo), and a woman holds a horn (Moon) in front of a crab (Cancer). (Heinrich Decimator in "De stellis fixis et erratici," Germany, 16th c.)

Inside the circle of Cancer was 'The Obelisk', whereas inside that of Leo was 'The Cove' (Fig. 43). This manifest pair of "phallus-womb" symbols suggests a masculine-feminine dichotomy at play, with the masculine element in the lunar circle and the feminine in the solar.[1] Some basic symbolism could help us to explain this apparent paradox. Thus, a phallus in Cancer could be symbolically interpreted as "life in queen," whereas a cove in Leo would mean "death in king."

Hierosgamos (from the Greek *holy marriage*) is a well-known anthropological custom among many cultures, where couples representing deities embrace in sexual union epitomizing the harmonization of opposites. The explained symbolism suggests that hierosgamos may have also been practiced by the Megalith Builders' monarchy, where the kings represented the Sun and the queens represented the Moon. If so, besides the ceremony to renew the monarchy, they would also celebrate the royal weddings or holy marriages.

Fig. 43: Left, the concrete pyramid indicating where The Obelisk was erected, in the center of the southern inner circle. Right, The Cove, in the center of the northern inner circle. (Both inside Avebury's henge.)

Given the proximity of Cancer to Leo, the Moon transiting over Cancer would be in the last days of its waning crescent phase, moving towards the new Moon that occurred while transiting over Leo (Regulus). The next new Moon after the heliacal rising of Rigel, when the Sun and the Moon were joined in the sky, would be the most propitious time for the kings recently crowned to celebrate hierosgamos. This ceremony would occur within the south circle ("life in queen"), at night and in complete darkness (new Moon), imitating their celestial models, who would also be joined below the horizon, "under them." This union would have the practical purpose of engendering the princes and princesses—the future kings and queens nineteen years later—according to a sacred ceremony related to the pair of brightest luminaries.

For the Megalith Builders, if Great Britain was sacred to some "celestial god," that would be Orion. Since we are supposing that the Neolithic inhabitants of this island were the Hyperboreans, it would be interesting to investigate the mythological relationship that exists between Orion and Apollo (the solar god worshiped by the Hyperboreans). In the Greek pantheon, Apollo & Artemis were two of the main gods, the twin children of Zeus (Fig. 44). Apollo was a male god of healing (life) associated with the Sun, whereas his sister Artemis was the goddess of hunting (death) associated with the Moon.

Fig. 44: Apollo and Artemis. (Attic red-figure cup, fifth c. BC.)

Both Apollo and Artemis were intimately related to Orion's fate, because Artemis fell in love with him but Apollo disapproved of the relationship. Orion was not a full god but a demigod, the result of the union of Poseidon—God of the Oceans—with a mortal woman. Apollo decided expediently to prevent his sister's "deviant love" for a non-pedigree god by sending a giant scorpion that killed Orion.[2] Artemis was very upset with her brother and translated Orion into a constellation. Later, Apollo also made the scorpion into the Scorpius constellation, so it could forever chase the demigod across the heavens. That is why, when Scorpio rises over the horizon, Orion goes down on the other side, and vice versa.

The fact that Apollo was a solar god but the Hyperboreans observed a lunar cycle to welcome his arrival to their land could be paradoxical; nonetheless, this mythological integration between

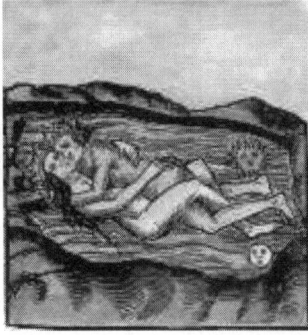

Fig. 45: Woodcuts of the alchemical treatise "Rosarium philosophorum." (Uncertain authorship, Germany, 16th c.)

solar and lunar principles seems very fitting to the solar-lunar integration at play in Avebury. In fact, the myth resolves the tension between the pair of twin gods, manifested in Apollo's disapproval of his sister's relationship with a demigod, in a way that would resonate with Avebury's ultimate function. Apollo's dislike of Orion would be a metaphor for the existence of a solar principle that is immortal, whereas Artemis's fondness for Orion would be the same metaphor applied to a lunar principle that is mortal. The dichotomy between these antagonistic principles (Apollo-solar-immortal vs. Artemis-lunar-mortal) is resolved by Orion's heroic journey in the sky, dying to be reborn again and again in a never ending cycle. This myth could therefore provide a glimpse into the Megalith Builders' understanding about existence, seen as a continuous cycle of births and deaths.

Spiritual Technology

We may now propose a deeper layer of meaning in the design of Avebury and Stonehenge. The Megalith Builders would have managed to gain some control over the process of death and rebirth, and they could have designed these monuments in order to make the kings "immortal" in the same fashion as Orion, i.e. dying to be reborn again as princes. The kings, like Orion, would consider themselves demigods, possessing an immortal spirit in a mortal body (Fig. 45).[3]

82 • SAILORS OF STONEHENGE

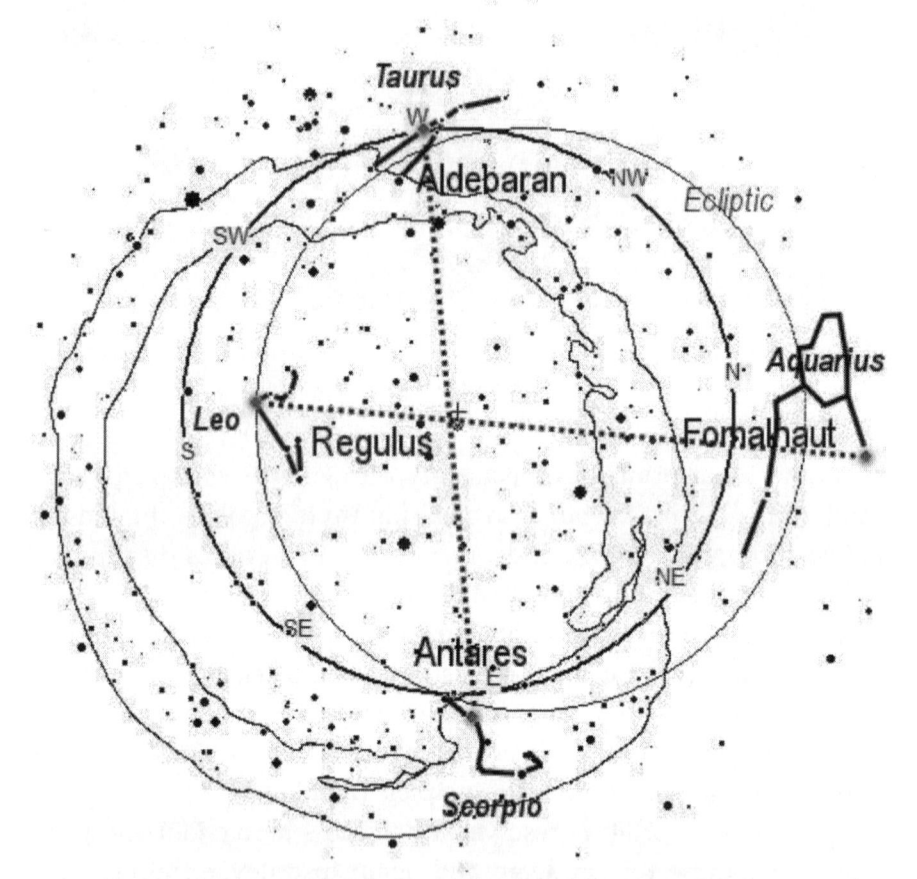

Fig. 46: Royal Stars: Regulus, Fomalhaut, Aldebaran and Antares, in the four sectors of the Zodiac, signaling the solstices and equinoxes in the megalithic epoch. (2300 BC, equatorial coordinates.)

At Avebury, the following full Moon after the kings were crowned would be seen skimming over the southern horizon. This peculiar full Moon would transit over Aquarius (opposite of Leo), a constellation that has no bright stars (third magnitude and higher); however, in the near one of Piscis Austrinus, there is a star of first magnitude called Fomalhaut—very similar in brightness to Regulus—that could have been perceived as the "lunar abode," likewise Regulus would be the "solar abode."

In fact, close to the Ecliptic, there are four first magnitude stars in each of the four quarters of the Zodiac which signaled the solstices

Fig. 47: Pair of stones in the southern inner circle inside Avebury's henge, with lozenge and elongated shapes.

and equinoxes during the megalithic epoch: Regulus, Fomalhaut, Aldebaran and Antares, in the constellations of Leo, Aquarius, Taurus and Scorpio respectively (Fig. 46).[4]

At Stonehenge, the following full Moon after midwinter would be part of a spectacular event, because it rose from its northernmost limit, over the entrance and Heelstone, while the Sun was setting on the opposite side. It seems reasonable to think that the Megalith Builders observed this celestial scene perhaps by celebrating the royal weddings, although they would still wait for the following new Moon two weeks later to begin hierosgamos.

The Megalith Builders might have designed these complexes using a sort of "spiritual technology" as a way to gain immortality. The henge would be designed, according to their beliefs, to contain the spirits of the sacrificed kings, so as to transfer them at the right moment to the conceived grandchildren.

At Avebury, The Cove would play the role of retaining the spirits, and The Obelisk the role of transferring them into the queens' wombs, which would resolve the paradoxical interchange of solar and lunar attributes between both circles.

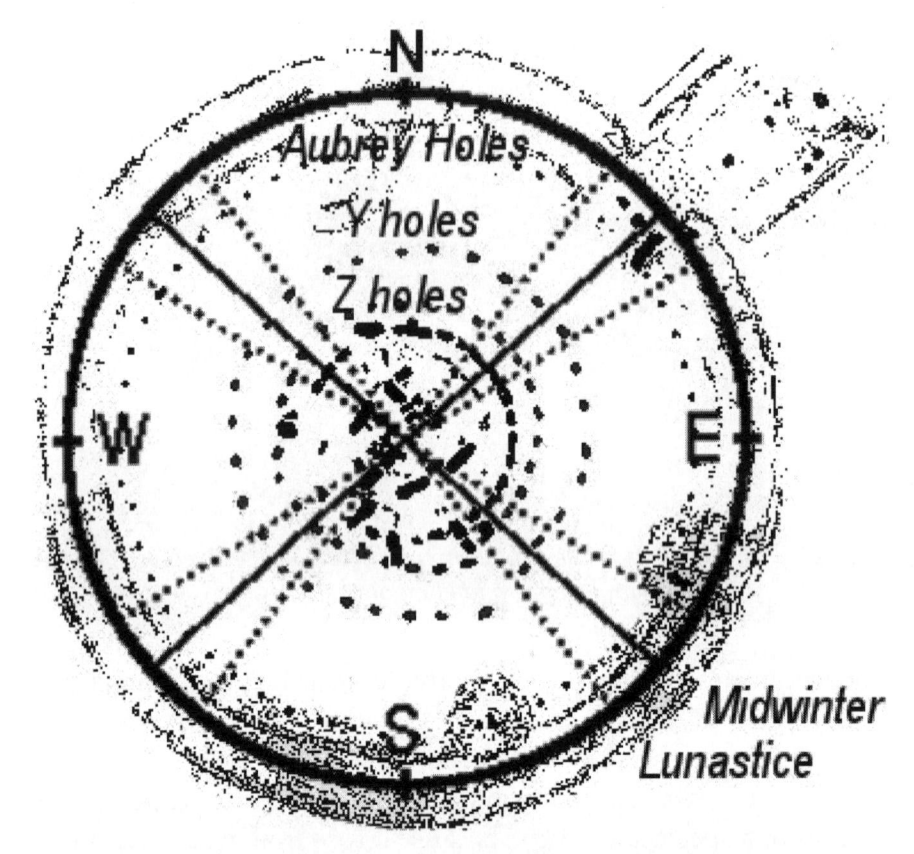

Fig. 48: The three rings of holes within Stonehenge known as Y, Z and Aubrey Holes. (Solstices and lunastices' directions are indicated.)

There are some minor details in the design of the henge that could also be explained under this "spiritual technology" hypothesis. The stones forming the avenues and some of the rings have the peculiarity of pairing one elongated stone with one with a lozenge shape, thus recreating the union of both solar (elongated-masculine) and lunar (lozenge-feminine) principles (Fig. 47).

Curiously, the avenues of Avebury do not join the henge directly but were deliberately crooked just at the juncture, perhaps as a way to prevent the entering or exiting of "spirits" in and out of the henge, channeled (or contained) by the stones forming the avenues and rings.

In the chapter dedicated to Stonehenge, we did not discuss the purpose of the last structural design introduced in the monument: two rings of pits dug around the Sarsen Circle, known as Y & Z Holes (ca. 5 ft / 1.5 m deep) (Fig. 48).[5]

There are 30 holes in the outer Y ring and 29 in the inner Z ring, numbers that immediately bring to mind the idea of a possible relationship with the Moon, on account of the days it takes to complete a cycle of phases (new to full, and back to new), known as the synodic period (29.5 days).[6]

The Y & Z rings have a manifest discontinuity about the direction of the lower lunastice moonrise (Fig. 48). Therefore, it could be proposed that one of the rings could serve to register the phases of the Moon day by day, starting from the new Moon indicated by the first hole in the direction of the low lunastice. But, why would they dig a second almost identical ring?

Gerald Hawkins—and later Fred Hoyle in more detail—proposed that both rings could have served to predict eclipses,[7] as a kind of "Neolithic abacus," but their provocative idea was proved inconsistent by its detractors and nowadays is completely abandoned. Nonetheless, these rings could have served, indeed, to monitor the phases of the Moon, but for a different purpose than predicting eclipses. Given that both Avebury and Stonehenge were the venues where the next princes and princesses were engendered, the careful observation of the Moon would be of crucial importance to guarantee the success of this goal, because the synodic period is almost identical to the menstrual period (a phenomenon noticed in most cultures).[8]

Since it was crucial that the queens got pregnant during the ceremony, the Megalith Builders should be precise and practical in choosing the time when the queens were most fertile. The window of women's fertility is located in the days farthest apart from the menstruation onset, so they only needed this piece of information to choose the optimum night for each couple. The construction of the Y & Z Holes rings would be, therefore, related to the issue of enhancing the chances of the queens getting pregnant during hierosgamos.

The outer Y ring could serve to track the Moon's phase, whereas the inner Z ring could serve to mark the menstrual phase of each queen. This could be done by recording the Moon's phase on the first day of their last menstruation, a day that would be signaled by inserting a special stone or pole in the corresponding hole of the Z ring. The week before and after this mark, the queen would not be fertile, whereas it would be crucial that the sexual union took place when the Moon's marker in the Y ring was transiting at the opposite side from the queen's marker in the Z ring. Each of the dozen or so queens would have their own marker in the Z ring, and all the procedures relating to the hierosgamos celebration would be planned according to specific rites of fertility aimed to enhance pregnancy.

From a political point of view, success in the queens' becoming pregnant as a result of this ceremony was of maximum importance, because it guaranteed that 19 years later there would be an adult successor to the crown.[9] But we should also keep in mind the possibility of deeper reasoning; since they might have believed that the spirits of the sacrificed kings were reincarnated into their first-born grandchildren, it was vital that conception occurred at this time and place.

The children engendered during the ceremony would be born nine months later. The ceremony at Avebury was celebrated in midsummer so the future kings or queens would be born around the next vernal equinox, arriving with the Spring (when the Sun visited Taurus). At Stonehenge, the midwinter ceremony would result in these special children being born around the next autumnal equinox (when the Sun visited Scorpio).

The Royal Necropolis

So far we have proposed that the Megalith Builders built in Carnac their royal representational mausoleum, in the Orkney Islands the headquarters of a priestly elite, and in Avebury and Stonehenge the venues where they renewed their monarchy. Obviously, they had to develop fluvial and maritime navigational skills to travel both across land and alongside the Atlantic European coasts. These

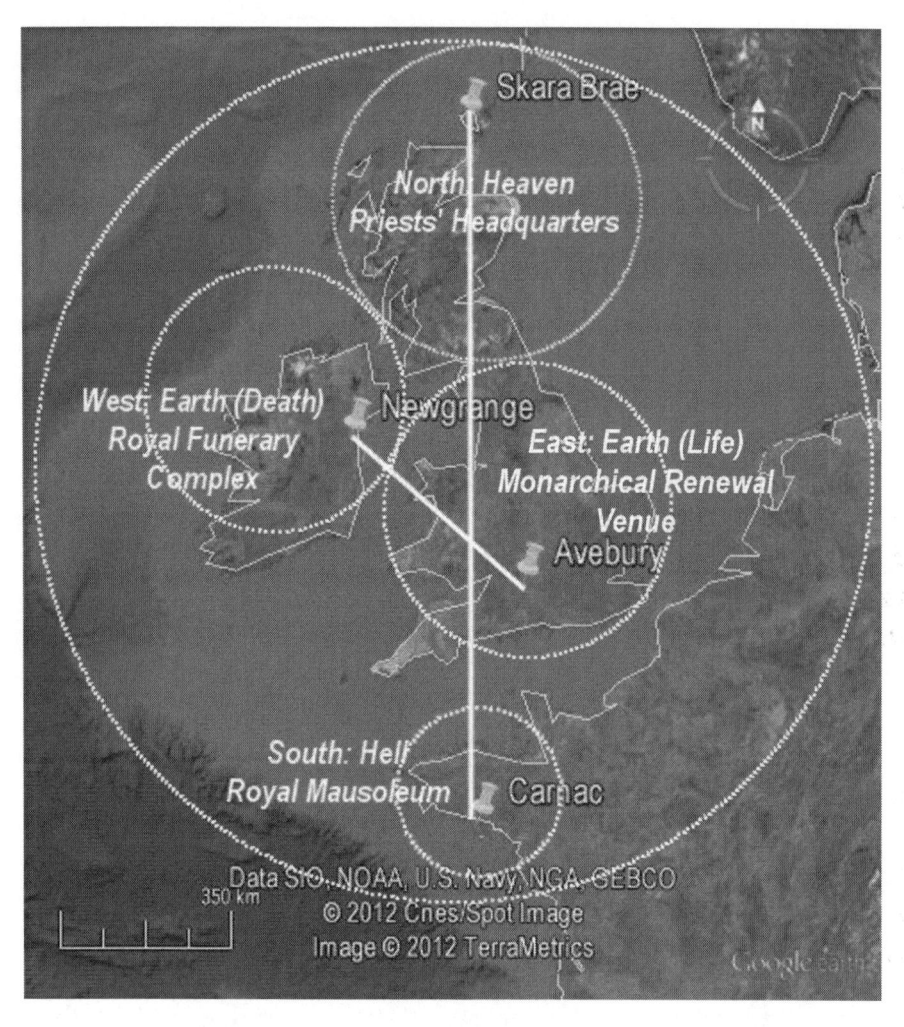

Fig. 49: Division of the Megalith Builders' territory in the NW of Europe. (The symbolism of the cardinal directions is indicated.)

skills needed to be developed enough to be able to create and maintain a more progressively interconnected network among locals.

By the fifth millennium BC, they began to dispose of their dead in communal graves constructed with large stones, a custom that spread throughout this and the next millennium. At the end of this period (end of the fourth millennium), the colossal royal monuments were erected, and half a millennium later—when Stonehenge was completed—a great sophistication in their designs was evident.

Fig. 50: Façade of Newgrange (Ireland).

The Orkney Islands and Carnac are aligned along the same meridian, a territorial disposition that suggests a division based on the cardinal directions, with a clear symbolism associated with each one (Fig. 49). Thus, the north with the priest's headquarters would be symbolically associated with Heaven, whereas the south and the royal mausoleum would be associated with Hell. The situation of Avebury and Stonehenge in between Orkney and Brittany suggests that England was part of the "realm of Earth," in between Heaven and Hell. In this middle-realm, the east and the renewal of the monarchy would be associated with life, whereas the west would be associated with death. If the Megalith Builders belonged to a solar culture that arranged their territory according to this basic symbolism related to the cardinal points, Ireland would be their western realm, the logical location for building the royal funerary complex or necropolis.

The passage mound known as Newgrange is, undoubtedly, one of the most spectacular megalithic monuments, and it was built, again, at the end of the fourth millennium BC (ca. 3100 BC) (Fig. 50). This monument is located in the northern inner side of a large meander of the Boyne River, where there are also other magnificent examples of passage mounds such as Knowth and Dowth (Fig. 51).

We may propose that, at the end of the monarchical renewal ceremony celebrated in Avebury in midsummer, the bodies of the sacrificed kings were transported by boat to Ireland, entered the

Fig. 51: Tumulus of Dowth and corridor of Knowth (Ireland).

mouth of the Boyne River and rowed up it for about 10 miles (15 km) until reaching Newgrange, where the corpses were disposed of. The fact that Newgrange is located in the exact direction of the midsummer sunset as watched from Avebury (azimuth ca. 310º) strongly supports their connection in purpose (see again Fig. 49).

Previously, we anticipated that the Megalith Builders could have designed Avebury—and very likely also Stonehenge—to transfer the spirits of the kings into the conceived grandchildren.

But, once the spirits were transmitted, why go through the tribulation of transporting their corpses to Newgrange? Why not, for instance, cremate them at the end of the ceremony? The dichotomy of the solar and lunar principles at play in Avebury could account for this.

The Megalith Builders understood life as a consequence of the union of two principles, one solar and one lunar, so they would understand death as the result of their separation. This belief would mean that they had two principles to deal with after death, that we may call "spirit" (solar principle) and "soul" (lunar principle) to better differentiate them. If the spirit was related to an immortal principle that begets life, then it would be the spirit that was transmitted during hierosgamos to engender a new royal life. Correspondingly, the soul should be related to the mortal principle of the flesh, so it would stay for a while within the mortal remains.

The Megalith Builders might also seek to gain some control over the transference of the souls from the corpses to some preferential destiny. If their intention was to transport the sacrificed kings to the most advantageous location at which to liberate their souls at the most favorable moment, then, very likely they would have developed a technique of mummification that prevented the decay of the corpses, so as to retain the souls inside until the optimum conditions for their liberation were met.

Newgrange is facing SE, towards midwinter sunrise (and towards Avebury). At this time of the year, the rays of the Sun penetrate through a box above the entrance to illuminate the rear chamber, which suggests that the funerary services were performed on that date. The kings were sacrificed at Avebury in midsummer, half a year before, so their corpses would be of necessity be mummified. This might be done at The Longstones, a kind of "cove" built in the Beckhampton Avenue, because this avenue lies to the west of the main henge and was for the exclusive use of the kings. Furthermore, The Longstones were built very close to the Beckhampton and South Street Long Barrows (Fig. 12, p. 31), perhaps recycled from pre-existing communal graves into chambers involved in the process of mummifying the kings (Fig. 52).

Fig. 52: Beckhampton Long Barrow. (Sketch by W. Stukeley, 17th c.)

The mummies would be transported to Newgrange where they would be kept inside until midwinter. Then, they would be taken out to liberate the souls, probably by cremation, sending them up to the sky with the smoke of the pyres. (In a following chapter we will argue that the final destiny of the souls may be Sirius, the brightest star of the night sky.)

If the Megalith Builders believed that after dying it was mandatory for the soul to visit hell, the purpose of the representational mausoleum at Carnac—in the territory symbolically associated with the hell—perhaps was not a memorial monument for the worship of ancestors, but a megalithic device designed to evade this terrible ordeal, by trading souls for rocks.

The change of dates in the celebration of the monarchical renewal ceremony, from summer to winter solstice (from Avebury to Stonehenge), had to cause an alteration in the customary dealing with the bodies of the sacrificed kings. As a matter of fact, the passage tombs of the Boyne River were not active from the second half of the third millennium BC onwards, so Newgrange and the rest of the monuments in this Irish "Royal Valley of the Kings" would serve as temporary royal tombs only for the kings sacrificed at Avebury. Once the monarchical renewal ceremony was moved to Stonehenge, they ceased to be used anymore; instead, the Megalith

Builders changed the final destiny of their mummified kings. (This issue is not discussed in this book, but we can anticipate that the new land of the west, where the mummies of the kings sacrificed at Stonehenge were transported, was America.)

Summary

In this chapter we have proposed that Avebury and Stonehenge were built with a deeper purpose than the mere political renewal of the monarchy. Their builders designed these monuments to transfer the spirits of the slaughtered kings to the princes engendered on site, in order to maintain the unbroken lineage of a single solar principle reborn in successive kings.

The Moon and the queens played a key role in the process. The royal weddings and hierosgamos served to engender the princes and princesses who would reign over the next lunastice. The Y & Z Holes of Stonehenge helped to determine the optimum moment to celebrate these unions.

The Megalith Builders divided the British Isles and the Brittany Peninsula into four quadrants, and built their main royal monuments on this territory in terms of a cosmic symbolism associated with each cardinal direction.

They considered that there were two principles (spirit and soul) whose union gave rise to life and whose separation resulted in death.

Newgrange and the rest of the Boyne Valley monuments in Ireland were the royal necropolis where the Megalith Builders deposited temporarily the mummies of the kings sacrificed at Avebury.

Endnotes

[1] The layout and principle contained in this arrangement would be similar to that in the Asian symbol of *yin & yang*, with each half containing a dot belonging to the other half.

[2] There are different versions of Orion's death. In one, Apollo challenges Artemis to hit with an arrow something over the sea, and she, unaware that the target was Orion's head, killed him. In another, it is Gaia (Mother Earth) who sent up the giant scorpion to kill Orion for bragging he could hunt down all the beasts on Earth.

[3] The "hierosgamos theme" appears frequently in the medieval alchemical tradition, where the more explicit regenerative purpose of the union goes along with a deeper and ultimately transformative purpose represented in Christian iconography as Christ reborn, a tradition that could have had its origins much earlier than currently supposed. Thus, the alchemical tradition can provide some "anachronistic" images to illustrate this process. The *Rosarium philosophorum* treatise contains 20 woodcuts, and those in Fig. 45 correspond to the first, fifth and last. In the first, the Sun, Moon and stars hover above a round fountain; the fifth shows the explicit union of a king and a queen in a pond with the Sun and the Moon discs, and the lasts depicts the Risen Christ holding a banner similar to St George's Cross.

[4] These stars were known in Persia as the Royal Stars, an appropriate name also for the Megalith Builders' culture of much earlier origin.

[5] There is another ring of holes, called Aubrey Holes, around the inside of the inner bank. The great difference in the time span between this and the Y & Z Holes seems to indicate that they were designed for different purposes. We proposed that the Aubrey Holes could be related to the inner bank functioning as an artificial horizon, so they could serve to monitor the evolution of the sky during the ceremony. There are 56 holes in the Aubrey ring, which could form an octagon of seven markers per side oriented towards the cardinal and intermediate directions.

[6] The synodic period is the time between two consecutive identical phases of the Moon (29.5 days), so it is a measurement of the Moon's illumination relative to the Sun as observed from the Earth. Since the Earth orbits around the Sun, the sidereal period measured against the stars is shorter (27.3 days) than the synodic.

[7] *Stonehenge: A Neolithic Computer*, by G. S. Hawkins, Nature, vol. 202, pp. 1258-61 (1963). *Stonehenge: An Eclipse Predictor*, by F. Hoyle, Nature, vol. 211, pp. 454-7 (1966)

[8] The information we have about Sabbats comes mostly from the reports of Catholic priests during the trials of witches, but, in spite of the obvious distortions, the elements mentioned: women, nights, mountains or forests, Moon, processions and dances in circle, banquets, hallucinogens, mass and orgies all seem to be arcane allusions to a hierosgamos celebration. The equivalent of Sabbat in Basque language is *Akelarre* which means "field of the goat," and the outstanding presence of a black goat in the Sabbats was also frequently mentioned. Later in the book, we will see the tremendous importance that Aries constellation—represented as a goat or ram—had for the Megalith Builders.

[9] Being a confederation of kingdoms guaranteed that, in case of infertility or fatality, there would always be enough royal progeny among them—brothers and sisters of the first-born—to solve a crisis of succession. If this endogamic practice was common among the monarchy of the dozen or so kingdoms, with the passing of generations it could be expected that they had to face genetic disorders, a risk that increases in the offspring of consanguineous relationships.

7
JASON & THE ARGONAUTS

IN this chapter we are going to learn about the Megalith Builders' mobility, by studying one of the oldest myths of classical Greece: *Jason and the Argonauts*.[1] This myth may contain information about the adventures of the princes, who, in imitation of Orion in the sky, sailed on Eridanus' reflection before being crowned.

The Expeditions

"Westerners have singularly narrowed the history of the world in grouping the little that they knew about the expansion of the human race around the peoples of Israel, Greece and Rome. Thus they have ignored all those travelers and explorers who in their ships ploughed the China Sea and the Indian Ocean, or rode across the immensities of Central Asia to the Persian Gulf. In truth the larger part of the globe, containing cultures different from those of the ancient Greeks and Romans but no less civilized, has remained unknown to those who wrote the history of their little world under the impression that they were writing world history."

Many would argue that historiography has advanced much from the time Henri Cordier wrote these words about one century ago,[2] but we are still far from admitting our great ignorance about the capacity to travel of prehistoric peoples. As we are going to expound, the Megalith Builders of Western Europe were fundamentally a maritime culture, and one of the first to develop the capacity to navigate in the open seas.

Several independent naval traditions — all already rooted in the Upper Paleolithic Age — appeared in the world. Frames of reeds coated with leather, like those carved in some Nordic regions, were among the oldest. Dugouts (hollowed tree trunks) were another line of evolution, and the oldest archaeological remnant of a boat is precisely that, a dugout canoe, dating from the eighth millennium BC (found in Holland). A third line of evolution was the use of intertwined plants such as reed, papyrus or totora. These three naval traditions appeared in different environments not necessarily connected in time or place, although the possibility of interactions and influences among them could have happened. The second of the traditions mentioned — dugout boats — is considered to be the precursor of plank-boats, a revolutionary breakthrough in naval technology that would be crucial in the ability to travel long distances.

One of the most important archaeological discoveries of boats took place in Great Britain, when three prehistoric boats were found in the mouth of the Humber River (North Ferriby, East Yorkshire). The boats were built using oak planks stitched together with yew withies, caulked with moss and capped with watertight oak laths.

Fig. 53: Prehistoric boat with sails, carved at Pedornes (Galicia, Spain).

The best preserved boat had room for up to eighteen paddlers and was adapted to seafaring in shallow waters. The radiocarbon dating indicates that this tradition of naval architecture had to be already mature by the end of the third millennium BC.[3]

The distance between Brittany and the Orkney Islands in the north is the same as between this French peninsula and the Strait of Gibraltar in the south (ca. 800 miles / 1,300 km), so the Megalith Builders would know perfectly where the gateway into the Mediterranean Sea was located. The Iberian Peninsula would first be explored by seafaring around its coasts. In fact, several prehistoric anchors made of stone have been found along the Atlantic coasts of Iberia, from Galicia to the Algarve. This is a good indication that seafaring navigation was already well established in the peninsula before the arrival of the Phoenicians in the first millennium BC.[4]

In addition, several carvings of boats have also been identified at these coastal regions. For example, at Borna Cove (Pontevedra, Galicia) there are boat-shaped petroglyphs similar to those that frequently appear in the Neolithic dolmens of Brittany.[5] Also, a more complex boat than those discovered in Borna—definitely able to navigate in the open-sea—was carved in Pedornes, also in Galicia (Fig. 53).[6]

Fig. 54: Probable painting of a boat in the Dolmen of Antelas (Portugal).

A painting could certify the antiquity of these naval representations. In the Dolmen of Antelas (north of Portugal), a probable boat was painted on one of its orthostats (vertical stones) (Fig. 54).[13] Since the image was painted instead of carved, the radiocarbon dating could be assessed from an organic sample taken directly from the painting, which eliminated the uncertainty about its antiquity. The analyses indicated that this dolmen was in use between 4340 and 3140 BC, i.e. between the fifth and fourth millennium BC. If we admit that this Neolithic painting represents a boat, it would be one of the oldest known, and would shift the onset of navigation in Europe back several millennia from the date at present estimated. (Moreover, the image resembles a planked boat adapted to navigate not only in the Mondego River that leads to the Dolmen of Antelas but also as a seafaring craft.)

There are also petroglyphs of boats with sails on the Iberian coasts besides that at Pedornes, such as those at Laja Alta near the Strait of Gibraltar, though their antiquity is more difficult to assess. Given the atmospheric conditions over the Atlantic Ocean—usually with winds blowing from northerly points of the compass—sails would help while navigating southwards, whereas rowing would be necessary to move northwards as well as in the rivers.

The Megalith Builders' ancestors, during the millennia that preceded Avebury's construction, would first explore their local habitat and would gradually travel into more distant regions by boats of regular size with mixed propulsion of sails and rowing, fit to navigate in the Atlantic Ocean. By the time they began to build their grandest monuments at Carnac, Avebury, the Orkneys and Newgrange, at the end of the fourth millennium BC, they should already have mastered the assembly of planked boats.

They certainly developed the technique of "mortise and tenon" joint, consisting of a "tongue" (tenon) that slots into a hole (mortise) cut in the mating piece, as it can be found in their most elaborate megalithic monument, at Stonehenge, where this kind of joint was used to secure the lintels above the standing stones (Fig. 55). If this technique was used with stones, the logical surmise would be that first they mastered it with wood prior to trying it out with stone. The framing of boats to assemble planks firmly would be one of its logical applications.

Fig. 55: The crow is perched on a tenon, in Stonehenge.

The main rivers would serve as ways to penetrate inland. For example, the Rhine River would be a route of penetration from the North Sea into central Europe and the Alpine regions. The Tagus River, the longest of the Iberian Peninsula, would allow sailors to penetrate into its interior. In particular, at the lower stretch of this river, in present day Portugal, the density of megalithic monuments is one of the highest in Europe, some of them dating from the early

Fig. 56: Megalithic temple of Tarxien (Malta).

fifth millennium BC, competing in antiquity with those in Brittany, which indicates that this location was another early hub of great importance for the Megalith Builders.

Besides the British Isles and the Peninsulas of Brittany and Iberia, the coasts of the Baltic and Mediterranean Seas would also be explored. Links would be established among the natives of all these lands reinforced by regular maritime routes, as the presence of megalithic monuments in all these territories witnesses (Fig. 2, p. 13). The Maltese group of islands, due to their position in the center of the Mediterranean Sea, had to have a great strategic value for a maritime culture. And, as expected, the Megalith Builders built on them some of their most spectacular temples between ca. 3500 and 2500 BC (Fig. 56). Diodorus even suggested a relationship between the Megalith Builders and the ancient Greeks when he wrote:[3]

"The Hyperboreans are most friendly disposed towards the Greeks, especially towards the Athenians and Delians [habitants of Delos, an early worshiping center of Apollo] who have inherited this good-will from most ancient times [...] **Abaris, a Hyperborean, came to Greece in ancient times** *and renewed the good-will and kinship of his people to the Delians."*

The Mediterranean coasts of Africa would offer fewer possibilities than the Europeans to go inland, with one great exception: the Nile River. They could navigate at least as far south as the First Cataract. This discovery would be a great breakthrough in their explorations because they could reach the Tropic of Cancer on the east side of Africa, as they would have also discovered that the Canary Islands lie near this tropic on the west side. A solar culture would give a profound symbolism to the geographic limit where the Sun reaches the zenith in midsummer, dividing the Earth above and below this parallel.

When the north seas were explored in their quest to find the northernmost point of Earth, they probably discovered Iceland, perhaps even Greenland. However, the cold weather at those high latitudes would prevent the establishment of long-term settlements and regular routes. Reaching the archipelago of the Azores in the middle of the Atlantic Ocean would be a great discovery.[7]

In general, we may advance the idea that the Megalith Builders would not arrive as conquerors, but as relatively small expeditions who would exchange goods, and overall knowledge, with the indigenous habitants of the lands they explored. Obviously, the monuments erected could not be uniform among such broad geographical locations, because they would depend heavily on the available materials and the degree of collaboration, demography and ingeniousness of the natives. Throughout centuries and generations, regular routes would be established connecting the most important destinations. Commerce would grow in importance and the bonds would grow tighter, particularly at those key places where priests settled among the natives.

The Myth

As we have already discussed, the myth of the Hyperboreans could be related to the Megalith Builders, yet there is also an equally ancient myth that contains even more explicit references to this correlation. That is the myth of *Jason and the Argonauts*, whose central theme is, appropriately, the renewal of the monarchy.

Succinctly, the kingdom of Iolcos (Thessaly, Greece) was reigned by Jason's uncle, Pelias, who had overthrown Jason's father, the

Fig. 57: Jason gives the Golden Fleece to Pelias.(Calyx, fourth c. BC.)

legitimate king. The myth begins with King Pelias receiving a prophecy which said that he was going to be deposed by someone wearing only one sandal.

Jason, on his way to meet Pelias to reclaim the throne, helped an old woman—the Goddess Hera in disguise—to wade a river, but ended up losing one of his sandals. Jason was later announced to Pelias as a man wearing only one sandal, so the king immediately knew that the man of the prophecy had arrived. Pelias agreed to cede the crown to his nephew under one condition, which Jason was forced to accept by means of a sly argumentation, and that was to fetch the Golden Fleece, a sacred ram's woolly skin (Fig. 57).[8] To fulfill this mission, Jason recruited a crew of about fifty great heroes who accompanied him aboard a ship called Argo, later immortalized in the sky as the Argo Navis constellation.

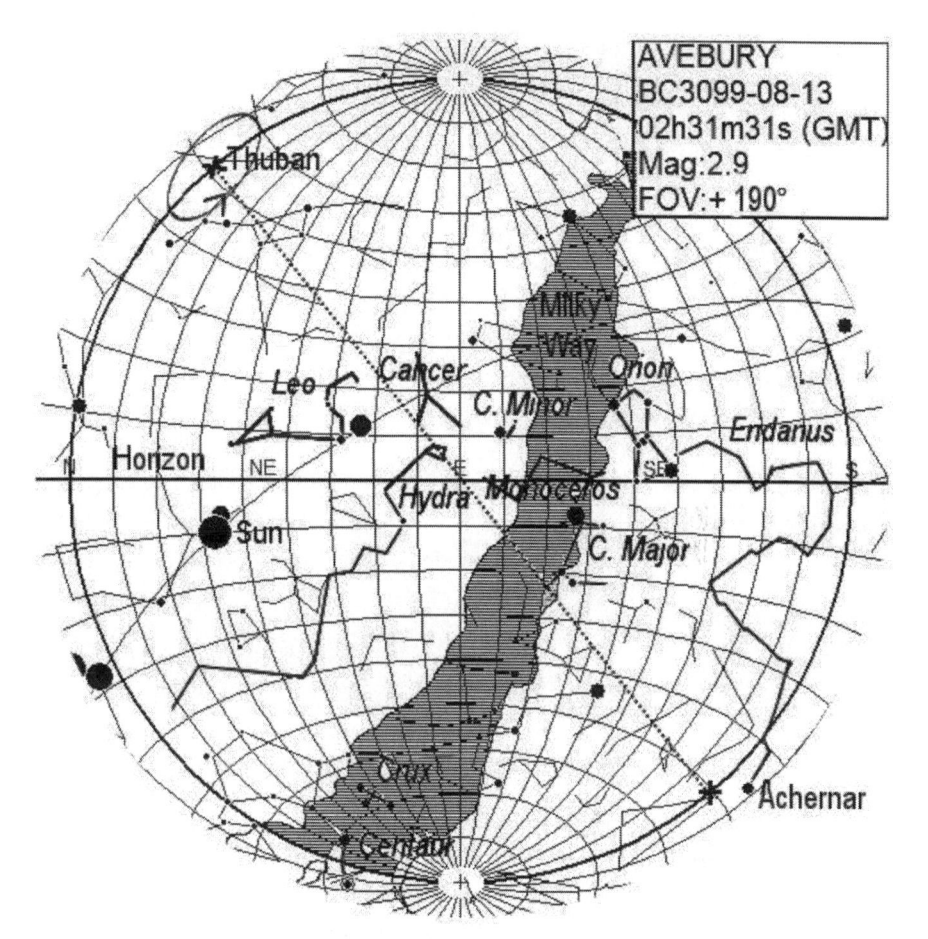

Fig. 58: The sky when Orion was rising tilted over the horizon of Avebury. (The poles of both hemispheres are also indicated.)

The eccentric prophecy of the "one sandal" gains its natural meaning when reconnected to its cosmic origin. The celestial scene that served as a template during the ceremony to renew the Megalith Builders' monarchy provides the link. The pair of stars that correspond to Orion's legs did not rise above the horizon at the same time, but Rigel rose ahead of Saiph (Fig. 58; Fig. 15, p. 34).

At Avebury, when one of "Orion's sandals" was still not visible, the princes left The Sanctuary heading towards the henge. Between Orion and Leo lies the Milky Way, which would explain why in the myth Jason loses his sandal while wading a river.

Fig. 59: "Dragon's teeth sown in furrows," or the Alignments of Carnac.

The connection between the Megalith Builders and the myth of *Jason and the Argonauts* is also detected in his trials. On one occasion, Jason must yoke a pair of fire-breathing bulls to plough and sow in the furrows some very unusual seeds: the teeth of a dragon. We could hardly find a more vivid allegory to describe the Alignments of Carnac than "dragon's teeth sown in furrows" (Fig. 59).

Moreover, according to the myth, prodigious warriors were born from each of the planted dragon's teeth, who Jason could defeat by throwing rocks among them. This could be again a reference to the mausoleum at Carnac, because it was built with rocks that represented the kings killed by the princes.

The allegorical picture begins to get clear. The myth of *Jason and the Argonauts* contains information pertaining to the Megalith Builders, particularly about the renewal of their kings, a very special event that unfolded according to their interpretation of some celestial cycles and constellations over a great expanse of territory.

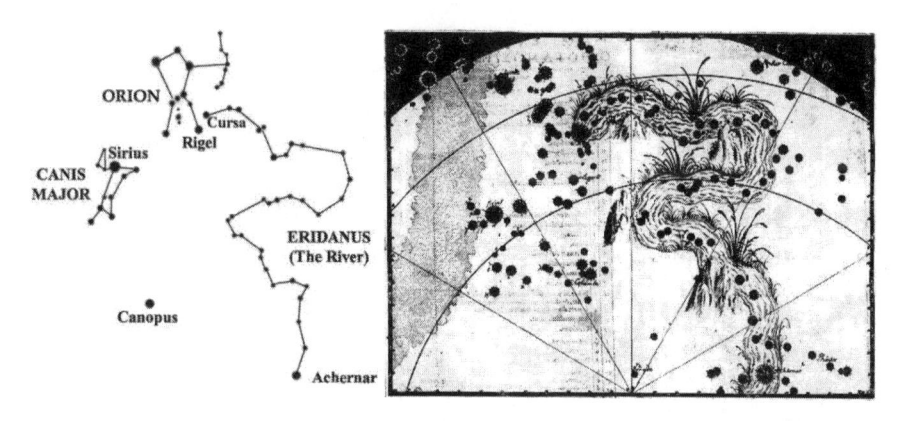

Fig. 60: Left, Eridanus in relation to Orion. Right, image by J. Bayer.

We have identified Avebury and Stonehenge as the ceremonial centers where the regicides took place, Carnac as the representational mausoleum, the Orkney Isles as the priesthood's headquarters, and Newgrange as the original necropolis. These locations serve to explain some of the megalithic royalty's movements, but, like Jason in the myth, the princes would also have to undergo an adventurous voyage before being crowned.

The Dark River

Eridanus is one of the constellations that cover the largest expanse of sky, represented as a meandering celestial river stretching between the stars Cursa—next to the left foot of Orion (Rigel)—and Achernar, a very bright star located at the bottom of the southern hemisphere (Fig. 60).[9] As a result of this celestial layout, Orion seems to arrive at his place in the sky after navigating along a celestial river born at the bottom of the celestial sphere.

The myth of *Jason and the Argonauts* was already mentioned by the early Greek authors, but Apollonius of Rhodes (Alexandria, third century BC) was who compiled, interrelated and elaborated the mythical material in the epic *Argonautica*. This epic voyage should contain information about the original one that gave birth to the myth, that of the Megalith Builders' princes previous to their crowning. Indeed Jason and the Argonauts had to navigate the Eridanus River.[10]

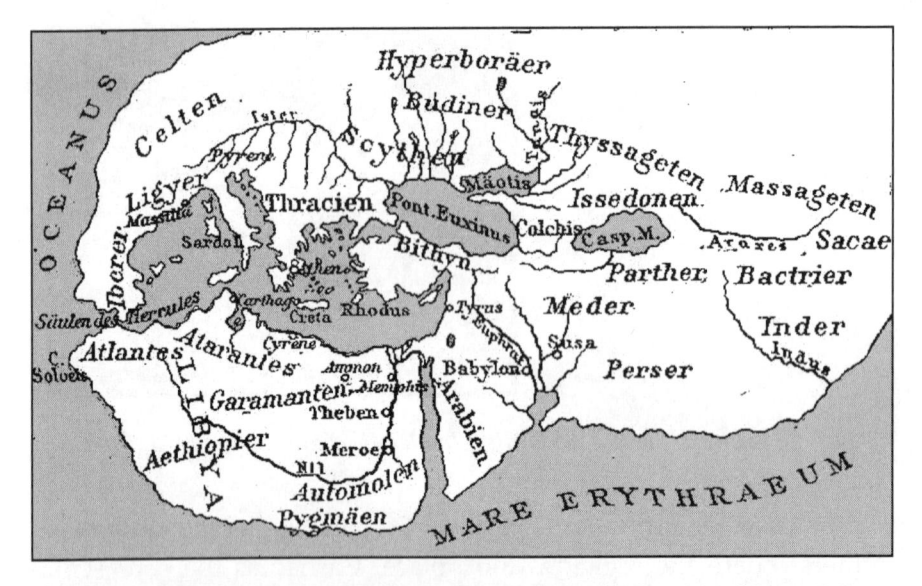

Fig. 61: World Geography according to Herodotus in the fifth c. BC.

Homer wrote that Eridanus was the Ocean River that surrounded the Earth, and other Greek authors wrote that it was a fabulous river in the NW regions of Europe.[11] However, this constellation belongs to the southern hemisphere, so it would be more logical to look for an equivalent river at lower latitudes. Following this reasoning, Eratosthenes and other erudite authors—Germanicus, Higinius, Alphonse X The Wise—proposed the Nile River as the equivalent on Earth of Eridanus. This consistent tradition of associating Eridanus with important real rivers could be more than a literary convention, perhaps it was a form of maintaining a tradition that had its origin with the Megalith Builders, for whom these stars reflected on the waters navigated by their princes before being crowned as the new kings.

Herodotus, the great geographer among the classical Greek authors, gave us a good idea about the limited geographical knowledge of the Greeks in the fifth century BC. The map in Fig. 61 is based on his descriptions. The Danube (Ister) and Nile (Nil) Rivers were supposed to divide the distorted European and African continents as if creating a fluvial ring, and the Hyperboreans still inhabited the undefined northernmost regions of the Earth.[12]

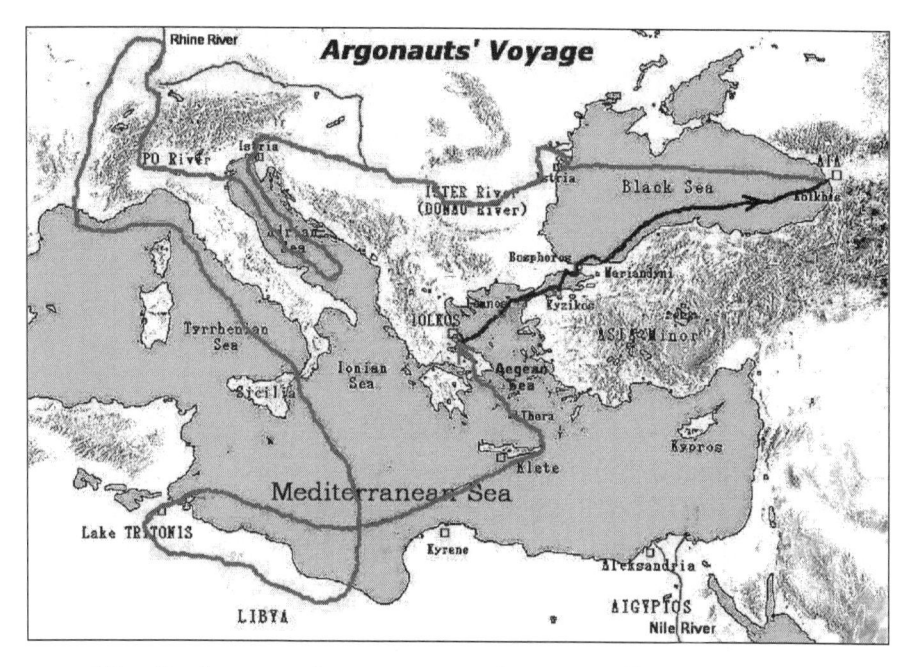

Fig. 62: Argonauts' voyage, according to Apollonius of Rhodes.

Although there are different proposals about the route that Jason and the Argonauts followed, it is generally agreed that the trip began in Thessaly (northern Greece) headed to the kingdom of Colchis on the eastern coast of the Black Sea, where they found and recovered the Golden Fleece (Fig. 62). However, the return trip was comparatively much longer. According to Apollonius of Rhodes, they had to deviate to the opposite coast of the Black Sea where they entered the mouth of the Danube River and rowed up into Central Europe. They reached the Adriatic Sea but had to return making a big loop back into the Po and Rhine Rivers. From central Europe, they proceeded southwards on the Rhone River into the Tyrrhenian Sea. They crossed the Mediterranean Sea to reach Libya, but they got lost along the sandy coasts. Finally, they found their way back home navigating north, through Crete and the Cycladic Islands, into the Aegean Sea.[13]

The similarity between the names of the main rivers that cross central Europe, Rhine-Danube, and the name of the celestial river

Fig. 63: Prehistoric carvings at Tanum (Sweden).

Eri-danus, triggered a question, "could the myth parallel the voyage of the Megalith Builders' princes?"

The Danube is born in the Black Forest and ends in the Black Sea; the name of the Thames River could derive from a Celtic expression meaning "Dark River," and the native name of Egypt (Khem) means "dark" due to the color of the fertile alluviums left by the Nile on its shores. But could all these "dark names," apparently unconnected and plagued with anachronisms, be derived from a unique "Dark River" reflection of Eridanus, extending from Great Britain to Egypt? Curiously, Eridanus was also labeled by the Greeks as the Melas River (the Dark River). We may speculate that the Megalith Builders were the people who originally named all these rivers and locations as a reflection of Eridanus, a celestial "Dark River" visible at night and born at the bottom of the sky.

Many of Jason's adventures took place at locations identified as part of this "Dark River," such as the Aegean and Black Seas, or the Danube and Rhine Rivers. Nevertheless, we have to take into consideration that the myth was probably grafted into the Greek geography from its original location in Western Europe.

For example, in the myth, the route makes a big loop in the Adriatic Sea, but in the original trip the Argo ship would have to have been transferred from the Danube to the Rhine,[14] from which point they would proceed northwards, so the loop should actually take place in the North Sea. This would imply that, once the princes reached the Rhine estuary in the North Sea, instead of heading directly to the mouth of the Thames in Great Britain, they would first make a loop into the Nordic regions.

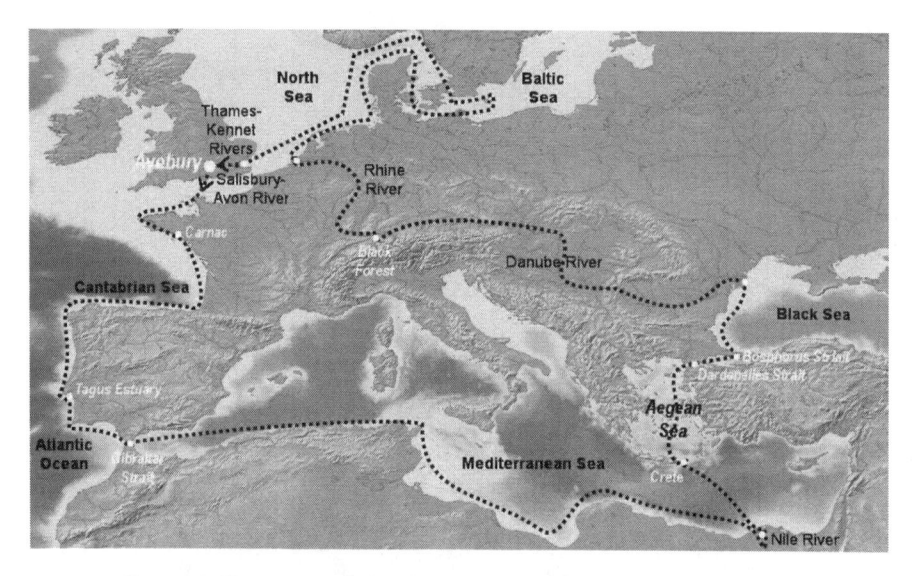

Fig. 64: Tentative map of the route followed by the princes.

This is interesting for several reasons. Firstly, Eridanus also makes a great loop in its upper part (Fig. 60, p. 105). Secondly, this loop could let them adjust the trip's duration by making the diversion shorter or longer. They had to arrive at Avebury or Stonehenge exactly on time for the crowning ceremony, in a year of lunastice and during a solstice (midsummer in Avebury, or midwinter in Stonehenge). And thirdly, the Baltic coasts were part of the Megalith Builders' original geography, as the numerous megalithic monuments in this region prove, including many petroglyphs of boats carved towards the late period of megalithism (Fig. 63).

In Jason's myth, the voyage starts and finishes in the same place (Thessaly, north of Greece), but the returning part is completely different and much longer than the initial one. Assuming that the "megalithic sailors" departed from somewhere in Western Europe, according to the myth, the initial part of the journey would be a comparatively short trip towards the NE where the Golden Fleece was located. Afterwards, since they would have to reach Egypt, they would enter the Mediterranean Sea through the Strait of Gibraltar and cross its waters from west to east. Once they reached the Nile and sailed as far as the First Cataract, they would turn around and navigate back to the Aegean Sea (Fig. 64).

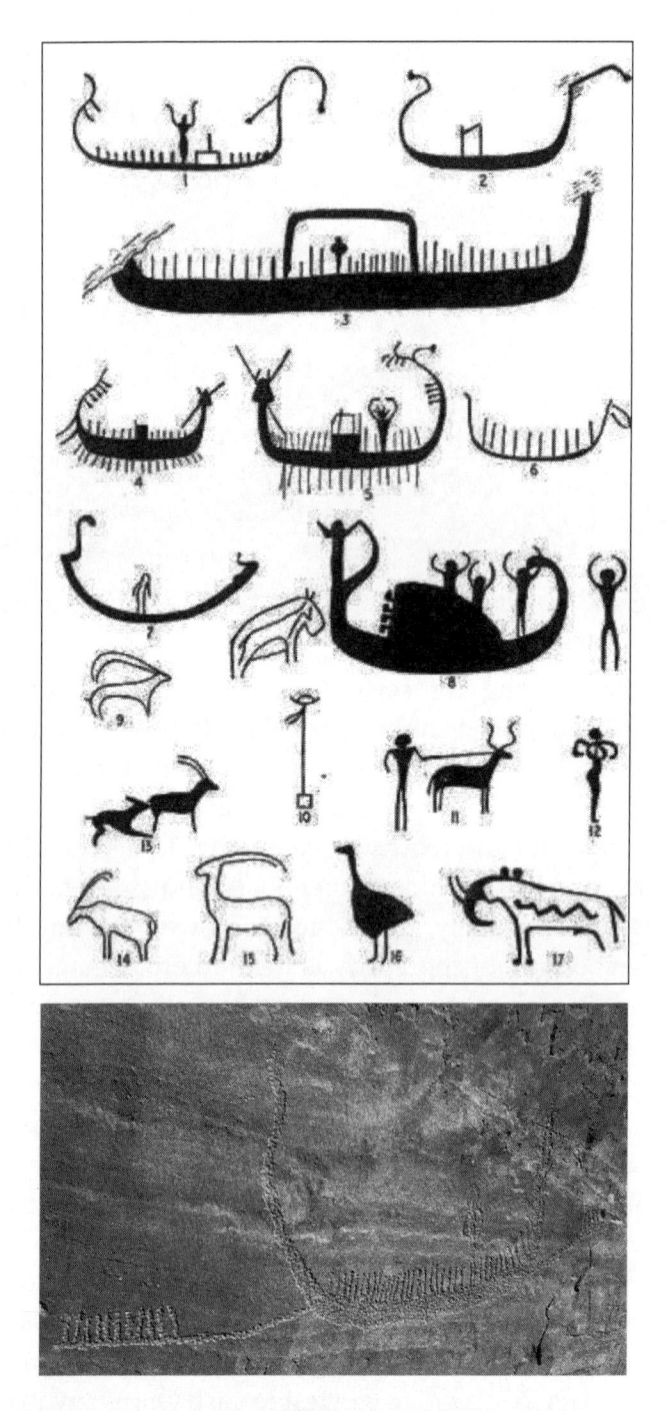

*Fig. 65: Petroglyphs in the wadis of the Eastern Desert.
Below, a large boat being dragged.*

Following the course of the "Dark River," they would pass from the Aegean to the Marmara Sea through the Strait of Dardanelles, and from there to the Black Sea through the Strait of Istanbul or Bosporus. Afterwards, they would enter the Danube's mouth and row all the way up to the Black Forest where they would have to transport the boat overland to the Rhine Basin (or change boats). They would follow the Rhine all the way to the North Sea, where they would turn east into the Baltic Sea. Somewhere over there they would make a U-turn back towards Great Britain. Finally, rowing up the Thames and Kennet Rivers, they would reach their destiny at Silbury Hill (Avebury).

The Circumnavigation

This route could have been in use for some generations, but we may now propose a substantial modification after the maritime and geographical knowledge, as well as the boat-building technology, had become more mature. The proposition is supported by very special Neolithic petroglyphs: hundreds of boats carved on the walls of the main "wadis" of the Eastern Desert in Egypt (Fig. 65).

The wadis are riverbeds dry-year-round except after unusual flash floods caused by sudden rains. The most important of them is Wadi Hammamata, being the conduit of communication between the cities of Qusays by the Red Sea with Coptos by the eastern shore of the Nile River. The ancient inhabitants on both sides of the Red Sea regarded this wadi as a prime-order strategic and commercial route, because it was the shortest distance (ca. 85 miles / 150 km) between the Nile River and the Red Sea (Fig. 66).

In Wadi Hammamata—and neighboring ones—the carvings of boats are more abundant. These petroglyphs are significant for our topic because they were carved during the Predynastic period of Egypt known as Haqada (ca. 4500 to 3100 BC).[15] Both these dates are momentous within megalithism, since the middle of the fifth millennium BC was when the first megalithic monuments appeared, and the end of the fourth millennium BC was when the largest monuments were built. In these wadis there are also numerous carvings of animals and hunting scenes, indicating that the artists were hunters in a more verdant landscape.

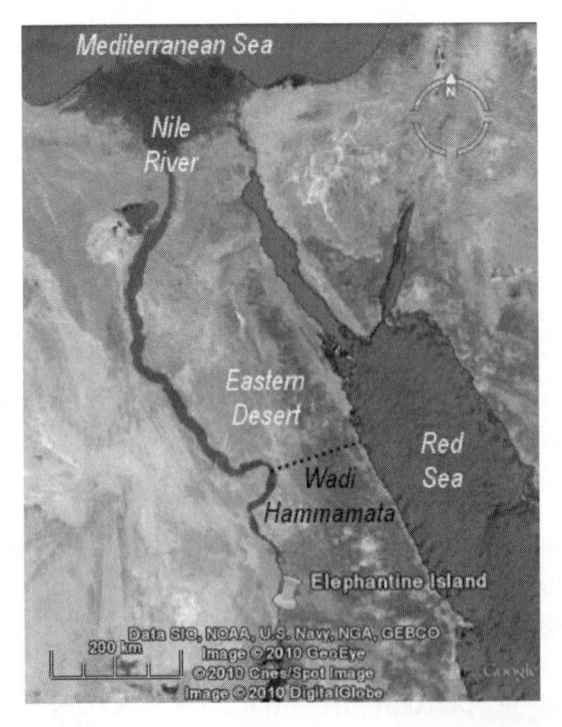

Fig. 66: Nile River. (The Wadi Hammamata is indicated.)

But, why would they carve such boats? It is not difficult to imagine the strong impression that the view of ships being dragged through their land would have produced in them.[16] Additionally, since they were carved in the Predynastic period—before the Egyptian civilization ruled by pharaohs—these boats had to be foreign. One possible origin might be Mesopotamia, but the Sumerians sailed in reed boats, whereas those in the carvings have high prows and sterns, powerful batteries of oars, and resemble more closely wooden-planked ships well adapted to maritime navigation. The other possibility is Western Europe, since the Megalith Builders were also very active in the fourth millennium BC. And we have a solid reason to expect their presence in that part of the world: the princes' rite of passage that preceded their coronation, in the form of a voyage along the reflection of Eridanus, between Egypt and Great Britain. If we admit that those boats could belong to the megalithic royal fleets, what need had they to cross that desert? The myth could clarify this atypical part of the journey.

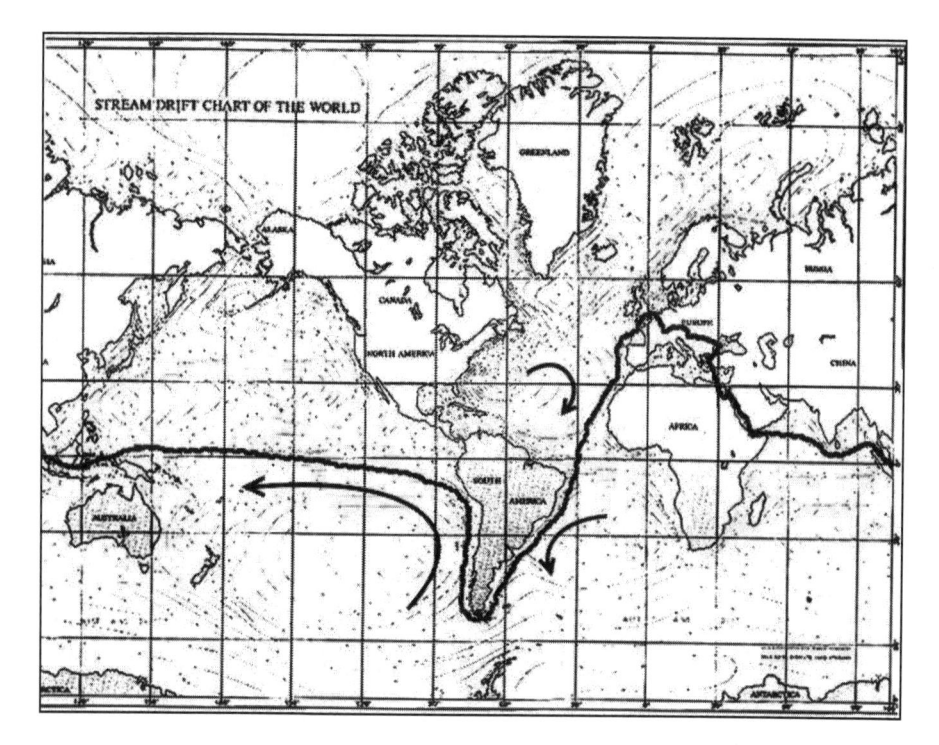

Fig. 67: Tentative route of the prehistoric voyages around the world.

As noted earlier, the Argonauts got lost in a Libyan desert before finding their way back home through Crete and the Aegean Sea. In classic literature, Libya is the generic name given to Africa, so this adventure had to happen in this continent though not necessarily in the actual country of Libya. The myth says that the Argonauts had to drag the Argo ship through the Libyan (African) desert for twelve days and their nights, which gives quite a realistic rate of progress to cross the Eastern Desert. Besides, since their destination was in Europe, the direction was from the Red Sea to the Nile River.

Eventually, the royal fleet would not enter the Mediterranean Sea through the Strait of Gibraltar but would continue to navigate southwards until they reached the Canary Islands. Once there, they had two options to reach the Red Sea, one shorter by circumnavigating the African continent, and another one much larger by circumnavigating the entire globe. The Megalith Builders learnt to sail around the world, by following the oceanic currents (Fig. 67).[17]

There is another interesting aspect of the myth that can easily be explained by this voyage. As mentioned, Jason and the Argonauts had to sail up the Eridanus River where Phaeton crashed his father's solar carriage. Various authors have interpreted this myth as the record of a cataclysm; however, this story could be explained in a much more benign way according to the subjective experience of those pioneering sailors who crossed the Equator and sailed farther south. Except for the lower regions of South America, the trip between the Canary Islands and the Elephantine Island—between both sides of the African continent—was mainly within the tropical region, where they had to endure an exceptional hot and humid climate, "as if the Sun's chariot fell into the waters."

Besides, crossing the Equator had to be equally shocking, because they would lose sight of the polar star, at that time Thuban, their familiar reference in the sky and of vital importance for sailing long distances. Instead, they found that "the north" seemed to have shifted to a different star, to the bright Achernar. In the "new realm governed by a different north," the Sun seemed to behave strangely, rising from the west and setting on the east, "as if the driver of the solar chariot had lost control."

Summary

In this chapter we proposed that the Megalith Builders developed a naval technology that allowed them to travel along the Atlantic and Mediterranean coasts of Europe and Africa.

The Megalith Builders represented Eridanus as a celestial river that connected the bottom of the sky with Orion. Since the princes were supposed to be incarnations of Orion, and this constellation seems to arrive from a celestial river, the princes also navigated on the waters that, according to their beliefs, reflected Eridanus, between the Nile and Kennet Rivers.

Like the myth of Hyperborea, the myth of *Jason and the Argonauts* had its origin in the megalithic culture, describing the great journey, a rite of passage, of the princes before being crowned as the new kings at Avebury (later at Stonehenge).

Finally, we have speculated on the possibility that this voyage was extended to circumnavigate the globe.

Endnotes

[1] Illustration on p. 95: *Nave Argo,* by Constantine Volanakis, 19th c.

[2] *Histoire Générale de la Chine,* by Henri Cordier (1920); available online at: gallica.bnf.fr/ark:/12148/bpt6k26604v

[3] A similar boat in antiquity and assembly technique but more adapted to fluvial navigation was found in Dover, in the Stour River.

[4] *Las naves de Kérné (II). Navegando por el Atlántico durante la protohistoria y la antigüedad,* by Victor Guerrero Ayuso. Proceedings of the IV CEFYP Symposium "Los Fenicios y el Atlántico." Available online: uib.es/depart/dha/prehistoria/docs/feb09.

[5] The term *dolmen* is of Breton origin, meaning *stone table*. A dolmen is a megalithic construction with three or more upright stones supporting a large flat horizontal capstone (table), usually covered with earth to form a barrow, or with smaller stones to form a *cairn*, though quite often the covering has weathered away.

[6] Reinoud de Jonge and Jay Wakefield have proposed that many Western European petroglyphs were geographic maps reporting ancient sailing discoveries in the Atlantic Ocean (*How the Sun God Reached America c.2500 BC,* 2002).

[7] Given the vigorous currents in the North Atlantic Ocean and the naval capacity of the Megalith Builders, it would be strange if they did not also reach America. The waters move in a clockwise gyre, connecting in its lower half the vicinity of the Canary Islands with the Antilles, and these American islands with Europe in the upper half of the gyre. It was precisely this Atlantic gyre that Columbus followed in 1492 to "rediscover" America.

[8] The represented image resembles a mythologized version of the original cosmic motif. Jason becomes the new king when he brings back the golden fleece, while a winged "victory" crowns him with a wreath. And the princes of the Megalith Builders were crowned as the new kings when the Corona Borealis was shining from the zenith of Stonehenge.

[9] Achernar is a zero magnitude star (m = −0.46, ranking 9). During the megalithic epoch, its declination was very close to the celestial South Pole (−83º in 3000 BC).

[10] The myths says that the Argonauts could still smell the charred body of Phaeton, the son of Helios who crashed his father's solar carriage in its waters.

[11] Historians and poets continued identifying it with the main rivers of the geography and historical moment in which they lived, as the Italian Po, the French Rhone, the German Rhine, or the Spanish Ebro.

[12] Herodotus also reported a Phoenician expedition under the patronage of Pharaoh Necao in the seventh century BC that circumnavigated the African continent. "Only" two millennia had to pass until the Portuguese sailor Bartolomeu Dias could validate this story, a great example of how going back in time does not necessarily imply doing so in knowledge.

[13] Hesiod (eighth c. BC) wrote that the return voyage circumnavigated Asia. An Egyptian version of the fifth c. BC, but probably derived from a pre-Hesiod epoch, stated that the Argo circumnavigated Europe, by sailing northwards along the Don River all the way up to the Frozen Sea, and then westwards, through Ierne (Ireland) heading to the Pillars of Hercules (Strait of Gibraltar).

[14] At present, the Danube is named so from the confluence of two short rivers, Breg and Brigach, the former originating near the watershed that divides the drainage of the NW (North Sea) and SE (Black Sea) basins.

[15] The name Haqada is taken from the city where more archaeological objects from this period have been found.

[16] The combination of animals and boats in the carvings is similar to the Iberian and Scandinavian ones (Fig. 53, p. 97; Fig. 63, p. 108), which may indicate that in all these cases the authors were hunters deeply impressed by the view of the foreign ships and sailors.

[17] The seas would not significantly favor a direction, but the rotation of the Earth causes major gyres in the oceans (Coriolis Effect), and predominant winds above, which determine preferential navigational routes. (The details of the Megalith Builders' voyages around the world—a book in itself—are out of the scope of this one, but will be published soon.)

8
ALMENDRES

IN this chapter we are going to investigate a stone ring even older than Avebury: the Cromlech of Almendres,[1] built in the Iberian Peninsula (central Portugal) in the fifth millennium BC. Based on astronomical considerations and the information provided by the myth of *Jason and the Argonauts*, we will speculate on the role this ancient monument could have played in the origin of megalithism.

The Iberian Connection

Once the general route of the princes' voyage has been exposed, the next goal should be to identify its origin, the equivalent of Thessaly in the myth, because this place would reveal where the Megalith Builders' confederation reunited.

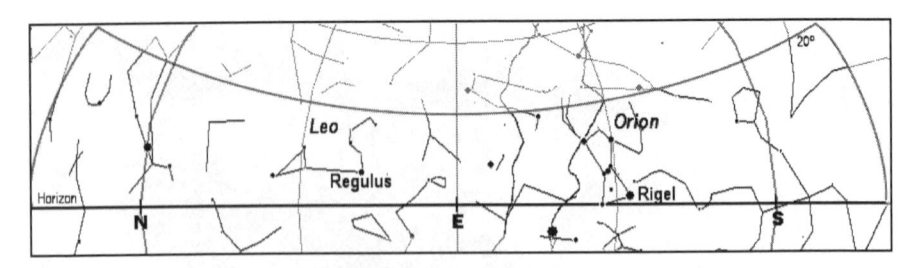

Fig. 68: Simultaneous rising of Leo and Orion, as seen from Avebury, at the time of its construction (end of the fourth millennium BC).

Obviously, the initial candidates to be considered as this special center would be among those megalithic complexes already mentioned, such as Avebury, Orkney, Newgrange or Carnac. In any of those cases—and others not listed but also studied[2]—there are good reasons to justify their special importance for the Megalith Builders.

Nevertheless, all of those lines of investigation were discarded in favor of a much more promising candidate that pinpointed the Iberian Peninsula. The main clue came from one of the initial figures of this book, the same one that had previously helped to unravel the mystery of Avebury: the scene of the heliacal rising of Rigel at the end of the fourth millennium BC (Fig. 68).

We already discovered the tremendous importance that the Megalith Builders conferred on this celestial scene. Leo and Orion were interpreted as divine characters playing on a terrestrial scenario formed by the eastern horizon and, for this scene to convey all its power, the two protagonists had to be synchronized, i.e. Leo and Orion had to show up on stage at the same time. This meant that their brightest stars, Regulus and Rigel, had to become visible over the horizon at approximately the same time.

The evolution of the rising times of both stars from two latitudes in Great Britain and Iberia, that of Avebury (51º) and that of Almendres or the Tagus estuary (39º), can be seen in Fig. 69. A great increasing disparity in the difference between the rising times of these two stars would be observed from Avebury when moving back in time from approximately 2000 BC (shown by solid lines), so this monument (or others at similar latitudes) could not be the original location from which Regulus and Rigel were contemplated ris-

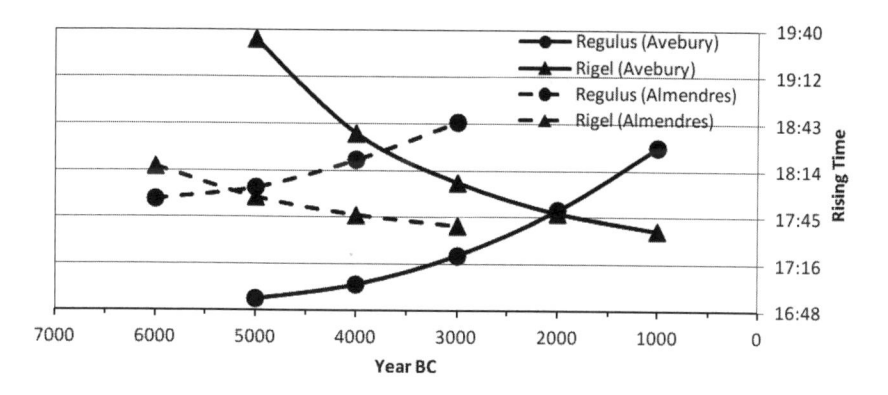

Fig. 69: Rising time vs. year for the stars Regulus (circles) and Rigel (triangles), from the latitudes of Almendres (dash lines) and Avebury (solid lines). (Arbitrary rising time scale in steps of ca. 30 min.)

ing at the same time over the horizon. It would, therefore, have been necessary to be at lower latitudes to witness the simultaneous rising of Regulus and Rigel.

From Almendres' latitude (dashed lines), both stars rose at the same time around 5000 BC; however, during the following millennium (fifth), Rigel began to rise increasingly further ahead of Regulus. That difference expanded to half an hour around the year 4000 BC, and to one hour around 3100 BC. By this time, the Megalith Builders' capacity of construction would have had to improve considerably, in consort with their geographical and astronomical knowledge, accumulated throughout centuries of maritime and "celestial" explorations. Consequently, if the Megalith Builders were originally centered at Almendres' latitude, this had to be the time (the end of the fourth millennium BC) when they were forced to tackle the problem of the divergence in rising times between Regulus and Rigel, which slowly but surely kept on growing and would continue to do so unless some drastic measures were taken.

The Megalith Builders would have observed that, at northern latitudes, the risings of these stars followed a reversed pattern, and in Great Britain it was Regulus which rose ahead of Rigel, though they would have also noticed that the time gap decreased considerably with the passing of generations (Fig. 69).

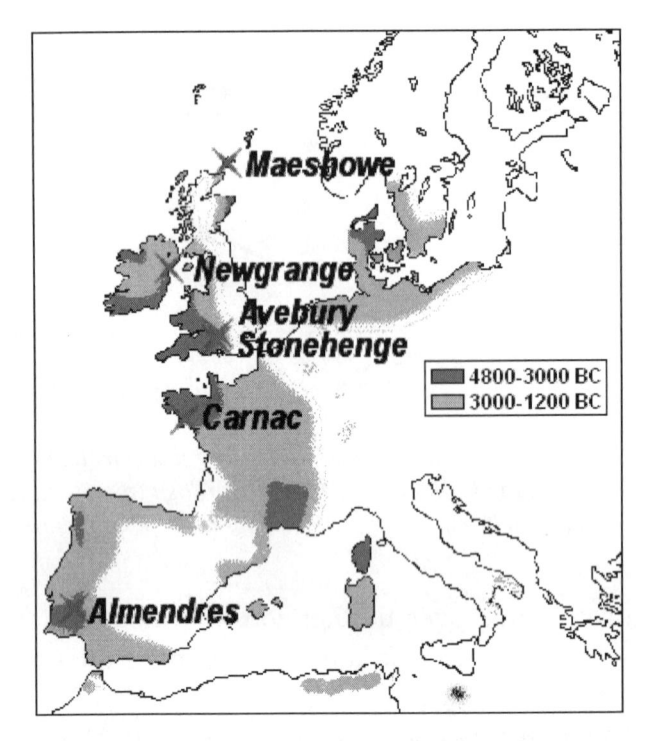

Fig. 70: Location of Almendres and the royal megalithic monuments.

The certain way to solve their problem was therefore quite simple: moving the ceremony to higher latitudes.

To move the ceremony from the Iberian Peninsula to Great Britain around the year 3100 BC implied that the divergence in time between the risings of both stars would remain similar (approximately one hour), but from then on the gap would be reduced progressively, and eventually both stars would end up rising at the same time (around the year 2000 BC). This phenomenon might have been anticipated by the Megalith Builders in finally choosing Avebury as the location at which to erect a new ceremonial center to continue renewing their monarchy, valid at least for the following two millennia. Seven centuries later, however, their successors would decide yet another change—not so much of geographical but of architectural nature—and they moved the ceremony to the neighboring site of Stonehenge, where it would continue for at least seven more centuries, until the end of the megalithic epoch.

Fig. 71: Almendres faces the far east.

To choose the best location would be decided only after careful exploration and evaluation of several geodesic, geographical, topographical and celestial factors. The latitude would affect the visibility of the stars; for example, some southern constellations such as the Crux and the Centaur would become invisible at higher latitudes than Avebury. The access by rivers would be a key factor since they arrived by boat from abroad. Also, the topography should permit a clear vision of the sky.

The Cromlech

The Cromlech of Almendres is the oldest stone ring in Europe, and one of the largest. It is located in the Portuguese region of Alentejo (ca. 60 miles / 95 km just SE of Lisbon) (Fig. 70), and it was built and remodeled several times during the fifth millennium BC. Additionally, in this region there is a high concentration of megalithic constructions, such as enclosures, menhirs and dolmens, indicating that this territory was an early megalithic focal point.

Could Almendres be the predecessor of Avebury, and so the monument where the monarchical renewal ceremony originated? Could it be the location from which the princes departed in a voyage "around the world" before being crowned?[3]

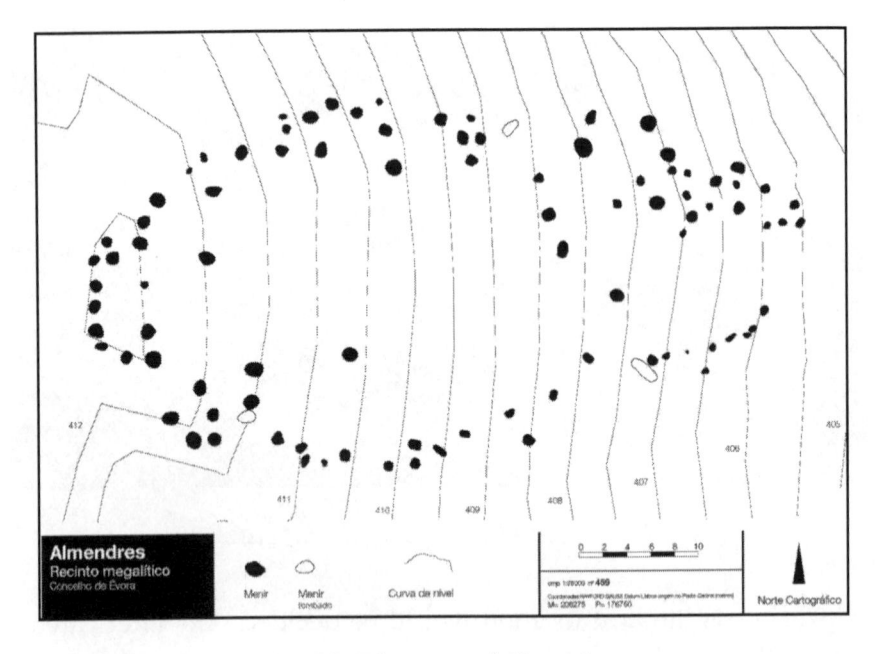

Fig. 72: Blueprint of Almendres.

Almendres is situated on a gentle hillside facing east (Fig. 71), with its western side at the top, where the larger rocks were erected. It seems to be formed by different clusters of rocks of varied sizes arranged in a general pattern that might resemble one or two elliptical rings aligned in an east to west direction (Fig. 72). There is hardly any resemblance between Almendres and Avebury, so, based only on their designs, the answer to the above formulated questions would be in the negative. However, before jumping to any conclusion, we should investigate what the sky above Almendres was like (Fig. 73).

The sky as it appeared in the middle of the fifth millennium BC at midsummer sunrise would be very similar to what could be seen from Avebury 1,400 years later. Rigel and Regulus rose at about the same time, but the main difference relative to Avebury was that the risings of these stars occurred considerably ahead of the midsummer sunrise. Even Sirius was able to rise heliacally in midsummer, and would be "the last of the protagonists to appear on stage" (eastern horizon) before the dawn would veil the stars.[4] This entire celestial configuration would function as a herald of midsummer.

ALMENDRES • 123

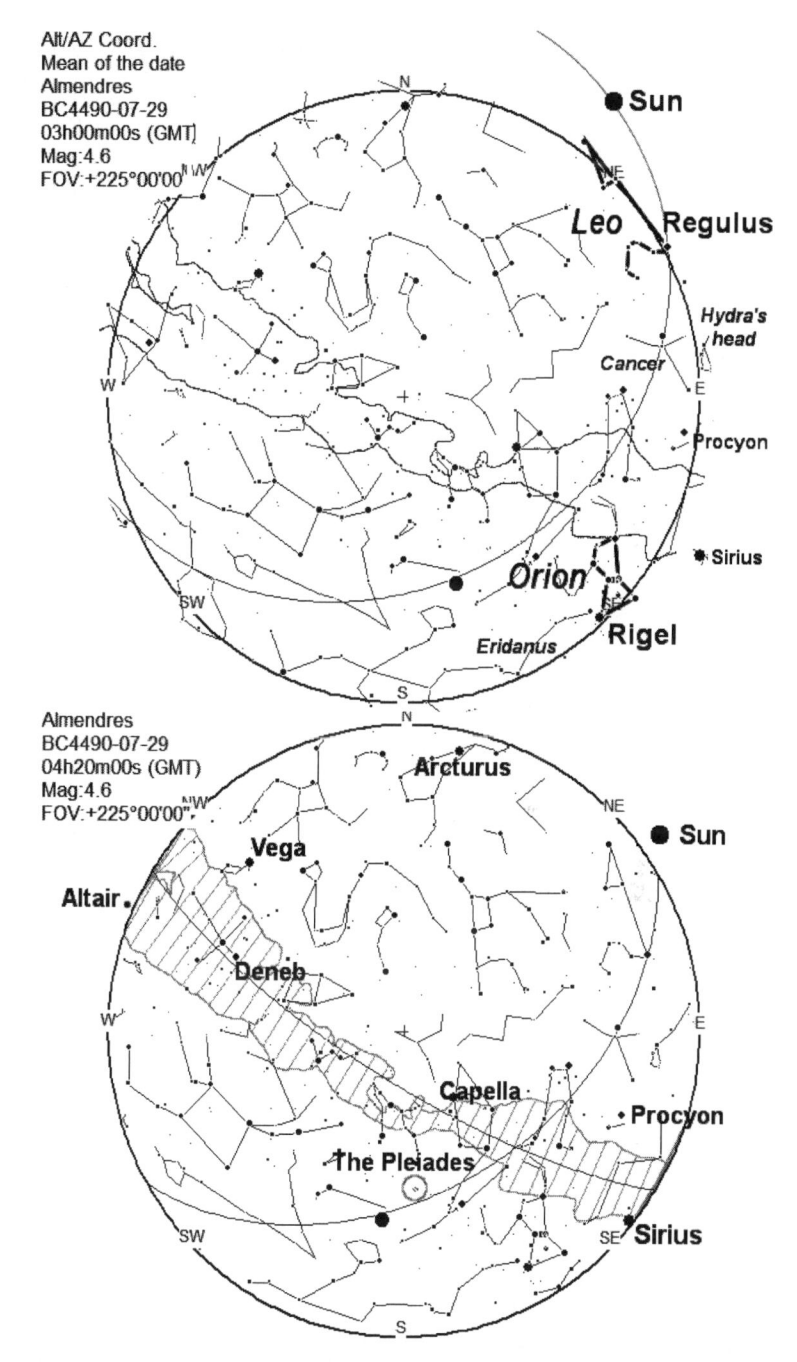

Fig. 73: The sky seen over Almendres (projected on it) before midsummer sunrise. Above, rising of Rigel; below, heliacal rising of Sirius, 1h 20 min later. (The area outside the circle remains below the horizon.)

Nevertheless, there is not any clear indication in the design of Almendres hinting that it could accommodate or reflect this scene, as it was the case in Avebury. The main axis of Almendres is not aligned south to north—the relative positions of Orion and Leo—but east to west which would fit better in an equinoctial setting.

The Victory of the Sun

There is a celestial event that could serve as a simple and practical method to determine the arrival of Spring, much easier to observe than the exact equinoctial day.

During midwinter, the Sun rises from the SE and the full Moon from the NE but, as the months pass by, the points of the horizon from where the Sun and the full Moon rise become progressively closer, the sunrises moving northwards and the full-moonrises moving southwards. The next full-moonrise after the vernal equinox is when, for the first time in the year, the Sun rises more to the north than the full Moon. (This cosmic event is still observed in Christianity, signaling the dates of Easter.)

Archaeologist C. Marciano da Silva suggests that the Cromlech of Almendres is oriented due East, and other enclosures and dolmens in the same region of Alentejo are oriented towards the first full Moon after the Spring equinox.[5]

The sky over Almendres in the middle of the fifth millennium BC, when the first full Moon after the vernal equinox was rising, can be seen in Fig. 74. As expected, the full Moon rose over the horizon slightly south of due east, and—inevitable for the Moon to be full—the Sun was setting in the opposite direction, slightly north of due west.

If the builders of this cromlech celebrated this night as the arrival of Spring, and therefore of the good weather and the renewal of life, then, they could have interpreted this celestial event as the annual episode in which "the Sun defeats the Moon." In that case, the most important moment would not be the moonrise but the following sunrise, approximately twelve hours later, when the positions of the Sun and the Moon were reversed (the full Moon was setting and the Sun was rising).

ALMENDRES • 125

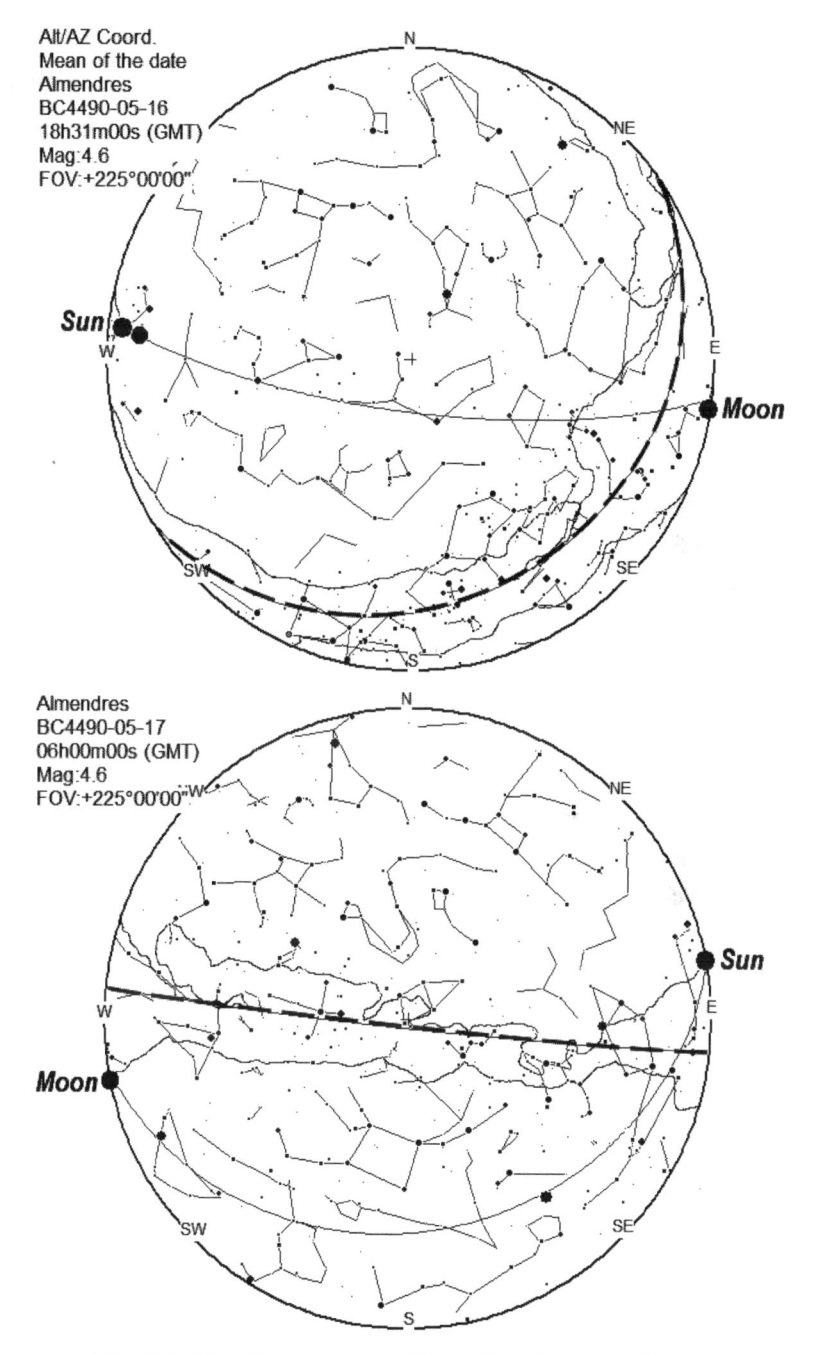

Fig. 74: The sky seen over Almendres (projected on it), when the first Spring Moon was rising, and the following sunrise. (The dashed line is the center of the Milky Way, the Galactic Equator.)

This configuration of the sky was quite remarkable: the Milky Way arched over the zenith in a direction slightly tilted from the east to west direction, as if creating a bridge between both luminaries just over their heads.[6]

The design of Almendres could be explained as a schematic reflection of the celestial layouts of this special night. The two crucial moments were the full-moonrise and its full-moonset about twelve hours later, when the Moon and the Sun interchanged their positions. The diffuse ring formed by the rocks could be a representation of the main features of the Milky Way surrounding the horizon during the full-moonrise, and the clear central axis of the cromlech as an avenue, also a reflection of the Milky Way, but at the full-moonset. At this critical moment, the builders would contemplate the light of the Sun, the Moon and the Milky Way, coming from the east, west and above respectively, focalized within the cromlech.

Earlier we proposed that the Megalith Builders could have designed Avebury playing with two principles, one solar and one lunar that we called spirit and soul, so the position of the Milky Way connecting these luminaries could be interpreted as a "celestial route." If the builders of Almendres held similar beliefs, then this cromlech could have been designed as a crucible in which these principles were fused together at Spring.

In summary, both Almendres and Avebury would be the products of builders very interested in the celestial cycles, from which they derived religious, social and artistic motifs for their megalithic constructions. In fact, we may propose that they were not from different cultures but different architectural manifestations of the same culture at different times of its evolution, separated by 1,500 years.

A shift of emphasis from equinoctial to solstitial ceremonies and from lunar to solar rites can be perceived.[7] There is also evidence of progress in stone building technology, as well as evolution in the architecture towards more stylized designs.

The Pyrenees and the Golden Fleece

Almendres can be proposed as a possible candidate as the center where the Megalith Builders reunited, and based on this hypothesis we can resume the investigation of the myth of *Jason and the Ar-*

Fig. 75: Jason retrieving the Golden Fleece from a tree guarded by a dragon lulled by Medea. (Apulian vase, fourth c. BC.)

gonauts. The goal of these heroes was to retrieve the Golden Fleece, the skin of a winged ram on which the prince Phrixus escaped from his step-mother, who was plotting to kill him. This prince arrived in Colchis, on the eastern coasts of the Black Sea, where he lived the rest of his life as the guest of Aietes, son of Helios. Soon after his arrival, Phrixus sacrificed the winged ram to Poseidon and hung its golden fleece on a tree guarded by a dragon sacred to the God Ares. This special ram was later immortalized as the Aries constellation.

The daughter of Aietes, Medea, was a priestess of Colchis. Upon seeing Jason she fell in love with him, became his lover and eventually his wife. She put the dragon to sleep with a magic potion, so that Jason could take the Golden Fleece from the tree (Fig. 75). Then she fled with Jason and helped him to be successful in his task of returning the Golden Fleece to Pelias. Medea played the feminine role and used magic, whereas Jason was the masculine counterpart who acted guided by Medea' wisdom, so both together represented

Fig. 76: The Pyrenees and Caucasus Ranges.

wisdom put into practice. Years later, however, Medea felt betrayed by Jason and became his nemesis, a logical consequence of the symbolism: action not based on wisdom brings failure.

This part of the myth contains a geographical reference to modern-day Georgia (the eastern region of the Black Sea), and an astronomical reference to Aries, the goat or ram of the Zodiac. Historically, Georgia had two halves, the western half known as Colchis, and the eastern known as Iberia—curiously, the same name as the European peninsula. The main geographical feature of Georgia is its mountains, particularly the Greater Caucasian Range that runs along its northern regions, its highest peak being Mount Elbrus (18,510 ft / 5,642 m, just on the Russian side of the borderline).

By transposing this information into its possible original location in the Iberian Peninsula during the megalithic epoch, we need to identify a range of high mountains in the far NE from Almendres. There are several candidates that could fit the specifications, from nearest to farthest: Sistema Central in the center of the peninsula, the Pyrenees—the natural partition between the peninsula and the continent, between Spain and France—and even the Alps in continental Europe.

However, there are clear indications coming from different considerations that seem to point to the Pyrenees as the original house of Aries. Thus, the Pyrenees form a linear mountain range between the coasts of the Cantabrian and the Mediterranean Seas in an east to west direction at about 42.5º N latitude, and this description fits that of the Caucasian Range, between the Black and Caspian Seas (Fig. 76).[8]

Even from a mythological point of view, the Pyrenees seem to be related to Aries, because Pyrene and Ares were the mythological parents of Cycnus (Cygnus constellation, represented as a swan).

Summary

The visibility of the celestial scene that the Megalith Builders observed during the renewal of their kings (the simultaneous rising of Leo and Orion) was the key factor that prompted a change in the place they celebrated this event, from Iberia to Great Britain.

The Iberian Cromlech of Almendres may have been the original place where the Megalith Builders and their ancestors gathered to celebrate the arrival of Spring, "when the Sun defeated the Moon." Due to the sacredness of this place, it would also be here where the different peoples of Iberia met for the first time to create the confederation of chiefdoms that evolved in time into kingdoms. Later they would choose the summer solstice as the time to renew their kings.

Almendres could be, therefore, the starting point of the long voyage that functioned as a rite of passage for the princes of the Megalith Builders, whose adventures originated the myths that arrived later in ancient Greece, such as that of *Jason and the Argonauts*.

Endnotes

[1] Above, a photo of the Cromlech of Almendres' upper part. (*Cromlech* is an obsolete term used to describe megalithic monuments with circular designs, in use only in a few cases due to tradition.)

[2] For instance, the Isle of Man, on account of its central situation in the overlapping of the different territories (Fig. 49, p. 87).

[3] There are only two latitudes where the elongations (range in degrees from due east) of the Moon at the lunastices are the same as the latitudes (ca. 52º and 38º), precisely where the largest stone rings in Europe were erected: Avebury-Stonehenge in Great Britain, and Almendres in Iberia (*Neolithic Cosmology: The Equinox and the Spring Full Moon*, Journal of Cosmology, by C. Marciano da Silva, vol. 9, pp. 2207-16, 2010). A culture interested in the celestial cycles, able to travel between Iberia and Britain, could have easily noted these special latitudes. Similarly, on extending the trips further, they could have discovered the latitudes at which that equivalence was also the case for the Sun, approximately at 28º and 62º (for example the Canary Islands and the Faroe Islands).

[4] Besides the heliacal rising of Sirius, a very bright asterism known as the "Summer Triangle," formed by the stars Vega, Deneb and Altair, was setting over the NW horizon. Also, a conspicuous cluster of stars known as the Pleiades—between Aries and Taurus—was culminating right before sunrise. The very bright star Capella was transiting close to the zenith, and Arcturus, the brightest star of the northern hemisphere, was close to the northern horizon.

[5] *The Spring Full Moon*, by C. Marciano da Silva, Journal for the History of Astronomy, xxxv, pp. 1-5 (2004)

[6] Obviously, the clarity of the dawn and the full Moon would not allow them to see the Milky Way, yet they would know indirectly from the position of the fading stars that it had to be arching above.

[7] Diodorus, writing about the Hyperboreans, said that, "*At the time of this appearance of the god [Apollo] he both plays on the cithara and dances continuously the night through from the vernal equinox until the rising of the Pleiades.*" This mythical celebration fits better with those proposed for Almendres during Spring.

[8] This may explain why Aries was represented by a goat or ram, since these are the archetypical animals that inhabits the mountains.

9
THE IBERIAN ZODIAC

THE Megalith Builders assigned some geographical features and constructions to several stars and constellations. For instance, Silbury Hill was erected as a reflection of the star Rigel, Eridanus was associated with several rivers stretching from Great Britain to Egypt, and now we have discovered a strong link between Aries and the mountains of the eastern Pyrenees. The logical question is, "were these isolated cases, or parts of a larger correlation?" In other words, could they be elements of a larger design that would function as a "celestial mirror" reflecting the heavens on earth?

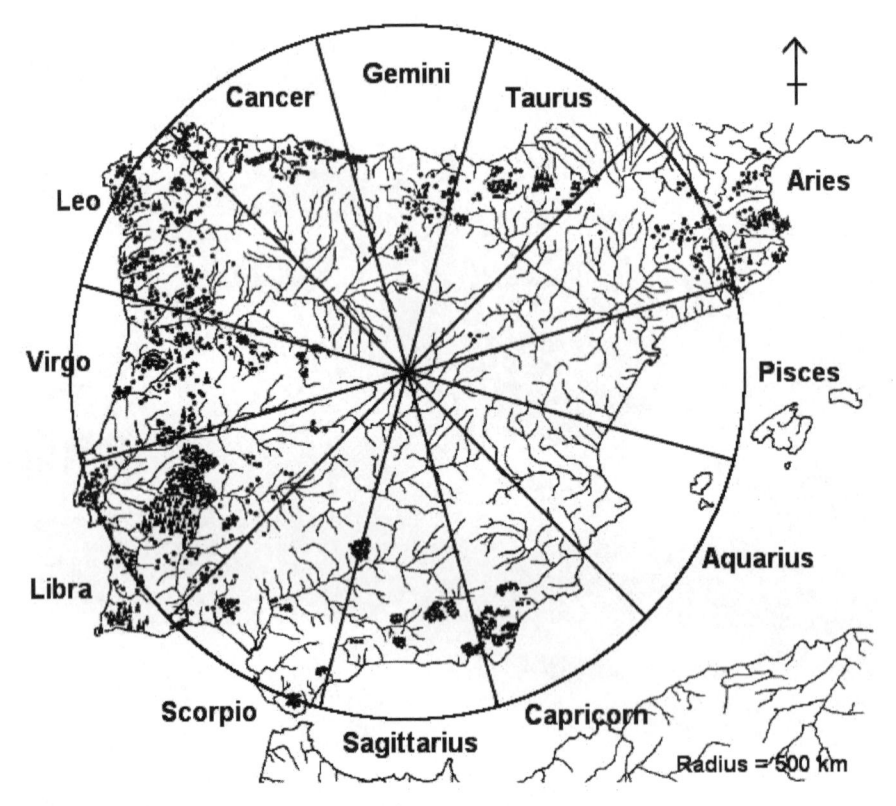

Fig. 77: The Iberian Zodiac. (The distribution of megalithic constructions on the peninsula is also indicated, after Philine Kalb.)

If Aries was assigned to a specific area, it seems logical to think that it was the same for the rest of zodiacal constellations. The regular shape of the Iberian Peninsula may confirm this supposition, because it seems perfectly to lend itself to designing a huge Zodiac around its coasts. The resulting Iberian Zodiac, with Aries assigned to the eastern Pyrenees, can be seen in Fig. 77.[1]

To validate or repudiate this idea, we should go back in time to study the distribution of megalithic constructions in Iberia, taking into account, however, that most of them would be cemeteries. The megalithic sites are located mainly in the coastal regions, while the interior remains mostly empty.[2] Also, the eastern region has a much lower density than the western, with no constructions in the vast territory corresponding to Pisces and Aquarius.

There is no simple archaeological explanation for the distribution of megalithic monuments in Iberia because the archaeologists are so focused on the details that they never contemplated a broader possibility: that the Megalith Builders could consider this peninsula as a whole. If we accept this possibility, then a simple explanation can be proposed, based on the analogy that relates sunrise with life and sunset with death. Given that most of the megalithic constructions seem to be related to funerary practices, a higher density should be expected on the Atlantic coasts, on the west, as is the case. It may even be speculated that the first builders of megalithic communal graves (dolmens) would not teach this construction technique to the inhabitants of the Mediterranean coasts because they considered it improper to build funerary monuments on the "Levant," in the land of sunrise. Likewise, the interior of the peninsula would reflect the circumpolar stars, which never set and are therefore "immortal," rendering this territory equally inappropriate for building funerary monuments. This hypothesis would imply that, by the time the first megalithic monuments began to appear in Iberia, the builders already had a sense of the peninsula forming a "geopolitical" entity.

The Axis mundi or Pillar

A deeper, older layer corresponding to the Sun's movements over the peninsula may lie beneath the design of the Iberian Zodiac. The directions of the solstices contemplated from the geographical center of the peninsular Zodiac can be seen in Fig. 78 (the angle formed by the solsticial axes at Madrid is 64.6º). The density of megalithic constructions is higher at both extremes of the axis formed by the midsummer sunrise and the midwinter sunset. In fact, the highest density can be found in the Portuguese region of Alentejo where Almendres is located, corresponding to the midwinter sunset extremity. The other extreme of this axis (midsummer sunrise) corresponds to the Eastern Pyrenees.[3]

This "solar axis or pillar" may have been set up by the Megalith Builders with its base in Almendres, its summit in the Eastern Pyrenees, and its middle section in the geographical center of the Iberian Peninsula.[4]

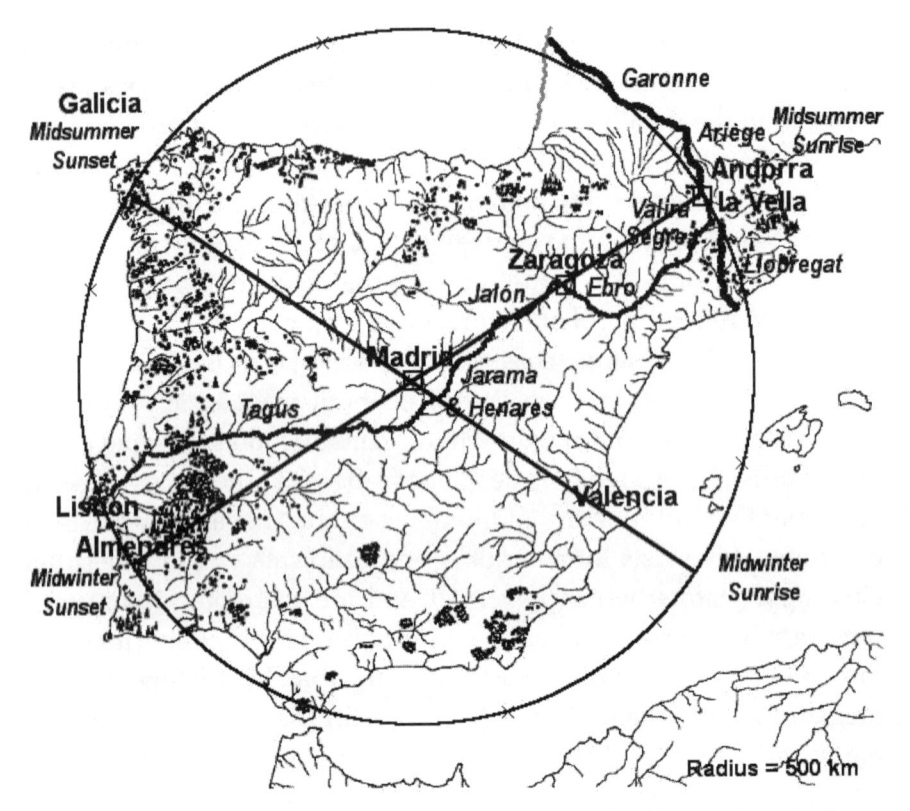

Fig. 78: Solstitial directions from the center of the Iberian Peninsula. (Some important locations and rivers are also indicated.)

The Tagus River could have served as a way to penetrate into the interior of the peninsula, and its tributaries Jarama and Henares would take them to the Ebro Basin. The Jalón and Ebro Rivers would be the next traversable waterways, and finally the Segre and its tributary Valira would be used as routes to penetrate northwards, into the Pyrenees. The circumference enclosing Iberia could be the reflection of the Ecliptic on the celestial mirror, as a stylized trajectory that corresponded to the seafaring route around the peninsula. The Megalith Builders seemed to have intentionally designed the reflection of the Ecliptic on water so that the luminaries were able to "navigate" around the Zodiac (Iberia) as they do in the sky. The Llobregat River on the southern side (Spanish) of the Pyrenees, and the Ariège and Garonne Rivers in the northern side (French), could have served to complete the encompassing of the

Ecliptic with a ring of water, connecting the Mediterranean and Cantabrian Seas through Andorra (Fig. 78).

This midsummer sunrise axis crosses one of the most important peninsular rivers, the Ebro, exactly at the point the city of Saragossa is located. Saragossa is a popular destination among Catholic pilgrims because it was in this city (known as Caesaragusta in Roman times) where the Virgin allegedly made her first appearance. According to the records, in the year 40 AD, while the Virgin was still alive, she appeared on top of a pillar to the Apostle St. James, who at that time was preaching in Iberia. It is from this episode that a sanctuary was built dedicated to the "Virgin of the Pillar" (in Spanish *Virgen del Pilar*), who later became the patroness of Spain (likewise, St. James became the patron) (Fig. 79).

Fig. 79: "Virgen del Pilar," the Patroness of Spain, in the Basilica of Saragossa, by the Ebro River.

The early fathers of Christianity, in their wish to convert people to their new religion, used to Christianize the most sacred local sanctuaries by imposing new iconography fitted to the original meanings, which made it easier for the locals to accept the changes instead of considering them too disruptive of their traditions. This was possibly why they placed the Virgin on top of a pillar in Saragossa, since it could be an excel-

Fig. 80: Dolmen in Roknia necropolis (Algeria).

lent way to Christianize the site where, according to ancient tradition, a sacred axis or golden pillar (solar) crossed the Ebro River.[5]

Ancient Astronomical Lore

The directions of the midwinter sunrise and sunset had to be also regarded as significant, since they point towards the minimum (Valencia) and maximum (Alentejo) density of megalithic constructions in Iberia, demonstrating completely different funerary practices at these regions, surely related to this solstitial circumstance.

The Ecliptic is equidistant between Iberia and the north of Africa, which suggests that the constellations in that zone of the Zodiac would reflect upon both sides of the Mediterranean Sea. Thus, Aquarius, visited by the Sun in midwinter, would reflect both upon the Valencian and Algerian coasts. Interestingly, Algeria, contrary to Valencia, has a high density of Neolithic dolmens. These dolmens are spectacular not in their dimensions but in their number, forming large necropolises such as those of Msila, Bou Merzoug, Bou Nouara and Roknia, the latter (halfway between the capitals of Algiers and Tunis) containing just on its own several thousand dolmens (Fig. 80). Could this antithetic distribution of funerary constructions on both sides of the Mediterranean Sea be related to the proper disposal of dead with respect to the celestial mirror?

THE IBERIAN ZODIAC • 137

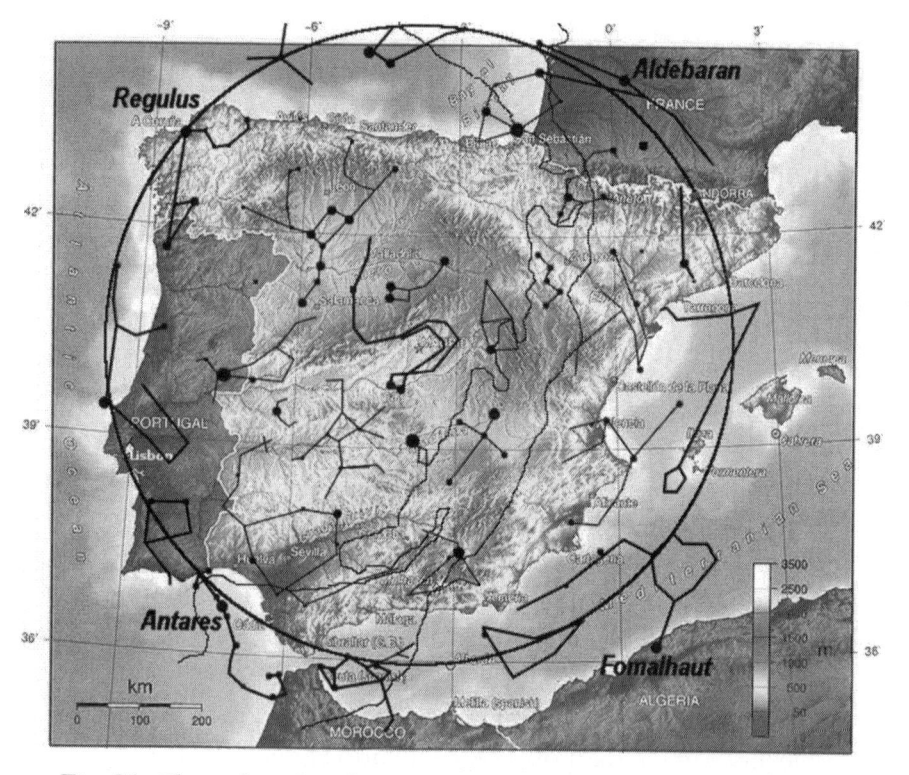

Fig. 81: The zodiacal and inner constellations projected over Iberia. (The "royal stars" are indicated.)

The Zodiac and its inner constellations can be printed over the Iberian Peninsula assuming that the Ecliptic corresponded to the circle (ca. 320 miles / 500 km of radius) that surrounds it (Fig. 81).

Earlier in the book, the stars Regulus and Fomalhaut were identified as "solar and lunar abodes" respectively. The former should be found on the northern coast of Galicia, and the latter on the Algerian coast. This supports the hypothesis that this part of the African territory was considered propitious for funerary practices because, in addition to being in the direction of midwinter sunrise (solar regeneration), it was also in alignment with the reflection of Fomalhaut, the lunar abode related to the soul's destiny. The inhabitants of SE Iberia could have developed the custom of carrying their dead (bones or ashes) to the African side across the Alboran Sea to deposit them in large necropolises.[6]

It is also noteworthy that the brightest star that reflects on Iberia, Arcturus, should be found in a mountain range of Portugal named Serra da Estrela (Range of the Star).

It is very tempting to go beyond these general comments and propose specific locations where the Megalith Builders could have assigned stars; however, several factors must be taken into consideration:

1) The geography distorts the mathematical projection.[7]

2) Some important megalithic monuments may have disappeared, particularly those that were built in places subject to continual settlements.

3) The singularity of the topography could make it unnecessary to signal the stars where there are conspicuous geographical features, such as special outcrops or mountain peaks.

4) Our ancestors surely were not as interested in assigning the stars on Earth mathematically as they were in assigning them according to the beliefs and stories associated with them. For instance, Orion and Scorpio may occupy comparatively larger extensions of the celestial mirror than other constellations because they played a major role in their social organization and religious beliefs.

"Yet men in Britain of 2000 BC must have known of some process by which the positions of the heavenly bodies could be expressed in terms of the terrestrial landscape. Anyone who stands within one of these circles or on a former astronomical hill such as St Michael's Hill at Montacute, Badbury Rings or Maeshowe in Scotland may become aware of a subtle symbolism in the surrounding landscape, where every eminence and furrow outlined on the horizon has some cosmological significance. Even today, the names of hills and mounds often reveal their former identification with an aspect of the Sun, the Moon or a star; or, rather, with the spiritual principle which it represents. The whole landscape of Britain has been laid out to a celestial pattern. Every hill has its astrological meaning, every district its centre of symmetry from which its hidden nature can be divined."[8]

The previous paragraph was written by John Michell, one of the most incisive and prolific authors of an alternative archaeology quite unacceptable to orthodox scholarship.

Fig. 82: Menhir at midsummer sunrise from Almendres (10 ft / 3 m tall).

To find "heaven on Earth" is, therefore, not a new occurrence, and several authors have outlined maps relating ancient constructions to the stars, from local arrangements to vast territories.[9] Nevertheless, most of these hypotheses have been received with great skepticism by the mainstream scientific community. Regardless of the strength of each case, they all vindicate the existence of an ancient cosmological legacy from cultures that in some cases predated historical civilizations and were much more "astronomically knowledgeable" than has been admitted.

The Knights of the Round Table, a Chimera?

The symbolism contained in the myth of *Jason and the Argonauts* again reveals its cosmic roots, because the dragon sacred to Ares that protects the tree where the Golden Fleece hangs seems to be a clear allusion to Draco and the axis that connects it with Aries. This "solar pillar," crossing the Iberian Peninsula from Almendres to the Eastern Pyrenees could be the Axis Mundi of the Megalith Builders, the pole sustaining the world (Fig. 82).[10]

Fig. 83: The Knights of the Round Table. (Modern rendering.)

The working hypothesis that Megalith Builders were politically organized as a confederation of about a dozen kingdoms was based on the number of rows displayed at Carnac. Now, it is reasonable to think that these kingdoms could be related to the signs of the Zodiac, reproducing its twelve constellations on Earth. The center of the Zodiac, called the Ecliptic Pole and located in Draco, had to reflect upon the peninsular center.[11] Its equidistance to each zodiacal sign and its location in the middle of the Axis Mundi would convert the center of Iberia into the *omphalos* (navel) of the confederation, the most suitable place where the "kings of the Zodiac" gathered periodically to reaffirm their alliance (Fig. 83).

In the Arthurian legend, the symbolism of the Round Table developed over time into a chivalric order known as the Knights of the Round Table, associated with King Arthur's court. There again seems to be an arcane coincidence between this legend and the royalty of the Megalith Builders, who would meet at the center of the Iberian Meseta—the inner plateau that literally means *table*—under the circumpolar stars, Arcturus being the brightest (Fig. 84).

THE IBERIAN ZODIAC • 141

Fig. 84: King Arthur presides over the Round Table. (Medieval codex.)

In summary, the Megalith Builders would have assimilated the coastal regions of the Iberian Peninsula—plus northern Africa and southern France—into a huge Zodiac divided into twelve kingdoms which tallied with each one of the zodiacal signs. They visualized the luminaries navigating around it in a counterclockwise direction. The Llobregat, Ariège and Garonne Rivers connected the waters on both sides of the Pyrenees (Mediterranean and Cantabrian Seas).

The center of Iberia would be a political and religious meeting point of extraordinary importance for several reasons: 1) it was equidistant from all the kingdoms, 2) it was the reflection of the celestial dragon that protected the immovable Ecliptic Pole, and 3) it was pierced by an "Axis Mundi" that rested on Almendres and culminated in the Eastern Pyrenees where Aries was reflected.[12]

The princes of each kingdom would gather at the center of Iberia to start their pre-crowning voyage together. They would first chase the midsummer sunrise direction (NE). Once they reached the Eastern Pyrenees, where they "recovered the Golden Fleece," they would descend on the north side of the mountains. They surely walked by the shores of the Ariège River, down to its confluence with the Garonne. This wider and plentiful river would allow them to board the large ships to be used throughout the rest of the voyage. Their main shipyard—one of the earliest and biggest in the world—would be there, at present day Toulouse.[13]

They would most likely depart during the vernal equinox, at the commencement of Spring, imitating the Sun's visit to Taurus (next after Aries) at this time of the year. Moreover, early Spring is when the depth of the rivers is higher due to the melt-water from the snow of the mountains. This would make the river journey easier, particularly along the Garonne River towards its long estuary in what is now the city of Bordeaux, the gate into the Atlantic Ocean.

The royal fleet would first pause at Carnac, in Brittany. Thereafter, they would sail across the Bay of Biscay and down the Atlantic coast of Iberia towards the Canary Islands. This archipelago, at the Tropic of Cancer, signaled the beginning of the arduous tropical circumnavigation of (eventually) the globe. Their final destiny was Silbury Hill (Great Britain), where they should arrive several years after their departure, in time for the crowning ceremony.[14]

Assuming the journey would take about four years, they would have to depart when the princes were around 15 years old, since they had to be crowned at the age of 19. The experiences of such an adventurous trip at that critical age would transform them completely. We could say that, through that rite of passage, they departed as children but arrived back in Western Europe transformed into trustworthy adults. During those years, the tutoring they received from the crew (surely recruited among the best sailors, warriors, astronomers-priests, musicians, etc.) would build up their personalities, not only to be able to control their emotions during the final test—when they would have to kill their parents just before their sacred marriage—but even more importantly to convert them into good kings and loyal members of the confederation.

If the Alignments of Carnac were a representational mausoleum of a confederation of kingdoms related to the Zodiac, the number of rows in the modules could reveal political changes along their millenary history. Le Ménec has 11 rows, Kermario 10 and Kerlescan 13. The extra row (13th) at Kerlescan (the module corresponding to the last centuries of the confederation) could be explained by

Fig. 85: The Chimera (tail as a dragon). (Kylix, 4th c. BC.)

adding a new kingdom to the 12 zodiacal ones (perhaps the center of Iberia, the reflection of Draco and equidistant from the others).[15] Explaining the number of rows at Kermario is more challenging because it suggests a reduction in the number of kingdoms. The traditional association of signs and luminaries can clarify this point.

In astrological lore, the Sun rules over Leo, and the Moon over Cancer, in total agreement with the symbolism proposed for these signs. The remaining ten zodiacal signs are ruled by the five traditional planets, each one ruling over a pair of signs.[16] Based on this, the ten kingdoms represented at Kermario could correspond to the five pairs of zodiacal signs ruled by the five planets. The territories associated with Leo and Cancer would perhaps have a special status, a sort of "parental condition" over the other ten, since they are ruled by the brightest luminaries, the poles masculine (Sun-Leo) and feminine (Moon-Cancer) of the sky. One of the ten kings would also have to rule over the territories associated with Leo and Cancer, and we have already demonstrated that Aries was particularly important for the Megalith Builders because it signaled the top of their Axis Mundi.[17] Consequently, this outstanding sign could be

Mercury Trilithon: Virgo-Gemini
Venus Trilithon: Libra-Taurus
Mars Trilithon: Aries-Scorpio
Saturn Trilithon: Capricorn-Aquarius
Jupiter Trilithon: Sagittarius-Pisces

Fig. 86: Zodiacal equivalents to Stonehenge's trilithons.

associated not only with the territory that reflected Aries (Aragon) but also with the territories that reflected Leo (Galicia) and Cancer (Asturias).

One of the most bizarre creatures that appears in classical mythology is the Chimera (Fig. 85). According to Homer, this fabulous animal was of divine origin and had the fore part of her body as that of a lion, the hind as that of a dragon, and the middle as that of a goat. The Chimera would fit perfectly with the representation of a "super-constellation" that combined Leo (lion), Aries (goat) and Draco (dragon)—and perhaps also Cancer although not explicitly indicated—as an echo of this very special megalithic kingdom.

The Cosmology of Stonehenge

This hypothesis can also help us to complete the description of Stonehenge's design. The five huge trilithons, i.e. the five pairs of columns linked with a lintel above placed at the center of the monument, would serve to represent the pairs of zodiacal kingdoms.

The trilithon in the middle is slightly taller than the others because it would represent Aries in the company of Scorpio (pair of standing stones), both ruled by Mars (lintel). The central situation of this special trilithon corresponds to the central location of Mars among the planets, so to one side would be the trilithons ruled in the heavens by the inner planets, Venus (Taurus & Libra) and Mercury (Gemini & Virgo), and to the other side those ruled by the most external planets, Jupiter (Pisces & Sagittarius) and Saturn (Aquarius & Capricorn) (Fig. 86).[18]

The ten traditional kingdoms would be represented by the five pairs of trilithons, but it would be necessary to design a plan that represented the "new kingdoms" of Leo and Cancer in a way that they did not break with the ancestral ten lines but also would reflect

Fig. 87: Section of the Sarsen Circle (also visible in the background), around the larger trilithons erected inside.

their "parental status." The Sarsen Circle, formed by thirty standing stones and as many lintels may have been that powerful new element that represented Leo and Cancer and associated kingdoms.

The design of a circle of standing stones and lintels would resemble that of a "never ending trilithon." Its circular shape around the trilithons would be a symbol of the eternal and infinite (without beginning or ending) union from which all is born (planets and associated kingdoms, represented by the trilithons) (Fig. 87).

From a more spiritual point of view, this special fusion of masculine (vertical stones) and feminine (horizontal lintels) poles would be part of the stone-technology implemented to channel the kings' spirits during the sacrifices and the hierosgamos, events that, obviously, had to take place within the Sarsen Circle.

There is also a numeric factor that would support this hypothesis, and that is the number of standing stones and lintels. The most natural and intuitive ways of keeping track of time and seasons are to count the number of days it takes for the Moon to complete a lunation or cycle of phases, what we call a month ("moonth") (ca. 29.5 days), and to count the number of days it takes for the Sun to go back to the same position in the sky, what we call a year (365 days). In one year there are 12 lunations and an incomplete extra one (365/29.5 = 12,37), so the division of the year into 12 periods or months is a very natural and intuitive form of creating a calendar based on the combination of the cycles of the Sun and the Moon.[19] The stars visited by the Sun in its annual trip—or by the Moon in its monthly one—would be divided, therefore, into 12 sectors or signs. From a practical point of view, the whole Zodiac would be divided into 360 degrees because that is the best approximation to a number divisible by 12 that reproduces the path of the Sun over the stars at approximately 1º per day (360º vs. 365 days).[20]

In conclusion, the use of 30 standing stones and 30 lintels in the Sarsen Circle would be related to the cycles of the Sun and the Moon around the Zodiac. It was a brilliant solution to implement in the monument the structures that represented Leo and Cancer, ruled by the brightest luminaries, and embracing the remaining ones ruled by the five planets.

We have provided, finally, an explanation to each of the features of Stonehenge (Fig. 88). Given that this monument was designed as a scenario, a reflection of the dynamic sky, some features correspond to the same stars at different moments of the ceremony.

As expected in monuments that played an identical role, the same elements that were identified in Avebury appear also at Stonehenge, although arranged differently. Avebury and Stonehenge exhibit different architectonical solutions to the same principle, that of the intimate union of masculine and feminine poles at all levels, celestial, human and terrestrial: Sun-Moon, solstice-lunastice, Leo-Cancer, king-queen, hill-valley, spirit-soul...

At Avebury, we proposed that two different stone rings representing Cancer and Leo were unified by a larger stone ring built around them. Moreover, this union was reinforced by placing at their centers the symbol of the other—the feminine Cancer had an obelisk, and the masculine Leo had a cove, thus creating a kind of prehistoric circle of the *yin & yang*. At Stonehenge, a unique circle of vertical stones (Leo-masculine) linked by horizontal ones (Cancer-feminine) formed an endless structure that also fused the pair of zodiacal signs of Leo and Cancer, at each degree of the Zodiac and day of the year.[21]

THE IBERIAN ZODIAC • 147

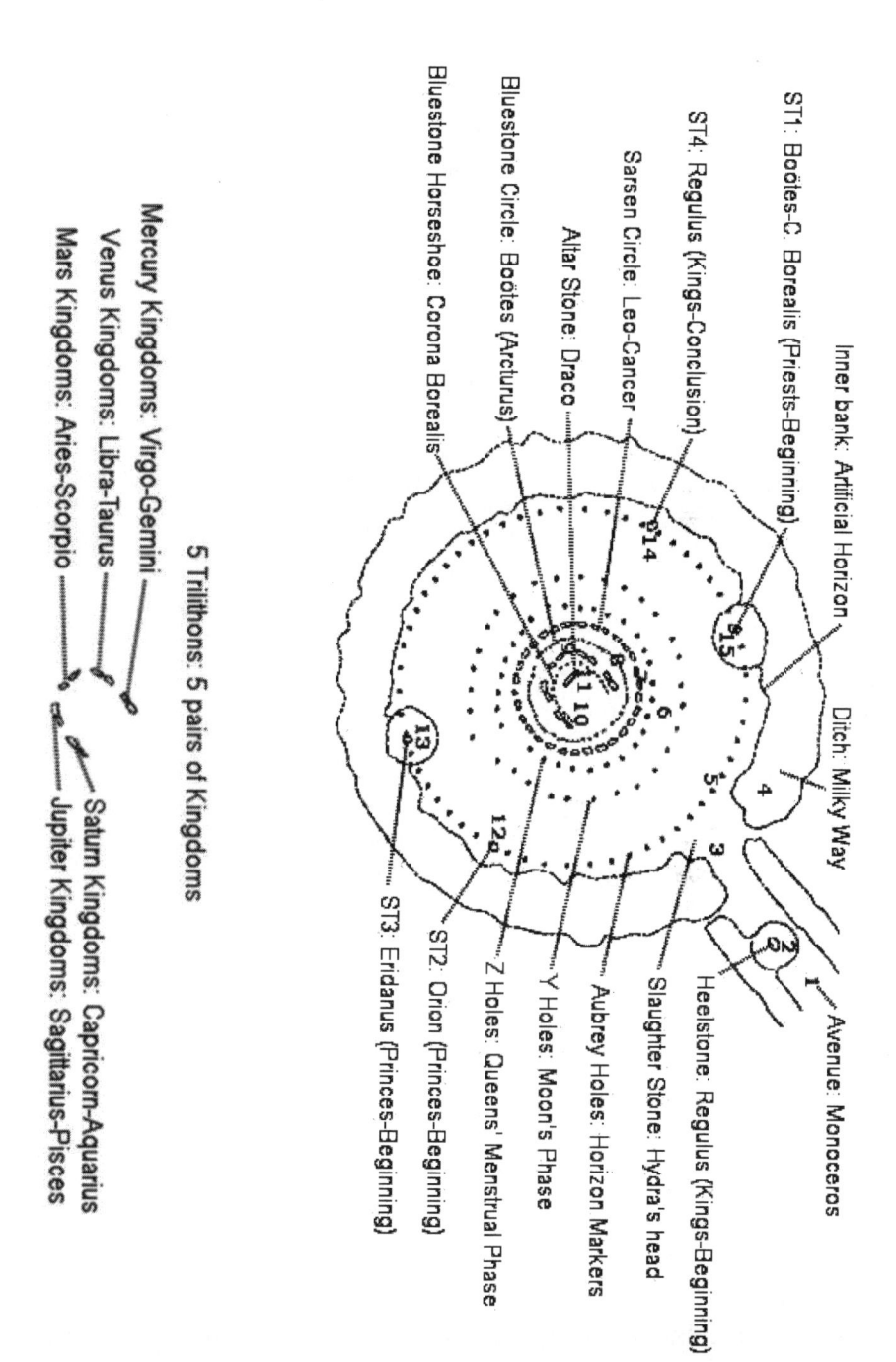

Fig. 88: Blueprint of Stonehenge indicating the function of each feature (the trilithons are explained in the insert below).

Fig. 89: The Heelstone (ca. 16 ft / 4.7 m tall).

As for the trilithons, the standing stones would represent the zodiacal signs associated with each one of the ten kingdoms, and the lintel above would represent the luminary that ruled and paired them from the sky.

Those elements of the entrance deserve a special mention because they are open to more than one valid interpretation. The Heelstone was present from the earliest phases of Stonehenge's construction (Fig. 89), and we proposed that its original function could be to signal the midsummer sunrises. However, once the monument was remodeled as a venue for renewing the monarchy in midwinter, this stone had to play a different role or else would have been removed. The rising of Regulus in midwinter may be the

Fig. 90: Stonehenge, with the Slaughter Stone in the forefront.

most logical choice, but not the only one. For example, the next full Moon after midwinter would rise a few degrees more to the north than the Heelstone's location (due to the lunastice), but it would transit directly over this stone some minutes later.

Also, the extrapolation of Avebury's design could suggest that a special gate was constructed at the entrance in representation of the stars Sirius & Procyon. If so, the Heelstone could represent Sirius, but then an additional stone should be placed alongside. Although no longer there, signs point to the existence of a stone exactly at that spot. (These explanations may not exclude one another, but were possibly the result of different initiatives on a monument that was active for many centuries.)

It should be expected an element representing the Hydra's head on the inner side of the entrance, and the Slaughter Stone could have played the role of signaling where the princes enacted the killing of the cosmic Hydra (Fig. 90).[22] Finally, Monoceros (the Unicorn) would be indirectly represented by the avenue, the path that the celestial hunter (Orion-princes) has to follow across the Milky Way tracking the celestial lion (Leo-kings).

Endnotes

[1] Based exclusively on geometrical considerations, the optimum circle would have a radius of approximately 320 miles (500 km) and would be centered on modern-day Madrid, the capital of Spain. This circle crosses the main peninsular harbors: Lisbon, Cadiz, Gibraltar, Barcelona and A Coruña. It also passes over Andorra la Vella, capital of the principality of Andorra, and approaches Palma de Mallorca (the capital of the Balearic Islands), as well as the southern French cities of Toulouse and Bordeaux, both by the Garonne River. This concatenation of modern cities could be regarded as a coincidence, an amalgam of founding dates that results in a grand anachronism, but perhaps also as a clue to the locations of some of the first proto-urban settlements established by the Megalith Builders in Iberia, thousands of years before they appear in the written records. The best bays, valleys or geographical circumstances that favor life at present would be equally appreciated in any epoch, at least since the end of the last glacial period (Quaternary Ice Age), about 10,000 years ago. Some of the most important Neolithic settlements may have been established in locations that were continuously inhabited in later times, in which, inevitably, the existing stones would end up being reused as part of new houses or in the masonry of temples and city walls. Consequently, we are not going to find megalithic monuments—or even clear archaeological evidence that they may have existed—in modern cities such as those mentioned above. Since archaeologists have access only to very limited physical evidence—mostly the cemeteries of the Megalith Builders—they can only propose limited hypotheses.

[2] The map does not distinguish between the diverse types and dimensions of megalithic constructions or their chronological differences (a very problematic issue that remains largely unresolved). Initial photo on page 131: entrance to the Dolmen of Menga (Málaga, Spain), one of the largest in the world.

[3] The modern regions associated with Aries are Aragon in Spain and Ariege in France, which are separated by Andorra. In these and neighboring regions, such as northern Catalonia, Roussillon and particularly at Languedoc, there are abundant megalithic constructions. An anachronism that surely will terrify the prudent etymologists concerns the similarity of the names Ariege and Aries (even Aragon, Andorra and Arga). The Argo ship was supposedly named for its builder, Argus, but perhaps it was taken instead from where it was bound for: Aries.

⁴ The Tagus River could have served as a route to penetrate into the interior of the peninsula. Its tributaries Jarama and Henares would take them to the Ebro Basin. The Jalón and Ebro Rivers would be the next navigable rivers, and finally the Segre and its tributary Valira would be used as ways to penetrate northwards, into the Pyrenees.

⁵ The desire to find the ultimate horizons, as seen from the center of Iberia, from which the Sun rose and set at the solstices (and the Moon at the lunastices) would have taken the Megalith Builders from one extreme of the peninsula to the other. The mountains of the Eastern Pyrenees would be considered especially sacred, and when the Megalith Builders decided to design a Zodiac around the peninsula, these mountains were assigned to Aries, represented as a goat or ram. During the megalithic epoch, Leo was the constellation visited by the Sun in midsummer. Leo was represented as a lion and assigned to the peninsular NW extremity, coinciding with the direction of the midsummer sunset. Both regions (modern-day Aragon and Galicia, reflecting Aries and Leo respectively) would be particularly sacred. The capital of Aragon is Saragossa, and it is located in the axis that signaled midsummer sunrise and Aries. The capital of Galicia is Santiago de Compostela, and it lies at the extreme of the axis that indicated midsummer sunset and Leo. It is quite a remarkable coincidence that both capitals are now considered the sanctuaries of the patroness and the patron of Spain (*Virgen del Pilar & Santiago Apóstol*). Santiago de Compostela is also the end point of an ancient pilgrimage known as The Way of St James. Are these mere anachronisms, or the manifestation of a deeply rooted solar culture that predates Christianity?

⁶ In Greek mythology, the Styx River formed the boundary between the world and the underworld, and all the souls had to be ferried across. This myth would fit perfectly with the Eastern Iberian custom of transporting their dead over to Africa (across the Alboran Sea). Perhaps they considered Iberia as the land of life (Earth or world), and Africa as the land of death (Hell or underworld).

⁷ For example, Cancer and Gemini reflected directly on the Cantabrian Sea, so they would have to be "pulled down" onto firm land, over the regions of Asturias and Cantabria respectively. On the other side of the Zodiac, Pisces would connect Catalonia and the Balearic Islands, and it becomes even more evident that Scorpio, Sagittarius, Capricorn and Aquarius would share both Iberian and North African coasts to accommodate their stars.

[8] *The New View over Atlantis*, by John Michell, Thames & Hudson Ed., pp. 46-7 (1983)

[9] For instance, in 1927 Katherine Maltwood claimed to have discovered the existence of a large celestial mirror in Glastonbury, near Avebury (*Glastonbury's Temple of The Stars*). This landscape-Zodiac was followed by new discoveries of at least half a dozen similar ones in Britain, such as those described by Grant Berkley in Wales (*The Discovery of the Ark of the Covenant: Based on the Works of Baram Blackett and Alan Wilson*). In Ireland, Anthony Murphy and Richard Moore link up the megalithic complex of the Boyne Valley with Cygnus (*Island of the Setting Sun: In Search of Ireland's Ancient Astronomers*), and Martin Brennan interprets the megalithic art of this Irish valley in cosmological terms (*The Boyne Valley Mission*). Andis Kaulins finds sky-maps connecting all kind of megalithic sites over large territories and all over the world (*Stars, Stones and Scholars*). Thomas Brophy discusses the relationship of a unique megalithic stone circle at Nabta Playa in Egypt with Orion (*The Origin Map: Discovery of a Prehistoric Megalithic Astrophysical Map and Sculpture of the Universe*). Robert Bouval proposed that the pyramids of Giza represented Orion's belt (*The Orion Mystery*), whereas Andrew Collins said they were built taking Cygnus as their celestial model (*The Cygnus Mystery*). Graham Hancock finds relationships between some constellations and many monuments of ancient civilizations; for example, the Giza complex would be related to Orion and Leo, or Angkor in Cambodia to Draco (*Heaven's Mirror: Quest for the Lost Civilizations*). In South America, Maria Reiche claimed that the famous Lines of Nazca were astronomical records of ancient Peruvians (*Mystery in the Desert*).

[10] This idea is present in the cosmologies of most cultures and civilizations, usually described as a pillar, pole, tree or mountain.

[11] The center of Iberia is almost on the same meridian as Carnac and the Orkney Islands; the longitude of Madrid is 3.7° W, and that of Carnac and the Orkneys is 3.2° W (only half a degree apart). Another "coincidence" suggesting that the Megalith Builders also considered this vertical axis along Western Europe to be a very special one.

[12] The Greek classical geography described in the myth of Jason and the Argonauts could be a reproduction of the original one existing centuries earlier in Western Europe. Classical Aries reflected on the Caucasus, and pre-classical or megalithic reflected on the Pyrenees. This could explain another curious anachronism, the existence of two

"Iberias" in such distant geographies. The courses of the Ebro and Kura Rivers both flow throughout the southern plains of their mountain ranges, the Pyrenees and the Caucasus, the first towards the Mediterranean Sea and the second towards the Caspian Sea (Fig. 76, p. 128). The Kura River would be the equivalent to the original Ebro River in Iberia (modern-day Spain), from where both "Iberians" got their name. Etymologically, *Iberian* derives from "the people who dwell by the Ebro River."

[13] Europeans still piece together their largest ships (Airbus airplanes and Ariane spaceships) at Toulouse, a good example of the strength of traditions. (Even the names seem to be uncannily related to Aries.)

[14] Herodotus reports that it took three years for a Phoenician expedition of the seventh century BC to circumnavigate Africa—though they went ashore for long periods to plant seeds and wait for the harvest.

[15] At present, Madrid is an autonomous region containing the capital of Spain, situated at the geographical center of the Iberian Peninsula. It is surrounded by Castilla (Castilla y León and Castilla-La Mancha) which occupies the high plains of central Spain known as Meseta, a plateau of ca. 2,000 ft (600 m) high on average (the Round Table) separated from the coastal regions by mountain ranges. León, meaning *lion* and with a rampant lion on its coat of arms, is the historical region situated in between Castilla and Galicia. Could this universal royal emblem have had its origin in the reflection of Leo upon Galicia? Notice how Leo's reflection adopts the posture of a rampant lion (Fig. 81, p. 137).

[16] To ascertain the order of the planets is very simple. The inner ones from the Earth (Mercury & Venus) always move in the sky not too far from the Sun, either ahead or behind, whereas the external ones (Mars, Jupiter and Saturn) move independently around the Zodiac, the slower its revolution the farther apart. To assign a pair of zodiacal signs to each planet is, therefore, a logical process. The closest luminary to the Sun, Mercury, would rule over the pair of signs contiguous to Leo and Cancer, i.e. over Virgo & Gemini. The next luminary, Venus, would rule over the next couple, Libra & Taurus. Following this pattern, Mars would rule over Scorpio & Aries, Jupiter over Sagittarius & Pisces, and Saturn—the slowest and farthest luminary—over Capricorn & Aquarius (logically, on the opposite section of the Zodiac from Leo & Cancer).

[17] This could be the real reason for Aries being the first sign of the Zodiac, and not because the vernal equinox took place on this sign during the first millennium BC, as is usually offered as an explanation.

[18] Eventually, the Altar Stone would be introduced at the center of the monument to indicate the single location of the "kingdom of the Dragon" at the center of the Zodiac. The eleven rows at Le Ménec could be explained either as the addition of the kingdom of the Dragon to the traditional ten or as the splitting of one of the three kingdoms that comprised three zodiacal signs (Aries, Leo and Cancer). An altogether different explanation for the numbers of rows at each of the modules of Carnac would be to consider the incorporation of "foreign kingdoms" into the confederation, adding to the ten traditional ones. In the last centuries of the confederation, represented at Carnac by the module of Kerlescan, it seems that the special kingdom that agglutinated the territories of Aries, Leo and Cancer split, and the confederation came to be formed by thirteen kingdoms. This political upheaval could have also contributed to the necessity of a new ceremonial venue that reflected the new idiosyncrasy, resulting in Stonehenge.

[19] The Sun and the phase of the Moon go back to the same positions every 19 years (Metonic Cycle), a quite elemental observance for a culture that studied their cycles, which Meton simply "rediscovered."

[20] The number 360 is divisible by all natural numbers up to 12 other than 7 and 11, which enormously facilitates measurements and simple mathematical calculations.

[21] This fusion was accomplished through several factors: 1) its concentric location at the center of the monument, 2) by enclosing the trilithons and bluestones, 3) by its circular shape, and 4) by the number of stones (30 standing and 30 lintels). In addition to being practical, the joint technique used to secure the lintels above the standing stones might have served another purpose, with the mortise and tenon fusing the masculine and feminine stones (and principles they represented) more intimately.

[22] There is also the possibility that the Slaughter Stone represented Procyon, since this star is on the inner side of the Milky Way, and the Slaughter Stone is on the inner side of the trench that represented the Milky Way.

10

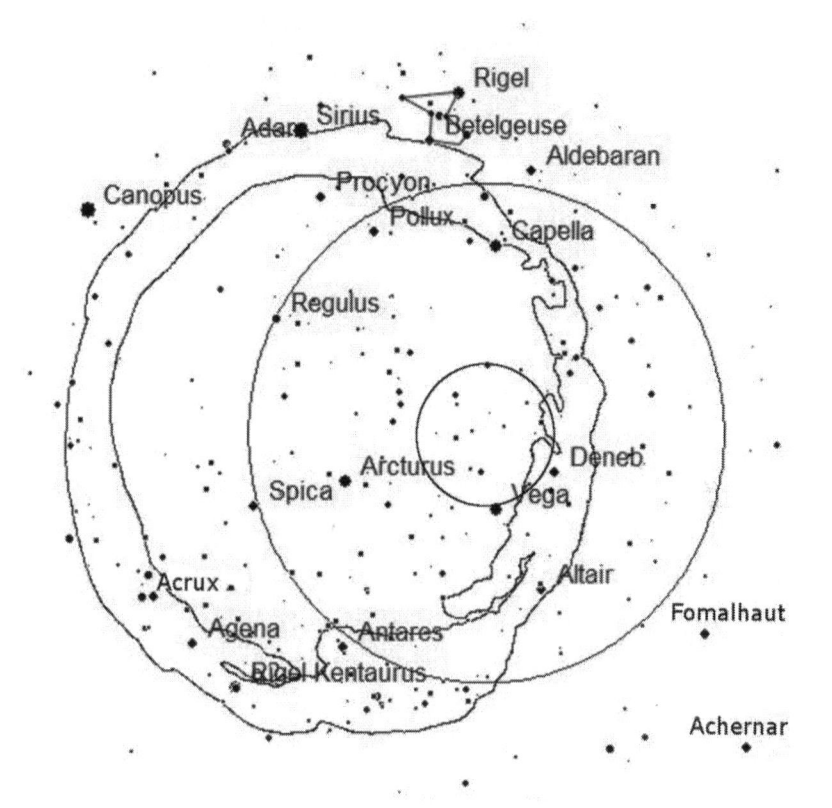

THE GREAT CELESTIAL MIRROR

WE have found the Zodiac and Orion's brightest star reflecting upon the geography of Western Europe, as well as Eridanus extending between the British Isles and Egypt. In this chapter we are going to find out that these were not isolated examples, but parts of a great celestial mirror that reflected the whole sky.

Fig. 91: The Centaur and the Crux projected on the Canary Islands.

To project the celestial sphere approximately onto a flat surface is not a difficult feat. The Megalith Builders may have used a sky map like that on the previous page to design a celestial mirror. Basically, there are two main rings: the Zodiac and the Milky Way.[1]

The Guanches

The Milky Way is a pale whitish band arching around the entire celestial sphere, more brilliant than the rest because that is where the galactic plane lies and the density of stars is highest.[2] The Megalith Builders were very interested in the Milky Way, as deduced from the designs of Almendres, Avebury and Stonehenge. The Centaur and the Crux are situated at the bottom of the Milky Way (lowest declinations), forming one of the most recognizable asterism of the firmament, so it could be expected that they assigned these stars to a remarkable location. The inevitable candidate had to be the Canary Islands, near the Tropic of Cancer. In fact, the main seven islands of this archipelago tally in number and arrangement with the brightest stars of these southern constellations (Fig. 91).

The two most eastern islands (Lanzarote & Fuerteventura) would reflect the pair of stars Rigil Kent & Agena, in the Centaur, among the brightest of the firmament. The remaining five islands of the archipelago would reflect the main five stars of the Crux: Acrux would reflect on Gran Canaria, Becrux on Tenerife, Gacrux on La Palma, Decrux on El Hierro, and Juxta Crucem on La Gomera.[3]

THE GREAT CELESTIAL MIRROR • 157

Fig. 92: Above, Roque Nublo, a "natural menhir" (ca. 260 ft / 80 m tall) in Gran Canaria. Below, Guanche megalithic sanctuary at Garajonay, La Gomera. (The silhouette of Teide Volcano appears in the background.)

The natives of Tenerife Island before Spanish colonization were the Guanches, a term that was later used to name the habitants of the whole archipelago. The Guanches were physically and culturally different from African people, they built megalithic sanctuaries (Fig. 92), engraved and carved rocks with complex geometric symbols, and mummified some of their dead.

The origin of this peculiar people remains controversial, but we can now easily solve the mystery. The Megalith Builders arrived at these islands because they were the best possible location to assign to the bottom of the Milky Way (the Centaur and the Crux).

The Guanches were therefore the closest we can come to observing the original Megalith Builders' culture, since their insularity and latitude prevented them from being too "adulterated" throughout history.[4] Some scholars have identified similarities between their language—unfortunately extinct though still present in the local toponymy—and those of Berbers and Basques, which has prompted them to suggest a migration in the past connecting these regions. There is, however, another reason that could provide a much simpler explanation to this phenomenon. These three cultures, on account of their geographical isolation—insularity in the case of the Guanches, and rugged terrain in the case of Berbers (Rif and Atlas Ranges) and Basques (Cantabrian and Pyrenees Ranges)—were able to preserve a common cultural substrate prior to historical times: that of the Megalith Builders. The origin of the Basque language (Euskera), so difficult to relate to any other, would come directly from that spoken by the Megalith Builders.

"The Hyperboreans also have a language, we are informed, which is peculiar to them," wrote Diodorus, in what may be one of the earliest references to the original Proto-Euskera.

The Canary Islands would be at the lowest part of the celestial mirror designed by the Megalith Builders on the Atlantic coasts of Europe and Northern Africa. According to the journey of the princes, these islands would represent the gate into the tropical regions situated at lower latitudes. Likewise, on the opposite side of Africa, the Elephantine Island in the Nile River would represent the exit gate. The island of Tenerife has at its center a great volcano, called Teide (12,198 ft / 3,718 m) after the Guanche term *Echeyde*, which means *Hell*. In the journey, the intertropical part would be considered as a "descent to Hell," corresponding to the "ascent to Heaven" the part that took place on the opposite section of the loop, in the Northern European regions (Fig. 67, p. 113).

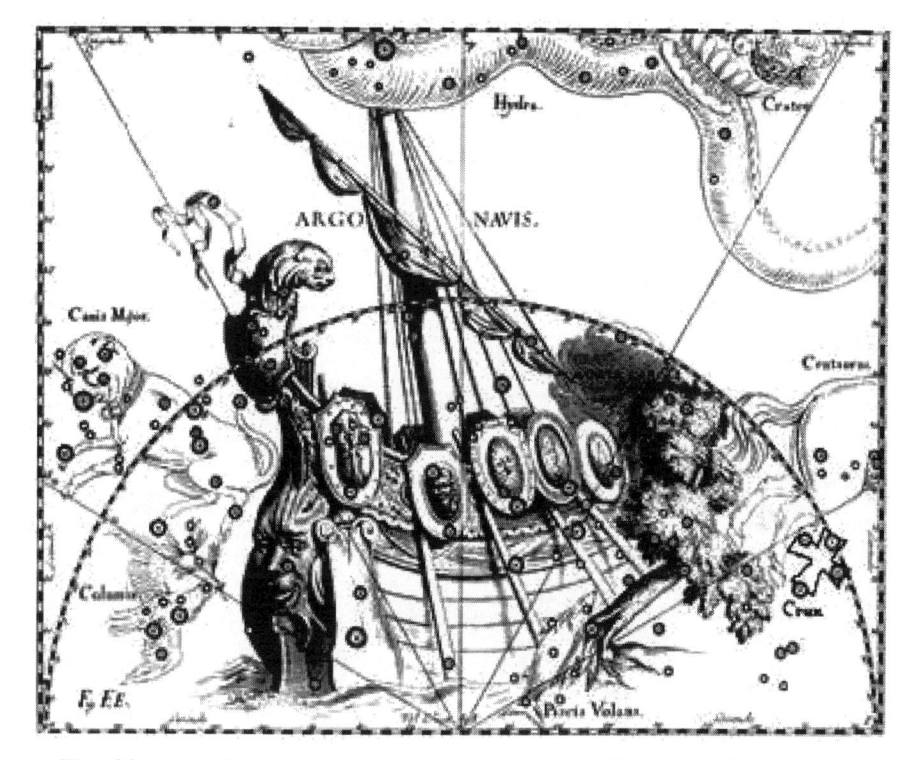

Fig. 93: Argo Navis (between Canis Major and the Crux) (J. Hevelius).

Argo Navis

Above the Canary Islands there is not so much land which could be assigned to the reflection of the following stars of the Milky Way, just the archipelagos of Madeira and the Azores. The section of the Milky Way that should reflect upon this part of the celestial mirror contains only one huge constellation: Argo Navis, the ship of Jason and the Argonauts (Fig. 93). It is striking, to say the least, that the stars which should reflect mostly upon the Atlantic Ocean are represented by a large ship.[5]

Argo Navis has its prow (front part) pointing towards the Crux. At its other end the stern contains the brightest star of the southern hemisphere, Canopus.[6] According to the celestial mirror, the Pico Volcano (1,600 ft / 2,351 m), in the homonymous island of the Azores, could be the special location where the Megalith Builders considered that such an especially bright star was mirrored.

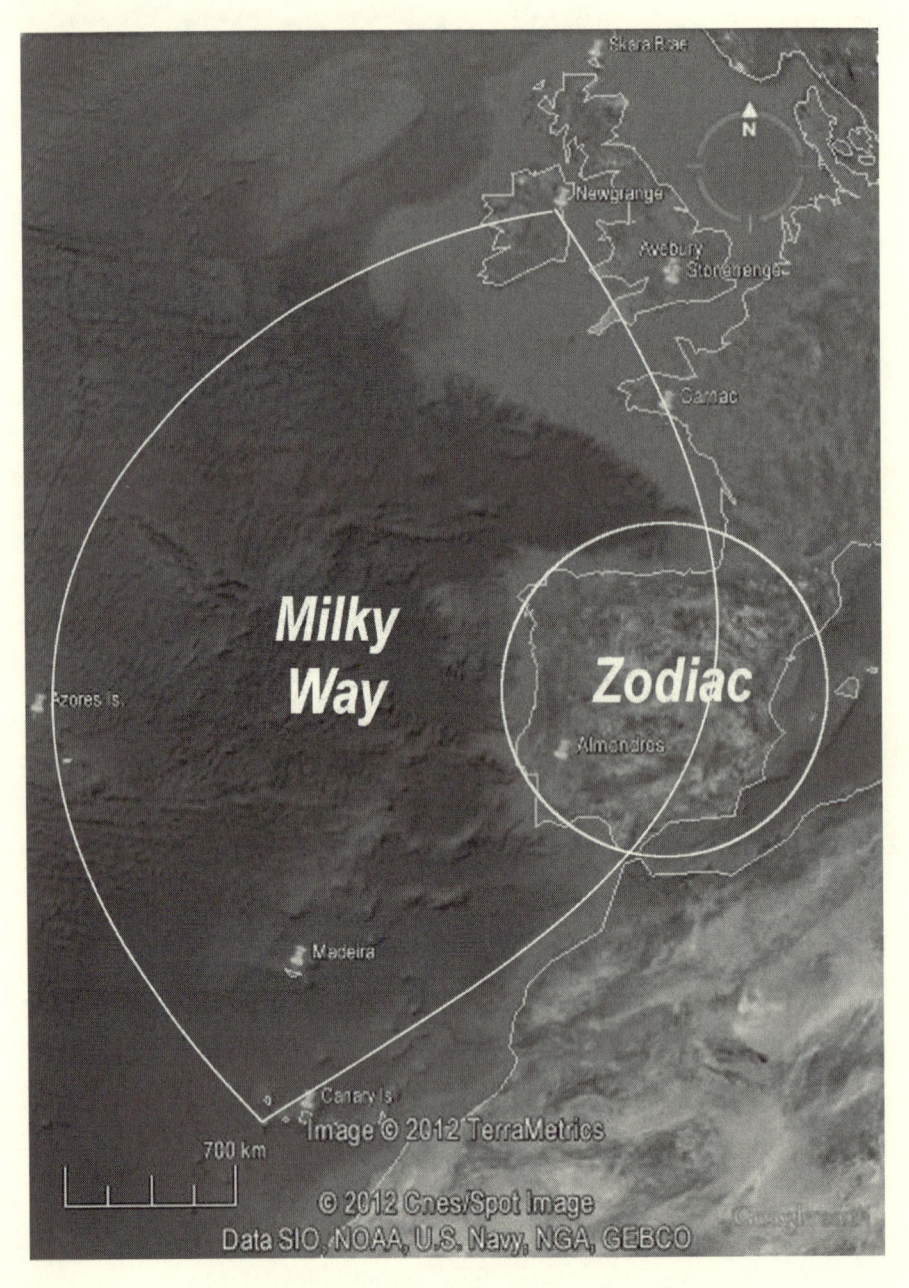

Fig. 94: Schematic plan of the great celestial mirror.

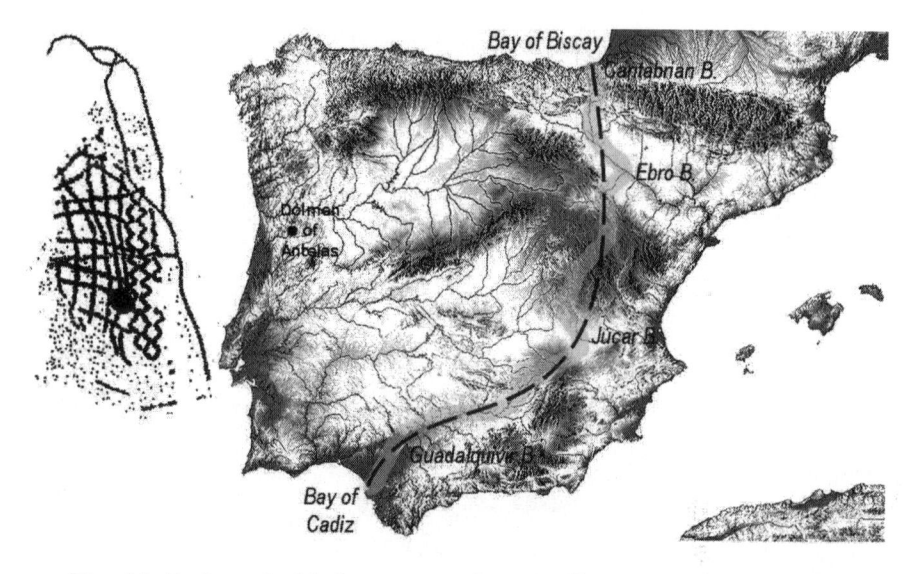

Fig. 95: Left, probable boat painted vertically on an orthostat of the Dolmen of Antelas (north of Portugal). Right, tentative course of the Milky Way throughout the Iberian Peninsula, between the Bays of Biscay and Cadiz. (The river basins crossed are indicated.)

The Milky Way

Following the Milky Way "upwards," the next constellation situated immediately after Argo Navis is Canis Major (the Greater Dog), and the only firm land "above" the Azores is Ireland.

The schematic map of the complete celestial mirror can now be projected, indicating the whereabouts of the two main celestial rings: the Milky Way stretching between the Canary Islands and Ireland, and the Zodiac encircling the Iberian Peninsula (Fig. 94).

The section of the Milky Way internal to the Zodiac had to reflect upon Iberia, between the Gulf of Biscay in the north and the Gulf of Cadiz in the south. If the Megalith Builders had assigned the rest of the Milky Way upon water, it seems reasonable to look for a fluvial course throughout the peninsula that connected these gulfs.[7] It should cross four river basins: those of the Cantabrian, Ebro, Júcar and Guadalquivir rivers (Fig. 95).[8]

Fig. 96: Entrance at Newgrange, with the roof-box above.

Finally, the section of the Milky Way that lay between the Zodiac (Iberia) and its bottom part, where the Centaur and the Crux are located (the Canary Islands), should reflect on the North Atlantic coasts of Africa. In this section of the Milky Way there is fundamentally one very bright constellation: Scorpius, and it should mainly reflect on what is nowadays Morocco.

Sirius

The Megalith Builders placed their royal necropolis in the Irish megalithic complex of the Boyne Valley, Newgrange being its most magnificent monument. Previously, we had conjectured that the bodies of the kings sacrificed at Avebury were taken there for proper disposal. Given that Sirius is a star in Canis Major and that this constellation should reflect on Ireland, the question naturally arose, "could Newgrange be the reflection of Sirius?"

The concurrence in Newgrange of function and celestial association reinforces that possibility, since building the royal necropolis under the brightest of the stars could be what the Megalith Builders had in mind when they chose to locate this monument in Ireland.[9]

Certainly, the round shape and the milky quartz used in the façade of Newgrange—some authors suggest that the whole cairn was originally covered with this type of rock—would fit with that of a monument built as the representation of the brightest star, and on the shore of the Milky Way.[10]

Perhaps the most noteworthy feature of Newgrange is the roof-box positioned above its entrance (Fig. 96). Its dimensions, the slightly upward inclination of the passage and the setting of some of the orthostats, create a very narrow view of the sky visible from inside the rear chamber of the structure. Newgrange is famous in that during midwinter days, a shaft of light radiating from the Sun just after sunrise illuminates the interior rear chamber.[11]

If Newgrange was built to represent Sirius on Earth, we surmise that it was the light of this star the builders actually intended to monitor. When the area of sky visible from inside Newgrange was analyzed through computer modeling, the result confirmed that Sirius could be seen through the window (Fig. 97).[12]

The visibility of this star from within the structure through such a narrow frame (ca. 4º azimuth x 1.5º altitude) is remarkable. We can conclude that it was most likely planned that way, and was not just a coincidence.

It could be expected that Sirius would traverse the window through its center instead of through the upper left corner. Perhaps the roof-box, in addition to monitoring the midwinter sunrise and

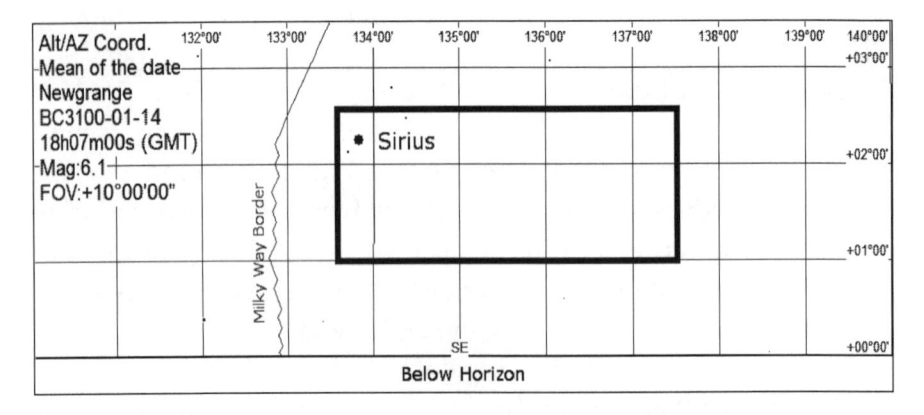

Fig. 97: Sky visible from the rear chamber of Newgrange in midwinter. (Azimuth vs. altitude. Sirius shone within the frame 1 h 35' after sunset.)

Sirius rising, was also designed to track other luminaries or stars and was built with several observatory purposes in mind (this is the opinion of Anthony Murphy, an expert on the monuments of the Boyne Valley).[13] Or perhaps Newgrange was designed and constructed a few centuries earlier than currently estimated, when Sirius' declination would fit better. For example, about 3400 BC, Sirius would have been seen crossing through the long diagonal of the window.

Endnotes

[1] The initial image on page 155 corresponds to the stereographic projection of the celestial sphere onto a plane using ecliptic coordinates with the same orientation as the celestial mirror. These coordinates accurately reflect the shapes of the constellations—the relative position of the stars to each other—within the Ecliptic, but distorts them as they are positioned farther away from the center. The band is the Milky Way, and the bigger circle is the Ecliptic (the Zodiac). The smaller circle is the route followed by the Celestial Pole in a Great Year cycle (ca. 26,000 years). The brightest stars are indicated. Also, notice how Orion—the only constellation signaled with lines as a reference—appears on the top facing downwards.

[2] Our solar system is located in a barred spiral galaxy whose galactic plane is inclined at about 60º to the plane in which the Earth rotates around the Sun (Ecliptic plane). The center of the galaxy is in the direction of Sagittarius, where the Milky Way is widest, to the point of including almost completely the adjoining zodiacal sign of Scorpius.

[3] Acrux and Becrux are first magnitude stars. To reproduce the shape of the Crux, the star Becrux should reflect on the north-eastern tip of Tenerife island, where the capital, Santa Cruz de Tenerife, is located. This is a curious anachronism, since the name of the capital means *Holy Cross*, and the flag of the archipelago is a white X on blue.

[4] For the very same reason, some degree of corruption from the original customs should be expected over its more than two millennia of isolation.

[5] Argo Navis appears nowadays redistributed into three smaller constellations: Carina (hull), Puppis (stern) and Vela (sails). Some authors also include Pyxis (compass).

[6] Canopus is a negative first magnitude star (m = –0.62; ranking 2).

[7] The Ecliptic (Zodiac) was designed over water to allow the luminaries to circulate. Likewise, the Milky Way seems to have also been designed over water to allow the movement of "something," which could support the idea of being considered as a celestial path for souls.

[8] Based only on geographical considerations, the four basins would be divided by three mountain ranges: the Basque, the Albarracín and the Alcaraz. The river in the Cantabrian Basin could be the Bidasoa; in the Ebro Basin the Arga, Aragón, Ebro, Jalón and Jiloca; in the Júcar Basin

the Júcar and Bazalote, and in the Guadalquivir Basin the Guadalmena, Guadalimar and Guadalquivir. The significance of the *Virgen del Pilar* sanctuary in Saragossa could now be refined because it was at this point where the Axis Mundi crossed the reflection of the Milky Way (Ebro River). If the Megalith Builders considered the Milky Way as a route for souls, then its logical anthropomorphic representation would be a celestial woman (the Milky Way) holding a child in her arms (the souls). Thus, the image of a celestial goddess holding her son in her arms could predate by several millennia the Bronze Age Goddess Astarte of the Eastern Mediterranean, considered the iconic precursor of the Virgin in Christianity.

[9] Sirius is not located within the Milky Way, but outside it. If we suppose that the Boyne River was intended to represent the Milky Way, that may explain why Newgrange was built on the northern shore of the river. Ireland would be crossed by the reflection of the Milky Way, probably along a fluvial path that corresponds roughly to the Shannon, Brosna and Boyne Rivers, connecting the Atlantic Ocean with the Irish Sea.

[10] If the painting found in the Dolmen of Antelas represented a boat, its vertical orientation—quite unnatural for a naval representation—could be a consequence of this stone being re-utilized from a previous site in which it was positioned horizontally. But if its orientation was intended to be vertical, it might represent Argo Navis, between Canis Major and Crux, reflected on the celestial mirror along a vertical direction between the Canary Islands and Ireland (across the Azores) and in front of the Iberian coasts where the Dolmen of Antelas is situated. The solid dot that appears on the stern of the painted boat might be a schematic representation of the star Canopus, the second brightest in the night-sky. (The insert in Fig. 95 is taken from *Passage-Graves of Northwestern Iberia*, by Maria de Jesus Sanches, Journal of Iberian Archaeology, vol. 8, pp. 127-58, 2006.)

[11] *The winter solstice phenomenon at Newgrange, Ireland: Accident or design?*, by Tom Ray, Nature, vol. 337, pp. 343-5 (1989)

[12] Sirius rising azimuth from Newgrange in midwinter 3100 BC was ca. 129º. (The sunrise azimuth was ca. 133º.)

[13] *Island of the Setting Sun: In Search of Ireland's Ancient Astronomers*, by Richard Moore & Anthony Murphy, Liffey Press (2009)

11
THE ARCHANGEL ORION

RIGEL is the star that corresponds to Orion's left foot, designated on the great celestial mirror by Silbury Hill. The head of this celestial hunter is close to Taurus, and the upper part of this zodiacal constellation was indicated by the Garonne River. Therefore, we can guess the territory the Megalith Builders assigned to Orion, a giant that rested his feet on the south of Great Britain and leaned his body over the western lands of France.

Based on these two simple conditions (Silbury Hill as Rigel and the Garonne River as the limit of Taurus), the right foot of Orion (star Saiph) had to be located on the Cornish Peninsula (SW of England). Likewise, his belt—three aligned stars Mintaka, Alnilam and Alnitak—had to be on the French coasts of the English Channel.[1] The number of megalithic monuments in both regions (Cornwall and Brittany) is overwhelming, but, in choosing the exact locations of these stars, there is a curious anachronism that may contain a clue.

Fig. 98: St Michael's Mount, in the Cornish Peninsula (SW of England).

The most famous site in the French region where Orion's belt should be mirrored is without any doubt Mont Saint-Michel. This is a granitic tidal island in the borderland of Normandy with Brittany, connected to the mainland through a thin natural land bridge, nowadays crowned with a magnificent abbey dedicated to the Archangel Michael (photo on previous page).[2] This attractive rocky promontory would certainly have come to the attention of the Megalith Builders, who would see in it a proper location to assign one of Orion's belt stars. The other two stars should, consequently, be along the Gulf of Saint-Malo. When another islet dedicated to the Archangel Michael (Ilot-Saint-Michel) appeared at the location where the other extreme of Orion's belt should be, a curious anachronism connecting this archangel and Orion began to become apparent. The central star of Orion's belt had to be on the cape where the city of Saint-Malo originated, called Aleth, perfectly aligned and equidistant between both Saint-Michel's islets. The confirmation of the association of St Michael with Orion became more evident when, along the coast of Cornwall, exactly where the right foot of Orion (Saiph) should be, appeared another mount dedicated to this archangel (St Michael's Mount), a tidal island with a castle on top and a chapel dedicated to him (Fig. 98).

Finally, as for Orion's shoulders, the star Betelgeuse should reflect above the Garonne estuary, near the present-day city of La Rochelle, and the star Bellatrix should be found not far from the fluvial island where the city of Tours is located.

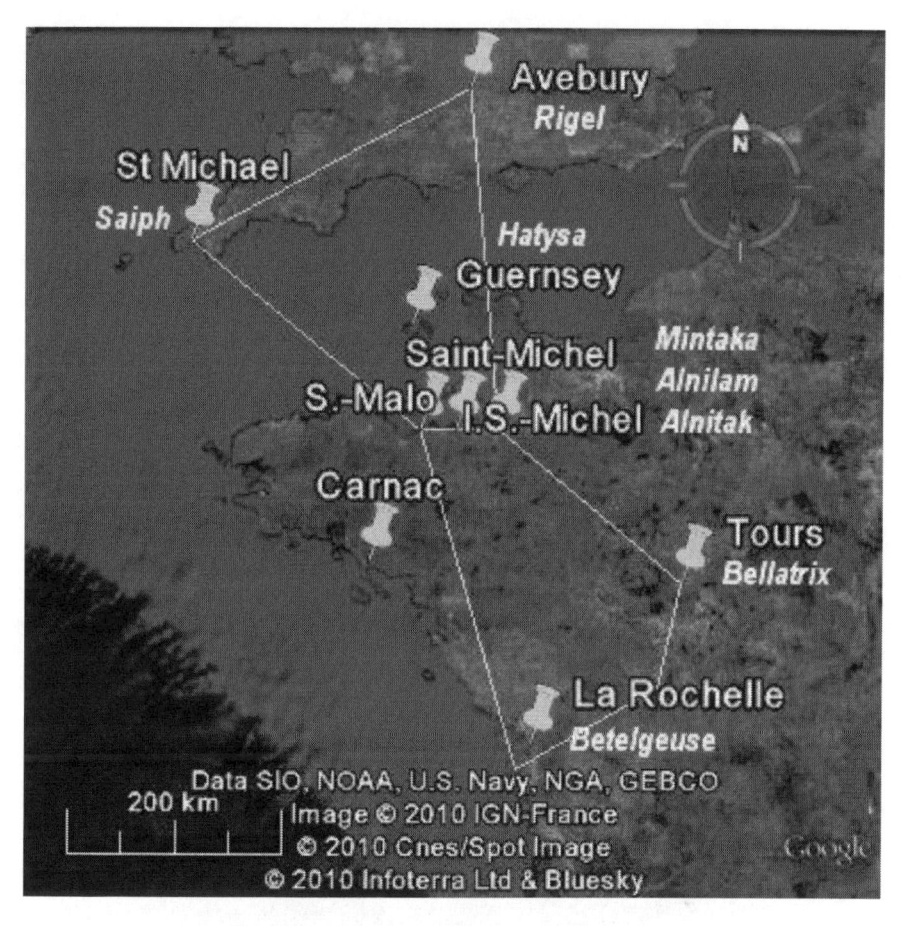

Fig. 99: Orion on the celestial mirror.

The Channel Islands would be the perfect location at which to assign the reflection of the stars dangling from Orion's belt, represented by a dagger or sword. In fact, these islands—particularly the larger ones, Jersey and Guernsey—are rich in megalithic constructions, including some magnificent passage mounds.

The final assignment of Orion can be seen in Fig. 99.[3]

Megalithic Lines

Alfred Watkins was an antiquarian who, in the first half of the last century, "discovered" that some megalithic monuments, churches, paths and prominent outcrops in the landscape of South Britain were aligned in straight lines that he called *Ley lines*.

Fig. 100: St Michael and the Devil. (Raphael, 16th c.)

Although Watkins considered these lines merely to be ancient paths, the concept has developed geomantic interpretations similar in concept to the Chinese *dragon lines* used in systems like *Feng-shui* (through which a vital energy called *qi* moves according to the laws of Heaven & Earth). Interestingly, the most important Ley line is called St Michael and goes from St Michael's Mount in the western

Fig. 101: Cairn of Barnenez, in the north of Brittany (France).

extreme of the Cornish Peninsula to the eastern coast of England, passing over Avebury and connecting tens of locations related to this archangel. The celestial mirror can provide an explanation to this phenomenon, because this axis was the bottom line upon which the great Orion rested his feet on Earth, and St Michael was no other than this constellation in Christian disguise, usually represented as an angel brandishing a spade or spear in the act of subduing a demon from above (Fig. 100).

Due to geodesic constrictions, Carnac could not reflect any of Orion's stars, so this unique megalithic monument had to belong to a different section of the celestial sphere. In the monarchical renewal ceremony, we saw that, besides Orion and Leo, there were other constellations that also played important roles, such as Canis Minor and the Hydra's head. These stars are located between the Milky Way and the Zodiac (Gemini & Cancer). The only land above the Iberian Zodiac is Brittany, so, if Canis Minor and the head of Hydra were assigned on the celestial mirror, there was no other option than on this peninsula.[4]

Brittany is extraordinarily rich in megalithic monuments, some of them among the oldest known, dating from the middle of the fifth millennium BC; however, the design of the celestial mirror seems to be of a later inception, around the end of the following millennium, when Avebury began to be remodeled as a new ceremonial center in substitution for the obsolete one in Almendres. Consequently, many megalithic monuments, particularly in Brittany, existed prior to the assignment of stars in the celestial mirror. This might be the case of Barnenez, a huge cairn with eleven passage graves in the north of Brittany (Fig. 101), the region where the brightest star of Canis Minor, called Procyon, should reflect upon. Perhaps it was remodeled to signal the reflection of this star.

The Celestial Beasts

The positioning of the Hydra's head on Brittany could explain why the animal chosen to represent this constellation was a water-snake, since most of its long body reflected on the Atlantic waters, arching along the western side of Iberia, from Brittany to the north of Africa, aligned with the Celestial Equator during the megalithic epoch (Fig. 102).[5] These celestial alignments constitute in themselves clear evidence of the true antiquity of the western representational system of constellations.

Only the head of Hydra would be on firm land (above the Celestial Equator), and it had to be on the west coast of Brittany. Megalithic alignments can be found in many sites, though not so vast and spectacular as those in Carnac. One of the reasons behind the shape of the Carnac stones could be to reflect the upper part of the body of a great celestial water-snake that rested its head on this land. A local folkloric legend says that the rocks go to bathe in the ocean at night, perhaps an allegory referring to its origins, when the builders understood that most of this long monument's "virtual body" stretched into the Atlantic waters, reflecting the stars of Hydra.[6]

During the monarchical renewal ceremony celebrated at Avebury, once the princes entered the henge, they would first encounter the Ringstone. The name and the shape of this stone suggest that the princes would pierce it with a spear or sword, the same way as Orion in the sky would have to gain access to Cancer and Leo.[7] This incident supports the hypothesis of the Alignments of Carnac being a representational mausoleum of a Hell or underworld "governed" by the huge snake that divided the celestial sphere into two hemispheres.

THE ARCHANGEL ORION • 173

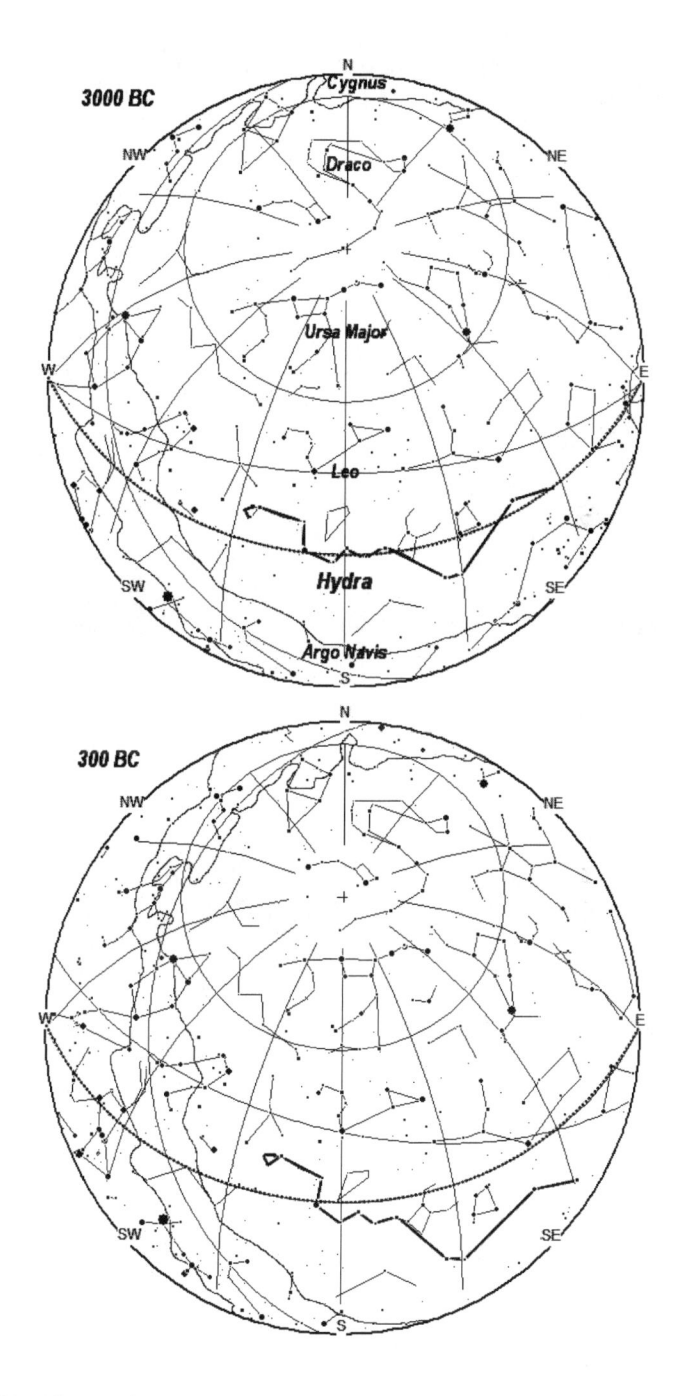

Fig. 102: The Hydra was aligned with the Celestial Equator (dotted line) around 3000 BC, whereas by 300 BC it already lay clearly off the line.

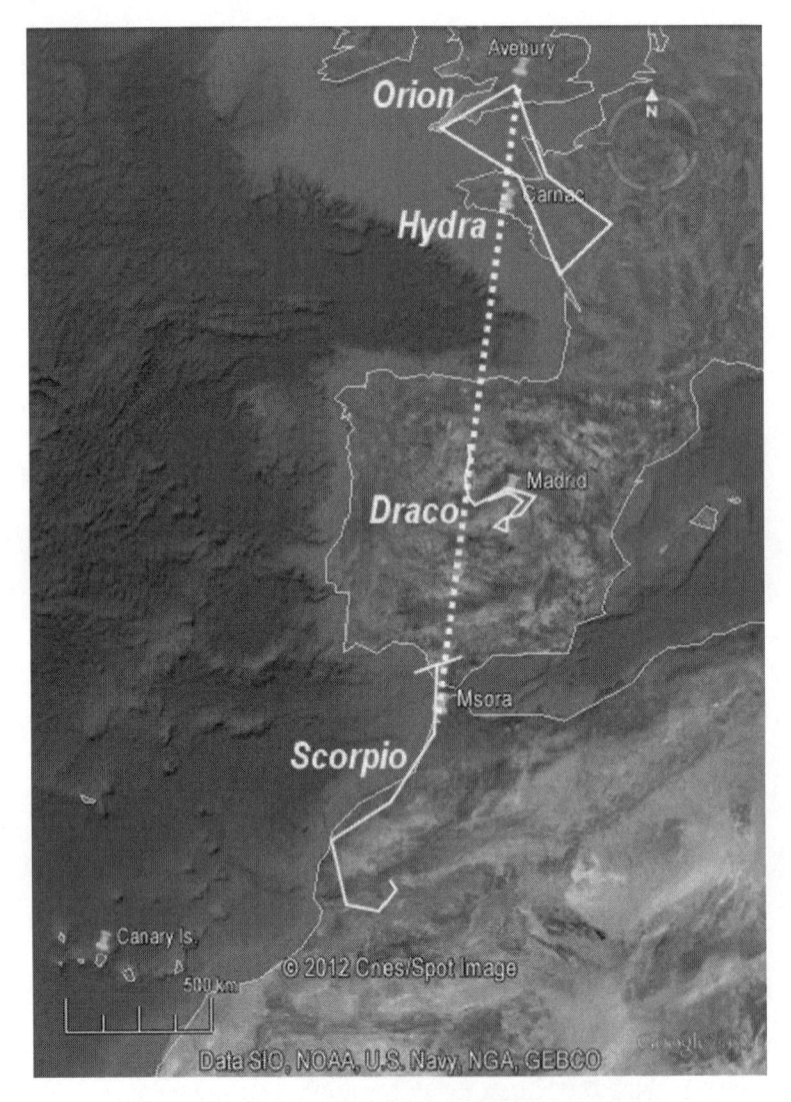

*Fig. 103: Axis connecting Avebury and Carnac.
Its prolongation crosses Iberia and hits the Strait of Gibraltar.*

Since we have identified the locations of Orion and Hydra's head on the celestial mirror, it is natural to check the line or "spear" that connected them, between Avebury and Carnac. Surprisingly, the prolongation of this axis hit the reflection of Draco (about where Thuban should be) at the center of Iberia; but even more revealing is the fact that it also hit the Strait of Gibraltar, a region that be-

Fig. 104: Cromlech of Msoura (Morocco).

longed to the reflection of Scorpio. This is the zodiacal sign whose stars have a lower declination, in fact, only its "head" shines close to the Ecliptic. Therefore, only the head should be assigned on the Iberian Peninsula (around the island of Cadiz), whereas its body and tail should be on African soil. The Moroccan coastal line seems to fit the curved body of Scorpio, which needs to reach the latitude of the Canary Islands, at the bottom of the Milky Way (Fig. 103).

The imprint of Scorpio according to these requirements reveals its lifted sting on the high Atlas Mountains, exactly where its loftiest peak is located: Toubkal (13,671 ft / 4,167 m), the tallest in North Africa.

There was still a greater surprise awaiting. The brightest star of Scorpio is Antares, and, right on the spot where it should be reflected (in the North of Morocco), there is a large Neolithic cromlech called Msoura (also Msora or Mzoura) (Fig. 104).

This cromlech has 167 rocks (ca. 5 ft / 1.5 m high on average) surrounding a slightly elliptical tumulus (190 x 177 x 20 ft / 58 x 54 x 6 m). On its western side there is a particularly tall menhir (ca. 16 ft / 5 m) called El Uted (The Pointer). According to a legend, this mon-

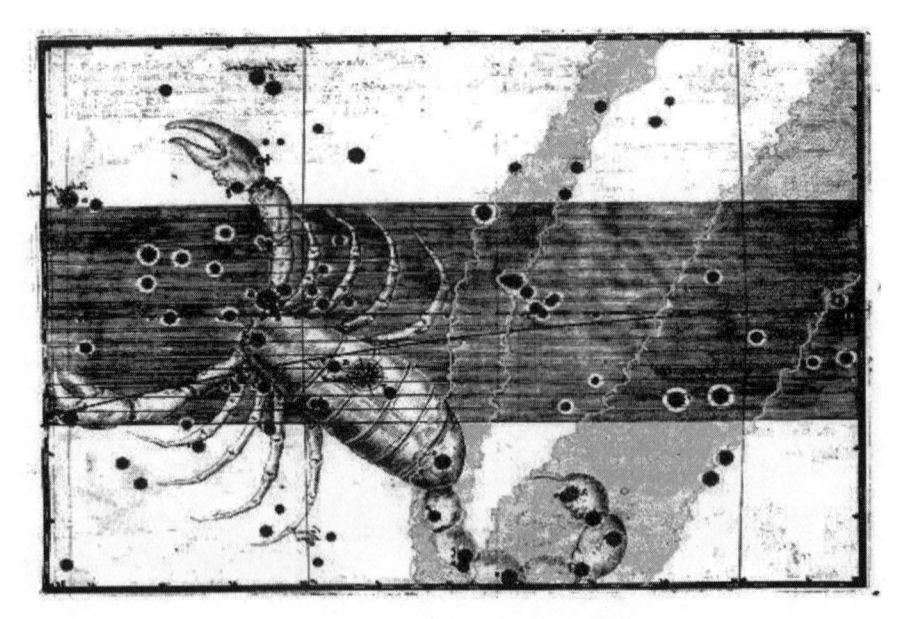

Fig. 105: Scorpio, across the Zodiac and the Milky Way. (J. Bayer).

ument is the tomb of the mythical giant Antaeus, son of Earth & Neptune. Could "the tomb of Antaeus" have been erected by the Megalith Builders to signal the spot where the red gleaming star Antares reflected?

Besides location, etymology and mythology associated with this stone ring, there is a clue in its design that strengthens the option of a positive answer. The Cromlech of Msoura has its entrance pointing to the west, signaled by a rectangular structure of small rocks and the outstanding presence of El Uted. If the princes symbolically killed the hydra—and by extension also the dragon and the scorpion—during the monarchical renewal ceremony, they would do the same during their voyage at the places where these "celestial beasts" were reflected.[8]

The Cromlech of Msoura faced the direction of the princes' arrival from the Atlantic Ocean once every 19 years, to ritualize in its interior the killing of Scorpio, the great enemy of Orion.[9] Both Orion and Scorpio constellations are mythological opponents, one always rising over the horizon when the other is setting on the opposite side. Therefore, they should be mirrored on opposite sides of Iberia, as shown in Fig. 103.

Orion and Scorpio occupy very special regions of the celestial sphere, in the vicinity of the places where the two great celestial bands—the Zodiac and the Milky Way—overlap. This circumstance can be clearly seen in the star atlases (Scorpio in Fig. 105; Orion in Fig. 16, p. 35). The darkest band corresponds to the Zodiac and the clear one to the Milky Way. (In the case of Scorpio, the Milky Way appears doubled due to the Great Rift, a dark band of dust that divides it lengthwise.)

The situations of Orion at the northern juncture, and Scorpius at the southern one, suggest that the Megalith Builders also perceived them as the cosmic guardians who supervised the flow of souls along the Milky Way, in and out of the Zodiac—Orion controlling the entrance and Scorpio the exit.

The celestial mirror reveals again a triple-layered cosmos divided into Heaven (Britain), Earth (Iberia) and Hell (Africa), similar to that already proposed for Britain (Fig. 49, p. 87). This fact suggests that this partition, based on the cardinal directions, was a recurrent model used by the Megalith Builders to organize the landscape on any scale, from local to global.

The Unicorn

Monoceros is a relatively modern constellation, however Richard Hinckley Allen hints at a much earlier origin:[10]

*"This [Monoceros] is a modern constellation, generally supposed to have been first charted by Bartschius as Unicornu; but Olbers and Ideler say that **it was of much earlier formation**, the latter quoting allusions to it in a work of 1564, as 'the other Horse south of the Twins and the Crab;' and Scaliger found it on a Persian sphere."*

Although this constellation was apparently unknown to the Greeks and Arabs, if we accept the previous report as genuine, the Unicorn could be of the same antiquity as the rest of traditional constellations. Given the critical situation of these stars—connecting Orion with Hydra's head across the Milky Way—the Megalith Builders must have had to identify and represent them with an an-

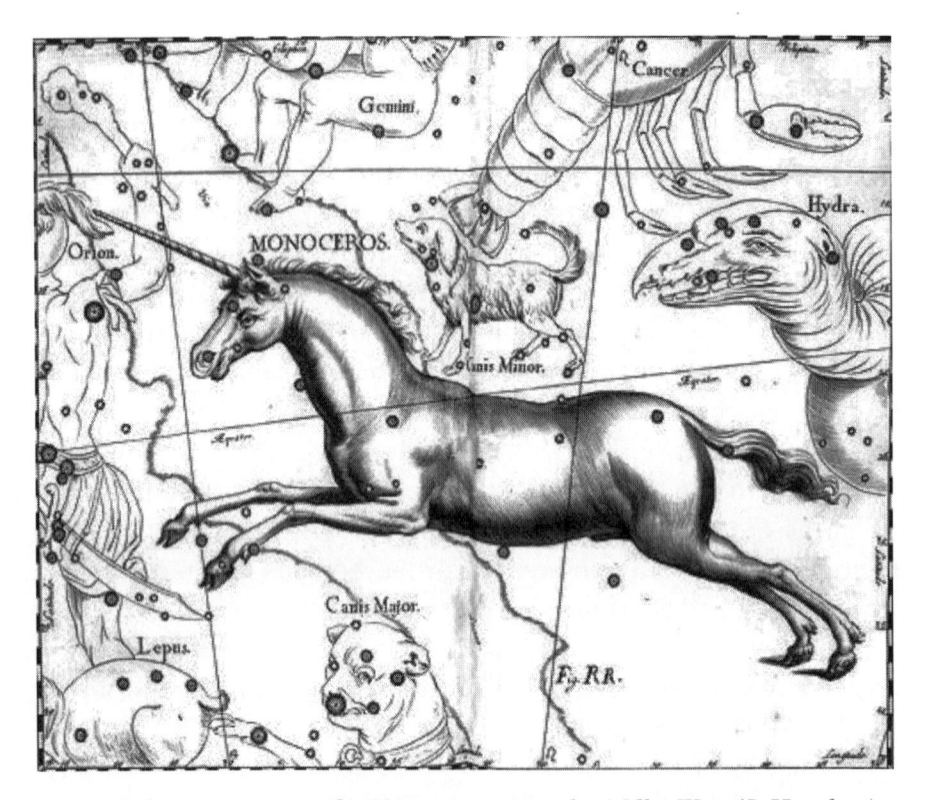

Fig. 106: Monoceros or the Unicorn, across the Milky Way (J. Hevelius).

imal that portrayed their function, and that fits perfectly with the unicorn, as we are about to see (Fig. 106).

During the monarchical renewal ceremony, the princes had to cross the Milky Way, represented by the ditches full of white water surrounding the henges of Avebury or Stonehenge. Monoceros is located exactly in the path that Orion would have to move across the Milky Way to fight against the hydra and to hunt the zodiacal lion.

Assuming the symbolism of the unicorn genuinely originated with the Megalith Builders, we may propose that the princes entered the henges not walking but riding upon white horses,[11] and that they did it holding spears, thus explaining the origin of the fabulous animal that results from combining a horse and a spear.

At Avebury, Leo and Cancer were represented by stone rings, and between The Sanctuary and the henge, next to the West Kennet

Avenue, there was a modest stone ring called Falkner's Circle that, following the same reasoning, had to be related to a constellation situated in Orion's path towards the Milky Way (Fig. 12, p. 31). Monoceros was the only candidate, so we can ratify that, indeed, Falkner's Circle represented this group of stars, perhaps having the practical function of keeping the white horses and spears (unihorns) inside it, waiting to be mounted by the princes on their way towards the henge.[12]

The Ringstone inside Avebury's henge, next to its southern entrance, represented Hydra's head, so, once inside the henge, the princes would first spear its hole, symbolizing the killing of the celestial beast—a combination of hydra, dragon and scorpion—that threatened to swallow the souls into Hell.

It would not be appropriate to use these spears later in the sacrifice of the kings, but there is another clue in the classical representation of Orion that could help us to infer more details about the sacrifices. Orion holds in one hand a lion skin, denoting that he is a lion's hunter whose main prey is not the bull (Taurus) above his head but the lion (Leo) inside the Milky Way (Fig. 16, p. 35). Orion also brandishes a club made of dull stars that cannot compare in brightness with those that signal the sword or dagger that hangs from his belt. These brilliant stars could represent the "ritual weapon" used to sacrifice the kings, very likely a flint dagger bequeathed from parents to sons (kings to princes), used exclusively once every nineteen years during the monarchical renewal ceremony.[13]

The princes would dress like Orion, i.e. with bright metallic adornments on their shoulders (stars Betelgeuse & Bellatrix) and sandals (Rigel & Saiph)—perhaps with a special detail on the left one (Rigel). A belt with three adornments (Alnitak, Alnilam and Mintaka) would fasten their clothes, from which hung a flint dagger (Hatysa), probably kept in a richly ornamented sheath. The princes would wear a hat with the horns of a bull in representation of Taurus, the constellation situated just above Orion's head, a symbol of life (Spring), and the sign under which they were born when conceived at Avebury. A ram's fleece would cover their backs (Aries), held by a golden brooch (the Golden Fleece).

Fig. 107: Icon of St George.

While the ceremony was celebrated in Avebury, the princes would parade along the West Kennet Avenue during the dawn of midsummer. Once the ceremony was moved to Stonehenge, they would parade along its avenue arriving at the henge in midwinter's afternoon, ahead of the kings who would arrive at sunset.

Earlier we postulated that St Michael was Orion in Christian form. There is also an equivalent on Earth: St George. The legend of St George and the Dragon provides the image most frequently used to represent this saint, riding a rampant white horse in the act of spearing a dragon in front of a maiden (Fig. 107).[14]

The image of St George killing the dragon fits with striking precision the cosmic scene acted out by Orion (St George), the Unicorn (white horse and spear) and the Hydra (dragon), in front of Cancer (maiden). (Remember that Inside Avebury's henge, next to the Ringstone that stood for Hydra's head, lay the south inner circle that represented Cancer, where the queens awaited for the new kings to celebrate hierosgamos.)

The Tower of Hercules

The localization of the Megalith Builders' kingdoms in Iberia implies that the final destiny of the princes' voyage had to be this peninsula. As already explained, after being crowned in Avebury or Stonehenge, the new kings descended by boat along the Salisbury-Avon River, and crossed the English Channel heading towards Carnac, where they stopped over to erect the menhirs in memory of their fathers, the late kings.

We can even estimate how long they would stay in Carnac because the precise moment and location they should re-enter their "zodiacal kingdoms" in Iberia had to be ruled by celestial cycles. Since Leo was associated with the monarchy, it is reasonable to think that the new kings would first touch Iberia where Leo reflected, and in midsummer, when the Sun transited over Leo.[15]

In Avebury, the ceremony was celebrated in midsummer, so the princes would have a full year, until next midsummer, before returning to Iberia, a time mostly to be spent working at Carnac. (The new kings did not only erect the stones in memory of their parents but also those corresponding to the most ancient kings.)

When the ceremony was moved to Stonehenge and to midwinter, the available time at Carnac would be reduced to half a year.[16]

The specific location in Iberia where they touched land had to be where Regulus, the brightest star of Leo, reflected. This constellation had been assigned to Galicia, the NW corner of Iberia. Since

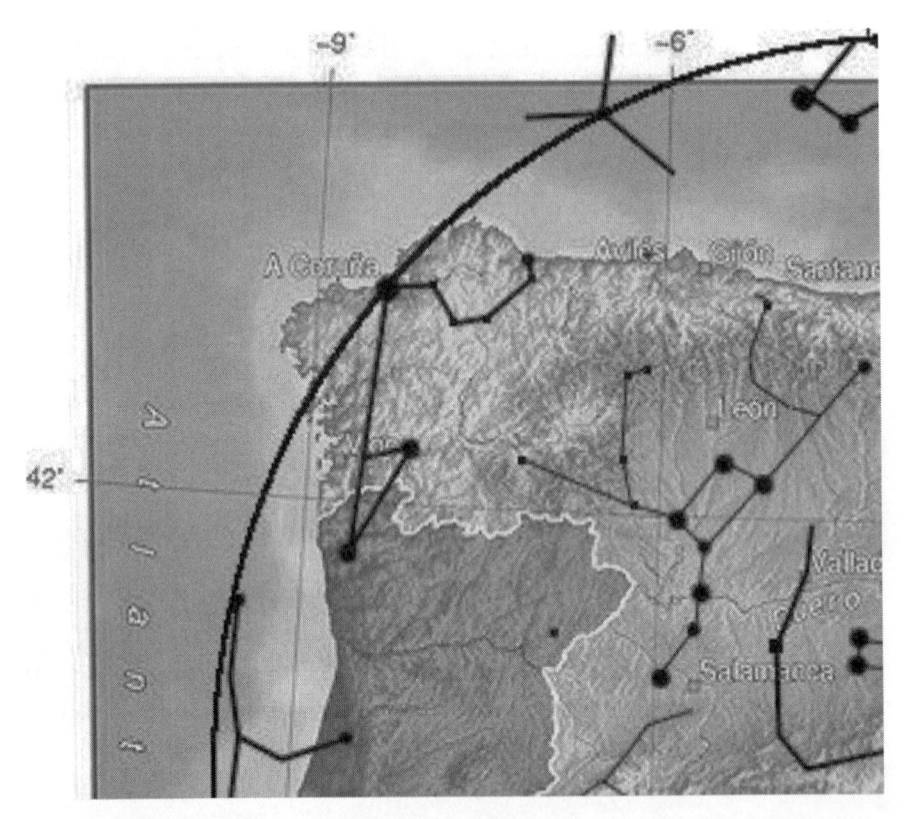

Fig. 108: Leo reflected on Galicia, with Regulus exactly on A Coruña.

Regulus is on the Ecliptic, and the Sun navigates around the peninsula, this star had to be signaled somewhere in the northern coasts of Galicia, not far from the present-day city of A Coruña (Fig. 108).

This place is famous for having the oldest existing lighthouse in the world, the Tower of Hercules, supposedly built by the Romans (Fig. 109).[17]

The location of this lighthouse is quite puzzling because it is in an indentation in the coast and, consequently, ineffective in guiding the ships navigating along either the northern or western coasts of Iberia, nor does it signals the westernmost extreme of the peninsula. It seems, therefore, built to guide only maritime traffic coming directly from the north, from the British Isles or Brittany.

An explanation for this oddity is to suppose that the original lighthouse was not built by the practical Romans but by the Mega-

Fig. 109: Tower of Hercules, in A Coruña (Galicia).

lith Builders based on religious reasons. The function would be obvious: to signal the star Regulus and the exact location at which the royal fleet coming from Brittany should land during midsummer sunrise. A great bonfire on its top would serve to guide and to celebrate the arrival of the heavenly "boat of the Sun" on the longest day of the year, symbolized by the royal fleet with the new kings on board.[18]

The Tower of Hercules is named after the greatest of Greek heroes, Heracles (Romanized as Hercules). Similarly to the myth of *Jason and the Argonauts*, an investigation of *The Twelve Labors of Hercules* could also reveal great insights about its "megalithic origin," as exemplified in the following discussion. According to a local legend, Hercules arrived at what is nowadays A Coruña in fulfillment of one of his famous Twelve Labors, the tenth.

Fig. 110: Heracles, dressed in a lion's skin, fighting Geryon, a triple-being giant. (Attic red-figure kylix, sixth c. BC.)

Succinctly, in this labor, Heracles has to travel to the island of Erytheia to obtain the Cattle of Geryon, a fearsome tyrant with the body of three men joined in one at the waist. Heracles had first to kill a two-headed dog called Orthus and its owner the shepherd Eurytion, before killing Geryon with an arrow dipped in the venomous blood of the Lernaean Hydra (Fig. 110).

The trip of the new kings to Iberia to take possession of their kingdoms reflects that of Heracles to Erytheia. The Cattle of Geryon would represent the animals of the Zodiac, which explains the bizarre form of this giant, having twelve limbs but only one waist, symbolizing the twelve signs of the Zodiac joined at the center. The two-headed dog would represent Canis Major and Minor (Greater and Lesser Dogs). The shepherd would be Orion, and the arrow poisoned with hydra's blood would be, most obviously, the Hydra. Correspondingly, in the final part of the "megalithic voyage," the new kings abandon Great Britain (the shepherd), cross the Milky Way between Ireland and Brittany (the two headed dogs), cross the Celestial Equator signaled at Carnac (the hydra), and finally arrive at Iberia (the "zodiacal cattle").

Fig. 111: Hercules in the Garden of the Hesperides. (Brass medallion, Italy, second c. AD.)

Erytheia was the "Red Island" inhabited by the Hesperides, the nymphs who tended a paradisaical garden in a far western corner of the world, at the edge of the encircling Oceanus River. The Garden of Hesperides contained the tree of immortality where golden apples grew, protected by a never-sleeping dragon (Fig. 111). The description of Erytheia fits perfectly that of the Iberian Peninsula, as the "Red Island" of the west, bathed by the Oceanus River (Atlantic Ocean). The tree of the golden apples would be the "solar pillar," the Axis Mundi that ended in the Eastern Pyrenees, and the never-sleeping dragon would be the reflection of Draco on the center of Iberia, coiled around that most sacred axis.

Hercules is directly related to Jason in the founding myth of Barcelona. After his fourth work, Hercules embarked with the Argonauts to help them to find the Golden Fleece, and they ended up in Montjuic, the hill next to Barcelona, adjacent to the mouth of the Llobregat River. The waters of this river lead to the Eastern Pyrenees, so the heroes were indeed not that far from finding the Golden Fleece.

Endnotes

[1] Saiph and the three stars of Orion's Belt are of second magnitude.

[2] Photo on p. 167: Mont Saint-Michel, in Normandy (France). During the megalithic epoch, it was not a tidal island because the level of the sea was ca. 20 ft (7 m) lower.

[3] All the locations that reflected Orion's stars could be related to places surrounded or proximate to water, a common denominator that could explain why the Megalith Builders erected Silbury Hill—the reflection of Rigel—and flooded its base.

[4] Since Canis Minor and Hydra are within the Milky Way, the Megalith Builders had to consider a fluvial route cutting through Brittany. The shortest distance between the English Channel and the Bay of Biscay is about 60 miles (100 km), and it would have to pass only one low mountain range. The Aulne River on the north side, and the Oulst and the final part of Vilaine Rivers on the south side, could have been considered as the water-thread of the Milky Way through Brittany.

[5] The same figure serves to illustrate the importance of the south to north axis connecting several constellations related to the ceremony of monarchical renewal: Argo Navis, Hydra, Leo, Ursa Major, Draco and Cygnus (the first and the last in opposing sections of the Milky Way). Due to the precession of the equinoxes, this axis slowly lost its accuracy with the passing of centuries.

[6] Similar legends are also associated with other megalithic monuments located by the seas or rivers, which could be derived from the original link established between the monuments and the nearby waters by the original builders, preserved in folkloric legends.

[7] It may be worth mentioning that, in the complete map of the sky during the megalithic epoch, the axis that connected both poles also pierced the head of the Hydra (Fig. 58, p. 103).

[8] Orion appears as a celestial hunter spearing the beasts of the sky—hydra, dragon and scorpion. The Archangel Michael, the substitute for Orion after the arrival of Christianity, also spears a beast with tail, wings, horns, scales and a trident, a "recast" of the celestial beasts into a single figure: the Devil.

[9] The outstanding presence of El Uted could symbolize the extreme of the imaginary spear that Orion wields from the opposite side of the celestial mirror to kill the celestial scorpion. Perhaps this could also

explain the purpose of the tallest menhir they ever erected: Locmariarquer (ca. 67 ft / 20 m tall)—now fallen and broken—driven into the ground near Carnac to kill the celestial hydra, ruler of hell.

[10] *Star Names: Their Lore and Meaning*, by Richard Hinckley Allen, Dover Publications Inc., p. 290 (1963, first published in 1899)

[11] The period at which horses became domesticated is disputed. There are chariot burials dating from 2000 BC, though an increasing amount of evidence supports the hypothesis that the Beaker People had managed to domesticate horses some centuries ahead of that, and even the people of the Eurasian Steppes did so as early as the fourth millennium BC.

[12] Its reflection on the celestial mirror should extend across the waters that separate Ireland (Canis Major) and Brittany (Canis Minor). Some minor islands could have been selected to reflect this zigzagging constellation; for example, Holyhead Island in Wales is at the exact location and has a very fitting name to be the island chosen as the reflection of the head of the Unicorn, while Bardsey, Lundy and Scilly islands in Britain, and Ouessant island in Brittany, could reflect its body. Although the coastal lines may be different from the actual ones, the singularity of the suggested locations would remain the same.

[13] This description evokes again the legend of King Arthur, in particular the episode of the sword Excalibur stuck in a rock, which only Arthur manages to extract proving himself to be the rightful heir to the throne.

[14] Evidences of St George's cult in Britain seem to go back to the sixth century AD, when he was introduced to Europe and the Levant by way of the Crusades. From this event many countries claimed the saint and his legend as their own, contributing to the proliferation of his cult. Curiously, St George is the patron saint of several countries and regions that formed a key part of the celestial mirror such as England, Portugal, Aragon and Catalonia. Likewise, the patron saint of Spain, St James, is usually represented as the "Moor-Slayer," killing an infidel instead of a dragon but ichnographically very similar to St George. During the Middle Ages, the images of St Michael, St George and St James were reduced to mere representations of "good defeating evil," but, could their persistence be the manifestation of an ancient tradition deeply rooted in the Megalith Builders' cosmology?

15 This would also be the optimum time of the year to cross the Gulf of Biscay, more perilous in other seasons (with a higher risk of storms).

16 The construction technologies with wood (boats) and stone (megalith) would have improved considerably, so this period would be more than enough to fulfill their filial duty at Carnac before heading to Iberia. Besides, moving the ceremony from midsummer to midwinter (from Avebury to Stonehenge) reduced to half the time that the kings were away from their kingdoms, diminishing considerably the potential political instability caused by such long absence, a factor that certainly had also to be taken into consideration when they decided to reform their millenary tradition.

17 The building was stone-coated in the 17th century AD to protect its old masonry, though still reflecting the original ramp that spiraled around to its top where bonfires were lit to guide the ships.

18 A Latin inscription in one of the stones of the Tower of Hercules and the fact that it is not mentioned in some chronicles serves to justify the Roman authorship of this ancient lighthouse. Both—epigraphic and by omission—are quite feeble arguments. The only justification is the actual pre-historical paradigm, within which it is inconceivable that pre-Roman people could erect a lighthouse. But the Megalith Builders were great sailors, and this corner of Galicia was tremendously important for them because it was where they celebrated the arrival of midsummer, and also every 19 years of the new kings, with a great bonfire on top of a tumulus, on the spot where Regulus reflected. The actual intervention of the Romans could be to remodel it. This explanation legitimates the posing of the following question, "could some of the Roman constructions, such as roads, bridges or even aqueducts be remodeled constructions of the Megalith Builders?" The Beaker People (the latest cultural expression among the Megalith Builders) could have had contacts with Egypt, Crete, Greece and Mesopotamia, with which places ideas could have been interchanged. How many pieces of so called Iberian art were actually made by the Megalith Builders, or modeled after them, in advance of the arrival of the Phoenicians in the first millennium BC? The oriental influences so frequently identified in Iberian art—supposedly introduced into the peninsula by expeditions coming from the eastern Mediterranean territories during this millennium—could have another explanation based on exactly the opposite direction of influence, created in a much older epoch, millennia ahead.

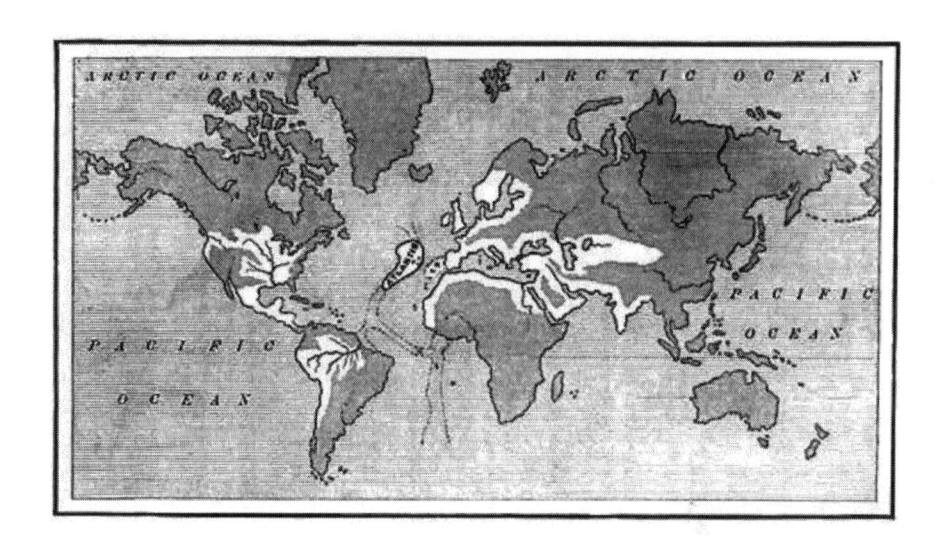

12
ATLANTIS

PLATO, in his dialogues *Timaeus* and *Critias* (fourth century BC), mentions for the first time the existence of the most legendary of civilizations: Atlantis. Ever since Plato's account, scholars have argued whether this story was based on the existence of a genuine Atlantis, or whether it was the product of his imagination, inspired by older traditions but no more than an allegory useful to enliven the narration of his dialogues.

More recent essays, such as *New Atlantis* (1624) of Francis Bacon, and particularly the book of the American congressman Ignatius Donnelly, *Atlantis: the Antediluvian World* (1882), spurred an interest in Atlantis that had waned during the Middle Ages.[1] In the late 19th and first half of the 20th centuries, the idea of Atlantis was mixed with esoteric teachings related to a very advanced civilization located on an island-continent of the Atlantic Ocean that disappeared after a great cataclysm.

Fig. 112: Fountains of Neptune (Romanization of Poseidon, God of the Oceans), and Cybele (a Goddess of the Earth), the most important and central to Madrid.

When the theory of plate tectonics became widely accepted, and the "lost continent" hypothesis was harder to sustain, other contenders to Atlantis kept on appearing. Dozens of sites all over the world have been proposed, though none convincingly demonstrated its validity.

In the myth, according to Plato, Atlantis was a confederation of ten kingdoms. This is so strikingly like the Megalith Builders' political organization that, just in itself, is a powerful hint that requires further research.

To compare the myth and what we have discovered about the Megalith Builders:

1. Atlantis had its mythological origin in the union of Poseidon (God of the Oceans) with Clito (a Goddess of the Earth) (Fig. 112). This couple distributed its territory among their children: five pairs of twins. The Megalith Builders considered that each of the five visible planets ruled over two zodiacal constellations (five pairs of twin signs), "children" of Leo & Cancer, and divided their territory into those five pairs of kingdoms.
2. The eldest son was named Atlas. The Megalith Builders emphasized Aries over the rest of signs because it was at the top of

their Axis Mundi. In Greek mythology, Atlas is also a titan who holds the celestial sphere, a fitting anthropomorphization of the Axis Mundi that supports the cosmos (Fig. 113).

3. The divine couple bequeathed to Atlas the "mountain surrounded by water rings" and gave him authority over his brothers. On the celestial mirror, Aries reflected on the Pyrenees Range, surrounded by the water rings of the Zodiac & the Milky Way (so the luminaries and the souls could navigate on the mirror as they do in the sky).

4. In honor of Atlas, the whole island was called Atlantis and the ocean surrounding it was called the Atlantic. The celestial mirror extended over islands (the British, Canary, Madeira and Azores) and peninsulas (those of Brittany and Iberia), all of them surrounded or bathed by the Atlantic Ocean.

5. Atlantis was beyond The Pillars of Hercules, the name by which Greeks knew the Strait of Gibraltar, the natural entrance into the main megalithic territory for Mediterranean sailors.

6. The twin brother of Atlas was named Gadeirus, and he ruled the region beyond the Pillars of Hercules. In the Megalith Builders' cosmology, the "twin sign" of Aries is Scorpio (both ruled by Mars) and, in the celestial mirror, Scorpio reflected on both sides of the Strait of Gibraltar. The city of Cadiz is one of the oldest in the Iberian Peninsula, and it is located on the island where the head of the celestial scorpion should reflect. Its etymology derives from a Phoenician outpost called Gadir that in Greek times came to be known as Gadeira. The geographical and etymological match between Gadeirus (Atlas's twin brother ruling beyond The Pillars of Hercules) and Gadeira (Cadiz's original name, above the Strait of Gibraltar) are so amazingly accurate that it cannot be merely a coincidence.

7. Atlas & Gadeirus were the first pair of Atlantean twins and, as a consequence, they were slightly senior in the hierarchy. In the Megalith Builders' cosmology the kingdoms associated with Aries & Scorpio, both ruled by Mars, had an especial status due to their relationship with the Axis Mundi.[2]

Fig. 113: Sculpture of Atlas in Santiago de Compostela (Spain).

8. Atlantis was designed according to a remarkable morphology: three rings of alternating earth and water. The structure of the celestial mirror could explain this feature, since it consists of two overlapping rings of water in representation of the Zodiac and the Milky Way. The third and innermost ring could be that where the celestial North Pole moves in a cycle of 26,000 years (Platonic or Great Year) around the Ecliptic Pole, making it concentric to the Zodiac.[3]

9. The water rings that surrounded the capital of Atlantis were coated with brass, tin and orichalcum respectively. The Megalith Builders could have constructed their capital using the celestial mirror as the blueprint. Brass is an alloy of copper and zinc with a bright gold-like appearance, and would be the best choice to represent the Zodiac, the Sun's path. Tin is a silvery malleable metal not easily oxidized, and therefore a good op-

tion to coat the wall that represented the whitish Milky Way.[4] Finally, orichalcum could have been bronze, an alloy of copper and tin well known from the late third millennium BC onwards that considerably improved the mechanical properties of materials known at that time. This would be the best choice to coat the innermost ring that surrounded the most "durable center," the immovable Ecliptic Pole, signaling the change of eras.

10. The Atlanteans kings reunited every five and six years alternately to reaffirm their bonds, come to a consensus on some important decisions, and to pass judgment upon those who had disobeyed the laws. The Megalith Builders renewed their monarchy following a calendar based on the Metonic Cycle (235 lunations, equivalent to approximately 19 years). The Metonic Cycle incorporates a subcycle of 136 lunations that reproduces the positions of the Sun and the Moon's phase within only 1.5 days of accuracy, and those lunations correspond precisely to 11 years. Therefore, they could have observed this subcycle to regulate their meetings. If they met every 5, 6 and 5 years, the last meeting would be for the princes to depart together on a voyage that would last for about 3 years.

11. Atlantis disappeared 9,000 years before the time of Solon. This does not match the disappearance of megalithism, which occurred in the second millennium BC, more fitting to 900 instead of 9,000 years before Solon. Could it be an error introduced while writing down or translating the original information?

12. The kings of Atlantis governed with justice and virtue, but with the passing of generations their divine nature diminished in inverse proportion to their increased thirst for power. They initiated a policy of expansion along the Mediterranean coasts, subduing Libya (Africa) as far as Egypt, and the Tyrrhenian Peninsula (Italy). However, when they tried to conquer Athens they were defeated. The simple enumeration of all these places is in itself a clear indication that the Atlantean raids should come from the western Mediterranean. The Iberian Peninsula is not mentioned in the list of conquered territories, logically if it was a land that already belonged to the conquerors.

*Fig. 114: Santorini Island, in the Aegean Sea.
(The missing part is where the Thera Volcano was before exploding.)*

According to the *Critias*, the gods decided to punish the Atlanteans, but the dialogue is interrupted at the moment Zeus and the rest of the gods have a meeting to dictate the sentence. Nevertheless, it is habitually assumed that the penalty was a great earthquake followed by a flood that caused its main city to disappear swallowed by the sea, *"in a terrible day and night"* says the *Timaeus*. The cataclysm also destroyed the Athenian fleet, which implies that it had to happen within the Mediterranean Sea.

There are also other authors who have connected the Atlanteans and the Megalith Builders.[5] Based on this equivalence, we could speculate about the details that might have surrounded their downfall. With the beginning of the second millennium BC, their interest in the Mediterranean Sea would gradually substitute that for the Atlantic Ocean, gravitating more towards the richer civilizations that had developed along the Mediterranean coasts. They may have built a maritime capital on one of its islands, which would have served them as a commercial and military outpost. Although placed outside the celestial mirror, it would be designed based on its structure, with several rings of water around it. The conflicts with Egypt and Athens could have originated from the control of the route—the reflection of Eridanus—that the royal fleet had to traverse every nineteen years. The tension would escalate and a war against the Athenians would finally break out, ending with the defeat of the Megalith Builders.[6]

The cataclysm that destroyed their maritime capital would be the final blow that precipitated their collapse, followed by a vacuum of power particularly severe in Iberia. As is always the case when civilizations collapse, pillage and plunder would break out, and a "dark age" would fall upon Europe.[7]

Minoans, Iberians, Celts and Tartessians

There is a candidate for the cataclysm that could have provoked the collapse of the Megalith Builders: the explosion of a volcano called Thera in the 17th century BC, on an island close to Crete known at present as Santorini (Fig. 114). This terrible explosion also caused the downfall of the Minoan culture, which might have been the final expression—the most refined artistically—of the Megalith Builder's society during the Bronze Age.[8] The Minoan culture was remarkably different from the Mycenaean, which is considered the historical setting where the myths of Classical Greece originated. The Mycenaeans would be the direct descendents of those who fought against the Megalith Builders, whilst also being the preferential inheritors of their cosmic knowledge.

The wealth of the main settlements in Western Europe would be completely sacked in a few generations. The religious knowledge would be preserved and transmitted orally in narratives progressively more disconnected from their original cosmic meaning. The Iberians & Celts would eventually appear as the main inheritors of this lore. The Celts never forgot that their ancestors immigrated from Iberia, and that the NW corner of that peninsula was the land of their mythological parents (the Leo & Cancer territories ruled by the Sun & the Moon). This is why they would undertake pilgrimag-

Fig. 115: Tartessian sculpture of a winged feline.

es to present day Galicia & Asturias coming from all corners of Europe, creating a spiritual movement that in the Low Middle Age would be Christianized as The Way of St James.

After a long struggle, the people in the southern part of the Iberian Peninsula would reorganize themselves into the legendary Tartessia (Fig. 115).[9] In the course of the first millennium BC, the arrival of different Mediterranean peoples to Iberia (Phoenicians, Greeks and Carthaginians) would gradually veil the Atlantean legacy, and the Romans & Christianity would finally cover it almost completely.

Chronology

"Today, I believe that the collapse of the economic model is not sufficient to explain, on its own, the deep social and mental ruptures which are detected in the context of the regional neolithisation. In the words of A. Whittle, 'becoming Neolithic may have been much more a spiritual conversion than a matter of changing diets.'"

The above paragraph is an excerpt from the conclusions of Calado.[10] This archeologist wonders whether the ultimate reason behind the distribution of regional megalithic constructions was of a different nature than economic, perhaps religious. The existence of a broad geographical perspective imbued with religious-cosmic beliefs would, in fact, explain the distribution of megalithic monuments not only on a local scale but all over the area of manifestation of the megalithic phenomenon.

A loose network of Mesolithic chiefdoms in Iberia would be the embryo of what would over time give birth to a confederation of Iberian peoples. This confederation would be ruled by kings renewed according to the Metonic Cycle, dictated by an elite of priest-astronomers.

In the fifth millennium BC, this confederation would become the Megalith Builders, a geopolitical entity with a common solar-cosmic religion, centered in Iberia but extending mainly across Western Europe. By then, they already had developed a naval technology that allowed them to send maritime expeditions to far reaching territories.

They would decide to build their first megalithic monuments in Brittany (France) and Alentejo (Portugal), lands of immortality (north) and rebirth (west) respectively. During the following centuries this custom would gradually spread not only geographically but also socially, from local ruling elites to lower socials echelons.

By the end of the fourth millennium BC they designed a huge celestial mirror over the Atlantic territories which served to regulate themselves politically and religiously (implementing Heaven on Earth). The largest and most unique constructions, such as those at Carnac, Avebury, Stonehenge and Newgrange, were royal monuments, erected at key sites of this celestial mirror according to a megalithic technology designed to attain the rebirth of the sacrificed kings as princes, thus preserving an unbroken royal lineage.

Before being crowned, the princes had to undergo, as a rite of passage, a long and arduous voyage that would be preserved in the myth of *Jason and the Argonauts*. Much of the knowledge contained in the classical mythology could have had its origin not so much in the Mycenaeans but in the Megalith Builders.

The most legendary of the civilizations, Atlantis, could be exactly where Plato said that it was, the Megalith Builders being the legendary Atlanteans: the sailors coming from the Atlantic Ocean.

The civilization of the Megalith Builders disappeared midway through the second millennium BC due to war and a geological cataclysm that coincided with the transition from the Age of Taurus to the Age of Aries.

The approximate timeline of the main events which occurred in Western Europe is shown in a table on the last page of the book.

Corollary

There are still many questions about the Megalith Builders or Atlanteans that need further investigation (subject of the next book, *Voyage Zero*), such as their role in spawning the classical civilizations, their presence in America, the specific sites in the Pyrenees and at the center of Iberia where they established some of their most sacred sites, or the celestial mirror transposed onto the geography of Classical Greece.

In conclusion, this book sheds new light on the megalithic phenomenon, going into detail about the timeline, design and purpose of its greatest surviving architectural manifestations, revealing a society much more organized, interconnected, mobile, advanced and, overall, influential in western civilization than currently recognized. In fact, I propose that the Megalith Builders were the initiators of Civilization, remembered as the legendary Atlanteans.

Endnotes

[1] Picture above, on p. 189: *Map of the Empire of Atlantis*, by Ignatius Donnelly.

[2] This fact explains why the central trilithon of Stonehenge—related to Mars—is slightly taller than the other four, because it corresponded to the kings that were descendants of the first pair of mythological royal twins.

[3] It is possible to consider several fluvial rings at the center of Iberia, around the mountain range called Guadarrama, a name of Arab origin that, curiously, means *Stone River*.

[4] Both brass and tin would substitute for gold and silver, too precious to be used in large quantities.

[5] Tony O'Connell, in his compilation of Atlantis theories, lists the authors who have recently related Atlanteans and Megalith Builders (*Atlantipedia.ie*):
"While not a new idea, a megalithic connection with Atlantis has recently [2007] been given further attention by the French writer Sylvain Tristan who was inspired by Jean Deruelle and Alan Butler. Alfred de Grazia also joined this club as well as the German author Helmut Tributsch who has added his support to the idea of a megalithic Atlantis, specifically locating its capital on the island of Gavrinis in Brittany. A similar claim has been made by Hank Harrison who also believes that the Morbihan region was an important Atlantean centre if not the location of its capital. Further support for a megalithic Atlantis has been given by Walter Schilling who places Plato's city in the Bay of Cadiz. Robert Temple has recently offered grudging support for the concept of Atlantean megalith builders [...] Ulf Erlingsson recently [2004] identified the empire of Atlantis with the megalithic cultures of Western Europe and North Africa and suggested its capital may have been in Ireland."

[6] The war against Athens seemed to have a deeper meaning, because it was not only a geographical dispute but the clash of two antagonistic modes of understanding the world. The Megalith Builders or Atlanteans were deeply religious, ceremonial, worshippers of the Sun and the luminaries, monarchical, deductive and subjective. The Athenians represented the seed of the opposite pole, a rational civilization, with man at the center of the universe, democratic, inductive and objective. Using modern jargon, we could say that it was a confrontation

between a civilization ruled by the right hemisphere of the brain against one ruled by the left.

[7] The construction of megalithic monuments ceased to a large extent around the middle of the second millennium BC. An Irish oral tradition has preserved the list of all the kings of Ireland, going back into prehistoric times. This list reflects the arrival of an invasion of people coming from Iberia, called Milesians, who would become the subsequent kings, and which also took place about this time. This migration would be just one among the many that would occur to different lands in the years following the collapse. They would mostly be affluent people who left Iberia seeking a more secure place to settle. The arrival of a new Age would be seen by the Megalith Builders with consternation, because that was going to profoundly alter the functioning of the celestial mirror upon which they had relied politically and religiously for the last 2,000 years. Perhaps, the priests-astronomers were not too surprised when they witnessed how the end of their era, the Age of Taurus, brought with it also the end of their civilization: defeat in war and destruction by the explosion of a volcano. Both were recognizable heralds of the new Age of Aries ruled by Mars, which marked the definitive abandonment of stone in favor of metal.

[8] Recently, the sailor Gavin Menzies proposed that the Minoans sailed to America, and that this civilization—comparatively advanced for the epoch—originated the legend of Atlantis. (*The Lost Empire of Atlantis*, 2011).

[9] The Tartessians were the pre-Roman people who lived in the western region of present-day Andalusia (southern Iberia), and whose capital was called Tartessos.

[10] *Standing Stones and Natural Outcrops*, by Manuel Calado (2005); available online at: crookscape.org/textjan2005/text_eng.html

APPENDIX: BRIGHTEST STARS

		Bayer Name*	Actual Declin.	(m)	Common Name	Site	Region & Country
1	α	Canis Majoris	−16.7	−1.44	Sirius	Newgrange	County Meath (EIR)
2	α	Carinae	−52.7	−0.62	Canopus	Pico Volcano	Azores Islands (POR)
3	α	Centauri	−60.8	−0.27	Rigil Kent	Fuerteventura	Canary Islands (ESP)
4	α	Boötis	+19.2	−0.05	Arcturus	Serra da Estrela	Central (POR)
5	α	Lyrae	+38.8	0.03	Vega	Jaén?	Andalusia (ESP)
6	α	Aurigae	+46.0	0.08	Capella	San Sebastian?	Basque Country (ESP)
7	β	Orionis	−8.2	0.18	Rigel	Silbury Hill	England (UK)
8	α	Canis Minoris	+5.2	0.40	Procyon	Barnenez?	Brittany (FRA)
9	α	Eridani	−57.2	0.45	Achernar	Elephantine Island	Aswan (EGY)
10	α	Orionis	+7.4	0.45	Betelgeuse	Oléron Island	PoitouCharentes (FRA)
11	β	Centauri	−60.4	0.61	Agena	Lanzarote	Canary Islands (ESP)
12	α	Aquilae	+8.9	0.76	Altair	Sierra Nevada?	Andalusia (ESP)
13	α	Crucis	−63.1	0.77	Acrux	Gran Canaria	Canary Islands (ESP)
14	α	Tauri	+16.5	0.87	Aldebaran	Toulouse?	Midi-Pyrénées (FRA)
15	α	Virginis	−11.2	0.98	Spica	Nazaré?	Centro (POR)
16	α	Scorpii	−26.4	1.06	Antares	Msoura Cromlech	Tanger-Tétouan (MOR)
17	β	Geminorum	+28.0	1.16	Pollux	Santander?	Cantabria (ESP)
18	α	Piscis Austrinus	−29.6	1.17	Fomalhaut	Algiers?	Capital (ALG)
19	β	Crucis	−59.7	1.25	Becrux	Tenerife	Canary Islands (ESP)
20	α	Cygni	+45.3	1.25	Deneb	Cuenca?	Castilla-La Mancha (ESP)
21	α	Leonis	+12.0	1.36	Regulus	Tower of Hercules	Galicia (ESP)

*Brightest stars, up to first magnitude (m < 1.5), and the locations they could be mirrored.

LIST OF FIGURES

Fig. 1: Old picture of Stonehenge (ca. 1850). 11
Fig. 2: Principal areas of megalithism in Western Europe. 13
Fig. 3: Zodiac with the classical twelve constellations or signs. (Equinoxes and solstices for the megalithic epoch.) 15
Fig. 4: Example of megalithic art engraved on a kerbstone of Knowth, a passage mound in Ireland. 17
Fig. 5: Map of south Brittany (Quiberon Bay) where the Alignments of Carnac are located. 22
Fig. 6: Saint-Michel tumulus, next to the Alignments of Carnac. (Christianized with a chapel on top.) 23
Fig. 7: Module of Kermario. 24
Fig. 8: Jupiter transiting over Leo. 26
Fig. 9: Retrograding of the Sun in midsummer during the 3,000 years of megalithism (47th to 17th c. BC). 27
Fig. 10: English Channel, separating the Peninsula of Brittany (Carnac) from the island of Great Britain (Avebury). 30
Fig. 11: Aerial view of Avebury's henge. 30
Fig. 12: Plan of Avebury's megalithic complex. 31
Fig. 13: Silbury Hill (ca. 131 ft / 40 m high). 32
Fig. 14: Eastern horizon of Avebury at midsummer dawn. 33
Fig. 15: Heliacal rising of Rigel from Avebury. (Top map with the stars' names, and lower with the constellations' and grid. August 13, 3099 BC.) 34
Fig. 16: Leo and Orion (J. Bayer). (Orion holds a lion skin.) 35
Fig. 17: Principal constellations visible directly over Avebury's S-N horizon, during Rigel's heliacal rising. (August 13, 3099 BC.) 36
Fig. 18: South entrance, flanked by two large stones across the ditch. 37
Fig. 19: Ringstone (Crowstone, Scotland), similar to the non-extant of Avebury. 38
Fig. 20: The Cove, in the northern inner circle. 39
Fig. 21: Plan of Avebury indicating the constellations, stars and characters involved in the ceremony of monarchical renewal. 40
Fig. 22: Artistic recreation of the Sarsen Circle and its inner elements. 44
Fig. 23: Plan of Stonehenge: 1) Avenue delineated by parallel ditches and banks, 2) Heelstone, 3) Entrance, with the Slaughter Stone inside, 4) Ditch with banks on both sides, the inner taller, 5) Aubrey Holes, 6) Y & Z Holes, 7) Sarsen Circle, 8) Bluestone Circle, 9) Five trilithons, 10) Bluestone Horseshoe, 11) Altar Stone, 12-15) Stationed Stones. 45
Fig. 24: Schematic plan of Stonehenge. 46
Fig. 25: Trajectories of Regulus, Rigel and Alphekka over Stonehenge in midwinter. (January 8, 2303 BC.) Three times: 1) Regulus rising, 2) Regulus culmination, and 3) Regulus extinction (Alphekka culmination). 47

Fig. 26: Projections of the celestial dome on Stonehenge the night before midwinter, when Regulus was rising (16:03) and culminating (00:19). (January 8 and 9, 2303 BC.) 49

Fig. 27: Projections of the celestial dome on Stonehenge in midwinter, when the Milky Way encircled the site (03:00), and Alphekka culminated (Regulus was setting) (06:40). (January 9, 2303 BC.) 50

Fig. 28: The Corona Borealis, between Boötes, Serpens Caput and Hercules (inverted and holding a lion skin) (J. Hevelius). 52

Fig. 29: Panel at the entrance to Stonehenge. 53

Fig. 30: Midwinter sunset seen from the entrance to Stonehenge. 54

Fig. 31: Map of Stonehenge's neighboring elements. 55

Fig. 32: Confluence of rivers in the area of Avebury and Stonehenge. (The Preseli Hills in Wales are in the opposite direction from the Kennet-Thames Rivers.) 56

Fig. 33: Above, Ring of Stennes. Center, a house of Skara Brae. Below, interior of Maeshowe. 62

Fig. 34: The movements of the main characters who participated in the ceremony to renew the Megalith Builders' monarchy. (Carnac and the Orkney Islands lie on the same meridian.) 64

Fig. 35: World map according to Herodotus. (Hyperborea is on the top. By S. Butler, 1907.) 66

Fig. 36: Apollo with the solar halo of Helios. (Roman mosaic at El Djem, Tunisia, second c. AD.) 67

Fig. 37: Ranges of risings and settings over the horizon, covered by the Sun between solstices (range on the circle), and by the Moon between lunastices (major and minor ranges, outside the circle). (The values are for Stonehenge's latitude.) 68

Fig. 38: Above, Recumbent Stone Circle of Easter Aquhorthies, with its recumbent stone flanked by a pair of standing stones. Below, Callanish Stones (Isle of Lewis). 69

Fig. 39: The Scottish megalithic sites, located "above." 70

Fig. 40: Phases of construction of Silbury Hill, between the 28th and 24th centuries BC. 71

Fig. 41: Alignments of Carnac. Each stone represented a king ruling during a Metonic Cycle. 72

Fig. 42: Traditional representations of the Sun and the Moon. A king holds a shining mirror (Sun) in front of a lion (Leo), and a woman holds a horn (Moon) in front of a crab (Cancer). (Heinrich Decimator in "De stellis fixis et erratici," Germany, 16th c.) 78

Fig. 43: Left, the concrete pyramid indicating where the Obelisk was erected, in the center of the southern inner circle. Right, The Cove, in the center of the northern inner circle. (Both inside Avebury's henge.) 79

Fig. 44: Apollo and Artemis. (Attic red-figure cup, fifth c. BC.) 80

Fig. 45: Woodcuts of the alchemical treatise "Rosarium philosophorum." (Uncertain authorship, Germany, 16th c.) 81

Fig. 46: Royal Stars: Regulus, Fomalhaut, Aldebaran and Antares, in the four sectors of the Zodiac, signaling the solstices and equinoxes in the megalithic epoch. (2300 BC, equatorial coordinates.) 82
Fig. 47: Pair of stones in the southern inner circle inside Avebury's henge, with lozenge and elongated shapes. 83
Fig. 48: The three rings of holes within Stonehenge known as Y, Z and Aubrey Holes. (Solstices and lunastices' directions are indicated.) 84
Fig. 49: Division of the Megalith Builders' territory in the NW of Europe. (The symbolism of the cardinal directions is indicated.) 87
Fig. 50: Façade of Newgrange (Ireland). 88
Fig. 51: Tumulus of Dowth and corridor of Knowth (Ireland). 89
Fig. 52: Beckhampton Long Barrow. (Sketch by W. Stukeley, 17th c.) 91
Fig. 53: Prehistoric boat with sails carved at Pedornes (Galicia, Spain). 97
Fig. 54: Probable painting of a boat in the Dolmen of Antelas (Portugal). 98
Fig. 55: The crow is perched on a tenon, in Stonehenge. 99
Fig. 56: Megalithic temple of Tarxien (Malta). 100
Fig. 57: Jason gives the Golden Fleece to Pelias.(Calyx, fourth c. BC.) 102
Fig. 58: The sky when Orion was rising over the horizon of Avebury. (The poles of both hemispheres are also indicated.) 103
Fig. 59: "Dragon's teeth sown in furrows," or the Alignments of Carnac. 104
Fig. 60: Left, Eridanus in relation to Orion. Right, image by J. Bayer. 105
Fig. 61: World Geography according to Herodotus in the fifth c. BC. 106
Fig. 62: Argonauts' voyage, according to Apollonius of Rhodes. 107
Fig. 63: Carvings at Tanum (Sweden). 108
Fig. 64: Tentative map of the route followed by the princes. 109
Fig. 65: Petroglyphs in the wadis of the Eastern Desert. Below, a large boat being dragged. 110
Fig. 66: Nile River. (The Wadi Hammamata is indicated.) 112
Fig. 67: Tentative route of the prehistoric voyages around the world. 113
Fig. 68: Simultaneous rising of Leo and Orion, as seen from Avebury, at the time of its construction (end of the fourth millennium BC). 118
Fig. 69: Rising time vs. year for the stars Regulus (circles) and Rigel (triangles), from the latitudes of Almendres (dash lines) and Avebury (solid lines). (Arbitrary rising time scale in steps of ca. 30 min.) 119
Fig. 70: Location of Almendres and the royal megalithic monuments. 120
Fig. 71: Almendres faces the far east. 121
Fig. 72: Blueprint of Almendres. 122
Fig. 73: The sky seen over Almendres (projected on it) before midsummer sunrise. Above, rising of Rigel; below, heliacal rising of Sirius, 1h 20 min later. (The area outside the circle remains below the horizon.) 123
Fig. 74: The sky seen over Almendres (projected on it), when the first Spring Moon was rising, and the following sunrise. (The dashed line is the center of the Milky Way, the Galactic Equator.) 125
Fig. 75: Jason retrieving the Golden Fleece from a tree guarded by a dragon lulled by Medea. (Apulian vase, fourth c. BC.) 127
Fig. 76: The Pyrenees and Caucasus Ranges. 128

206 • SAILORS OF STONEHENGE

Fig. 77: The Iberian Zodiac. (The distribution of megalithic constructions on the peninsula is also indicated, after Philine Kalb.) 132
Fig. 78: Solstitial directions from the center of the Iberian Peninsula. (Some important locations and rivers are also indicated.) 134
Fig. 79: "Virgen del Pilar," the Patroness of Spain, in the Basilica of Saragossa, by the Ebro River. 135
Fig. 80: Dolmen in Roknia necropolis (Algeria). 136
Fig. 81: The Zodiac and inner constellations projected over Iberia. (The "royal stars" are indicated.) 137
Fig. 82: Menhir at midsummer sunrise from Almendres (10 ft / 3 m tall). 139
Fig. 83: The Knights of the Round Table. (Modern rendering.) 140
Fig. 84: King Arthur presides over the Round Table. (Medieval codex.) 141
Fig. 85: The Chimera (tail as a dragon). (Kylix, 4th c. BC.) 143
Fig. 86: Zodiacal equivalents to Stonehenge's trilithons. 144
Fig. 87: Section of the Sarsen Circle (also visible in the background), around the larger trilithons erected inside. 145
Fig. 88: Blueprint of Stonehenge indicating the function of each feature (the trilithons are explained in the insert below). 147
Fig. 89: The Heelstone (ca. 16 ft / 4.7 m tall). 148
Fig. 90: Stonehenge, with the Slaughter Stone in the forefront. 149
Fig. 91: The Centaur and the Crux projected on the Canary Islands. 156
Fig. 92: Above, Roque Nublo, a "natural menhir" (ca. 260 ft / 80 m tall) in Gran Canaria. Below, Guanche megalithic sanctuary at Garajonay, La Gomera. (The silhouette of Teide Volcano appears in the background.) 157
Fig. 93: Argo Navis (between Canis Major and the Crux) (J. Hevelius). 159
Fig. 94: Schematic plan of the great celestial mirror. 160
Fig. 95: Left, probable boat painted vertically on an orthostat of the Dolmen of Antelas (north of Portugal). Right, tentative course of the Milky Way throughout the Iberian Peninsula, between the Bays of Biscay and Cadiz. (The river basins crossed are indicated.) 161
Fig. 96: Entrance at Newgrange, with the roof-box above. 162
Fig. 97: Sky visible from the rear chamber of Newgrange in midwinter. (Azimuth vs. altitude. Sirius shone within the frame 1 h 35' after sunset.) 164
Fig. 98: St Michael's Mount, in the Cornish Peninsula (SW of England). 168
Fig. 99: Orion on the celestial mirror. 169
Fig. 100: St Michael and the Devil. (Raphael, 16th c.) 170
Fig. 101: Cairn of Barnenez, in the north of Brittany (France). 171
Fig. 102: The Hydra was aligned with the Celestial Equator (dotted line) around 3000 BC, whereas by 300 BC it already lay clearly off the line. 173
Fig. 103: Axis connecting Avebury and Carnac. Its prolongation crosses Iberia and hits the Strait of Gibraltar. 174
Fig. 104: Cromlech of Msoura (Morocco). 175
Fig. 105: Scorpio, across the Zodiac and the Milky Way. (J. Bayer). 176
Fig. 106: Monoceros or the Unicorn, across the Milky Way (J. Hevelius). 178
Fig. 107: Icon of St George. 180
Fig. 108: Leo reflected on Galicia, with Regulus exactly on A Coruña. 182

LIST OF FIGURES • 207

Fig. 109: Tower of Hercules, in A Coruña (Galicia). 183
Fig. 110: Heracles, dressed in a lion's skin, fighting Geryon, a triple-being giant. (Attic red-figure kylix, sixth c. BC.) 184
Fig. 111: Hercules in the Garden of the Hesperides. (Brass medallion, Italy, second c. AD.) 185
Fig. 112: Fountains of Neptune (Romanization of Poseidon, God of the Oceans), and Cybele (a Goddess of the Earth), the most important and central to Madrid. 190
Fig. 113: Sculpture of Atlas in Santiago de Compostela (Spain). 192
Fig. 114: Santorini Island, in the Aegean Sea. (The missing part is where the Thera Volcano was before exploding.) 194
Fig. 115: Tartessian sculpture of a winged feline. 196

Credits

Note: For the full text for each figure, please see the preceding *List of Figures*. Images from Wikimedia Commons are indicated by WC followed by category and author (within brackets). PD stands for *Public Domain*, and WB for *work based upon*.

Photo p. 9: WC: Milky Way (PD). Fig. 1: WC: Stonehenge (PD). Fig. 2: Adapted WC: Cultura Megalítica de Europa (TharkunColl). Fig. 3: Unidentified original. Fig. 4: WC: Knowth (PD).

Photo p. 21: WC: Carnac (PD). Fig. 5: Unidentified original. Fig. 6: WC: Tumulus du Mont-Saint-Michel du Carnac (Yolan Chériaux). Fig. 7: WC: Carnac Stones (marek69). Fig. 8: WC: Leo (T. Credner). Fig. 9: WB Cartes du Ciel map.

Photo p. 29: William Stukeley: WC: Avebury: PD. Fig. 10: Own picture. Fig. 11: Google Earth. Fig. 12: Own work. Fig. 13: Own work. Fig. 14: WB Cartes du Ciel map. Fig. 16: WC: Uranometria (PD). Fig. 15: WB Cartes du Ciel map. Fig. 17: WB Cartes du Ciel map. Fig. 18: Own work. Fig. 19: Unknown source. Fig. 20 & Fig. 21: Own work.

Photo p. 43: Own work. Fig. 22: Own photo of a panel at Stonehenge. Fig. 23: Unknown source. Fig. 24 & Fig. 25: Own work. Fig. 26 & Fig. 27: WB Cartes du Ciel maps. Fig. 28: WC: Uranographia by J. Hevelius (PD). Fig. 29: Own photo of a panel at Stonehenge. Fig. 30: Photo by Amen-Ra. Fig. 31: Own work. Fig. 32: WB Google Earth map.

Photo p. 61: WC: Ring of Brodgar (PD). Fig. 33: WC: Stennes (Drewcorser), WC: Skara Brae (PD), and WC: Maeshowe (Islandhopper). Fig. 34: WB Google Earth map. Fig. 35: WC: Heródoto (PD). Fig. 36: WC: Helios (Mathiasrex). Fig. 37: Own work. Fig. 38: WC: Aquhorthies (Bill McKelvie), and WC: Callanish (PD). Fig. 39: WB Google Earth map. Fig. 40: Own. Fig. 41: WC: Carnac (Steffen Heilfort).

Photo p. 77: WC: Newgrange (Shira). Fig. 42: Henricus Decimator (PD). Fig. 43: Own works. Fig. 44: WC: Apollo in ancient Greek pottery (PD). Fig. 45:

WC: Rosarium philosophorum (PD). Fig. 46: WB Cartes du Ciel map. Fig. 47: Own work. Fig. 48: WB unidentified map. Fig. 49: WB Google Earth map. Fig. 50: WC: Newgrange (Aligatorek). Fig. 51: WC: Dowth (PD), WC: Knowth (S. Schachner). Fig. 52: WC: Beckhampton (PD).

Picture p. 95: WC: The Argonauts (PD). Fig. 53: Unidentified author. Fig. 54: Elisabeth Shee-Twohig (taken from endnote 4). Fig. 55: Own work. Fig. 56: WC: Tarxien (PD). Fig. 57: WC: Jason (PD). Fig. 58: WB Cartes du Ciel map. Fig. 59: WC: Carnac (Above: Marek; below: Steffen Heilfort). Fig. 60: WC: Johann Bayer: Uranometria (PD). Fig. 61: WC: Herodotus, (Map by F. Putzger, 19th c. PD). Fig. 62: WC: Argonauts (Based on Maris Stella's map). Fig. 64: WC: Europe (Demis Mapserver map). Fig. 63: Unidentified author. Fig. 65: Photo courtesy of Francis Lankester (eastern-desert.com; rock-art drawings by Arthur Weigall). Fig. 66: WB Google Earth map. Fig. 67: WB Google Earth map.

Photo p. 117: Own. Fig. 68: WB Google Earth map. Fig. 69: Own work. Fig. 70: Adapted from WC: Cultura Megalítica de Europa (Tharkun Coll). Fig. 71: Own work. Fig. 72: downloaded from Concelho Évora homepage. Fig. 73 & Fig. 74: WB Cartes du Ciel maps. Fig. 75: Archaeological Museum of Naples. Fig. 76: WC: Pyrenees (PD), and WC: Caucasus Mountains (PD).

Photo p. 131: WC: dolmen de Menga (Grez). Fig. 77 & Fig. 78: WB map of Philine Kalb. Fig. 79: WC: Virgen del Pilar (Ovidiocalvo). Fig. 80: WC: Roknia (Gasmi.M.). Fig. 81: WB map of unknown origin. Fig. 82: Own work. Fig. 83: Unknown source. Fig. 84: WC: Round Table (PD). Fig. 85: WC: Chimere (PD). Fig. 86: Own. Fig. 87: Own work. Fig. 88: WB unidentified original plan. Fig. 89: WC: Heelstone (PD). Fig. 90: WC: Slaughterstone (Old Moonraker). Fig. 91: WB Google Earth map. Fig. 92: WC: Roque Nublo (PD), and WC: Parque Nacional de Garajonay (Cardenasg). Fig. 93: WC: Uranographia by Johannes Hevelius (PD). Fig. 94: WB Google Earth map. Fig. 95: WB map of WC: Spain (Manuel GR), and boat picture taken from endnote number 4. Fig. 96: WC: Newgrange (PD). Fig. 97: WB Cartes du Ciel map.

Photo p. 167: WC: Mont Saint-Michel (PD). Fig. 98: WC: St Michael's Mount (PD). Fig. 99: WB Google Earth map. Fig. 100: WC: Raphael (PD). Fig. 101: WC: Barnenez (NewPapillon). Fig. 102: WB Cartes du Ciel maps. Fig. 103: WB Google Earth map. Fig. 104: Unknown author. Fig. 105: WC: Johann Bayer: Uranometria (PD). Fig. 106: WC: Monoceros (PD). Fig. 107: Unknown author. Fig. 108: WB partial map of unknown origin. Fig. 109: WC: Tower of Hercules (Csörföly D.). Fig. 110: WC: Geryon (PD). Fig. 111: Unknown author.

Picture p. 189: WC: Atlantis (PD). Fig. 112: Own works. Fig. 113: WC: Atlas (Luis M. Bugallo). Fig. 114: WC: Santorini (PD). Fig. 115: WC: Tartessos (Saiko).

INDEX

Note: Page ranges are intentionally not used, so the relevance of each term can be readily noted by the number of times it is indexed.

A

A Coruña, 150, 182, 183, 206, 207
Abaris, 100
Achernar, 105, 114, 115, 201
Acrux, 156, 165, 201
Adam and Eve Stones, 31
Adriatic Sea, 107, 108
Aegean Sea, 107, 108, 109, 111, 113, 207
Africa, 101, 106, 113, 114, 116, 136, 137, 141, 151, 153, 157, 158, 162, 172, 175, 177, 193, 199
Agena, 41, 156, 201
Aietes, 127
Akelarre, 94
Albarracín, 165
Alboran Sea, 137, 151
Alcaraz, 165
Aldebaran, 41, 83, 201, 205
Alentejo, 21, 121, 124, 133, 136, 197, 222
Aleth, 168
Alexandria, 105
Algarve, 97
Algeria, 136, 206
Algiers, 136, 201
Almendres, 117, 118, 121, 122, 124, 126, 129, 130, 133, 139, 141, 156, 172, 205, 206, 222
Alnilam, 167, 179
Alnitak, 167, 179
Alphekka, 47, 48, 51, 54, 58, 203, 204
Alphonse X, 106
Alps, 99, 129
Altair, 41, 130, 201
Altar Stone, 43, 154, 203
America, 7, 23, 92, 114, 115, 198, 200
Andalusia, 200, 201
Andorra, 135, 150
Angkor, 152
Antaeus, 175
Antares, 51, 59, 83, 175, 176, 201, 205
Antelas, 98, 166, 205, 206
Antilles, 115
Apollo, 66, 74, 79, 80, 93, 100, 130, 204, 207
Apollonius of Rhodes, 105, 107, 205
Apulia, 205
Aquarius, 20, 82, 83, 132, 136, 144, 151, 153
Aragon, 144, 150, 151, 187
Aratus, 16
Archangel Michael (see St Michael), 168, 186
archeoastronomy, 12
Arcturus, 34, 51, 54, 59, 130, 138, 140, 201
Ares, 127, 129, 139
Arga, river, 150, 165
Argo Navis, 2, 102, 108, 113, 115, 116, 127, 150, 159, 161, 165, 166, 186, 206
Argonautica, 105
Argonauts, 95, 101, 104, 105, 107, 113, 114, 116, 117, 127, 129,

139, 152, 159, 183, 185, 198, 208
Argus, 150
Ariège, river, 134, 141, 150
Aries, 20, 94, 127, 128, 129, 130, 131, 132, 139, 141, 142, 143, 144, 150, 151, 152, 153, 154, 179, 190, 191, 198, 200
Ark of the Covenant, 152
Artemis, 79, 80, 81, 93, 204
Arthur, King, 59, 140, 187, 206, 208
artificial horizon, 47, 69, 93
Asia, 96, 116
Assyria, 60
asterism (see star), 130, 156
Asturias, 6, 144, 151, 196
Aswan, 201
Athens, 74, 100, 193, 194, 195, 199
Atlantic Ocean, 86, 97, 98, 99, 101, 114, 115, 133, 142, 158, 159, 162, 166, 172, 176, 185, 189, 191, 194, 197, 198
Atlantis, 74, 152, 189, 190, 191, 192, 193, 198, 199, 200, 208, 222
Atlas: Mountains, 158, 175; Son of Poseidon, 190, 191, 207, 208
Aubrey: Holes, 43, 54, 60, 93, 203, 205; John, 41
Aulne, river, 186
Avebury, 1, 12, 27, 29, 30, 33, 34, 35, 36, 38, 39, 41, 44, 45, 46, 48, 51, 55, 56, 57, 61, 63, 67, 71, 72, 73, 77, 81, 82, 83, 84, 85, 86, 88, 89, 90, 91, 92, 98, 103, 105, 109, 111, 114, 117, 118, 120, 121, 122, 124, 126, 130, 146, 149, 152, 156, 163, 171, 172, 174, 178, 179, 180, 181, 188, 197, 203, 204, 205, 206, 207, 222
Axis Mundi, 139, 140, 141, 143, 166, 185, 191

Azores Islands, 101, 159, 161, 166, 191, 201

B

Babylonia, 14, 15, 23
Bacon, Francis, 189
Badbury Rings, 138
Balearic Islands, 150, 151
Balkan Mountains, 28
Baltic Sea, 100, 109, 111
Barcelona, 150, 185
Barclay, Gordon, 13, 14, 19
Barnenez, 172, 201, 206, 208
Basque, 94, 158, 165, 201
Bayer, Johann, 5, 201, 203, 205, 206, 208
Bazalote, river, 166
Beaker People, 33, 41, 187, 188
Beckhampton: Avenue, 31, 38, 40, 90; Long Barrow, 32, 90, 205
Becrux, 156, 165, 201
Bellatrix, 33, 168, 179
Berber, 158
Berkeley, 5, 6, 7
Berkley, Grant, 152
Betelgeuse, 33, 168, 179, 201
Bidasoa, river, 165
Big Bang, 9
Biscay, Gulf or Bay of, 142, 161, 186, 188, 206
Black: Forest, 108, 111; Sea, 107, 108, 111, 116, 127, 128, 129
Blackett, Baram, 152
Bluestone, 51, 203
Boötes, 34, 37, 51, 52, 54, 55, 59, 204
Bordeaux, 142, 150
Boreadae, 72
Boreas, 65, 72
Borna Cove, 97
Bou: Merzoug, 136; Nouara, 136
Bouval, Robert, 152
Boyne, river, 88, 89, 91, 92, 152, 163, 164, 166
brass, 192, 199
Breg, river, 116

Brennan, Martin, 152
Breton, 22, 115
Brigach, river, 116
Bristol-Avon, river, 53, 56, 57
Britain, 11, 14, 19, 22, 27, 29, 43, 59, 60, 61, 63, 65, 66, 67, 70, 73, 79, 92, 96, 100, 108, 111, 112, 118, 119, 120, 129, 130, 131, 138, 142, 152, 155, 167, 169, 177, 182, 184, 187, 191, 203
Brittany, 12, 18, 21, 29, 56, 59, 88, 92, 97, 100, 142, 167, 168, 171, 172, 182, 183, 184, 186, 187, 191, 197, 199, 201, 203, 206, 222
Brodgar: Ness of, 74; Ring of, 61, 67, 207
bronze, 53, 59, 193
Bronze Age, 41, 166, 195
Brophy, Thomas, 152
Brosna, river, 166
Browne, Bishop, 74
Buddhism, 6
bull, 20, 104, 179
Butler, Alan, 199

C

Cadiz, 150, 161, 175, 191, 199, 206
cairn, 61, 115, 163, 172
Calado, Manuel, 18, 20, 197, 200
calendar, 5, 10, 19, 22, 70, 146, 193
Calicut, 26
Callanish Stones, 69, 204, 207
Cambodia, 152
Canada, 6
Canary Islands, 101, 113, 114, 115, 130, 142, 156, 158, 159, 161, 162, 166, 175, 191, 201, 206
Cancer, 20, 27, 34, 37, 58, 77, 78, 79, 101, 142, 143, 144, 146, 151, 153, 154, 156, 171, 172, 178, 181, 190, 195, 204

Canis: Major, 34, 36, 161, 163, 166, 184, 187, 201, 206; Minor, 34, 171, 172, 186, 187, 201
Canopus, 159, 165, 166, 201
Cantabria, 151, 201
Cantabrian: Mountains, 158; Sea, 129, 135, 141, 151
Capella, 41, 130, 201
Capricorn, 20, 144, 151, 153
Carina, 165
Carnac, Alignments of, 12, 14, 21, 23, 26, 27, 29, 56, 61, 63, 72, 73, 75, 86, 88, 91, 99, 104, 105, 118, 140, 142, 152, 154, 171, 172, 174, 181, 184, 187, 188, 197, 203, 204, 205, 206, 207, 208, 222
Cartes du Ciel, 5, 58, 207, 208
Carthaginians, 196, 222
carving (see also petroglyph), 3, 16, 74, 97, 111, 112, 116
Caspian Sea, 129, 153
Castilla y León, 153
Castilla-La Mancha, 153, 201
Catalonia, 150, 151, 187
cathedral, 74
Caucasus Range, 128, 129, 152, 205, 208
celestial: cycle, 14, 45, 71, 104, 126, 130, 181; dragon, 141; drama, 60; god, 71, 79, 166; mirror, 131, 134, 136, 138, 152, 155, 156, 158, 159, 161, 165, 166, 167, 171, 174, 177, 186, 187, 191, 192, 195, 197, 198, 200, 206; orientation, 12; river, 35, 55, 105, 114; route, 48, 126; scene, 35, 39, 46, 48, 57, 58, 73, 83, 103, 118, 129; sphere, 10, 105, 156, 165, 171, 172, 177, 191
Celestial Pole, 20, 48, 59, 63, 74, 165
Celts, 2, 65, 66, 195, 222
Centaur, 121, 156, 158, 162, 206
Centro, 201

Channel Islands, 169
Chimera, 2, 139, 144, 206
China, 96
Christianity, 93, 135, 171, 181
Clito, 190
Colchis, 107, 127, 128
collective unconscious, 4
Collins, Andrew, 152
Columbus, Christopher, 115
Compostela, 151
Copernicus, Nicolaus, 10
copper, 53, 192
Coptos, 111
Cordier, Henri, 96, 115
Cornwall, 60, 167, 168
Corona Borealis, 37, 47, 48, 51, 52, 54, 55, 57, 59, 115, 204
cosmology, 9, 10, 17, 59, 152, 187, 191, 222
cosmos, 177, 191
Cove, The, 30, 31, 37, 78, 83, 203, 204
crab, 20, 204
Crete, island, 107, 113, 188, 195, 222
Critias, 189, 194
cromlech, 2, 117, 121, 122, 124, 126, 129, 130, 175, 176, 201, 206
Cross, 93, 165
crown, 26, 51, 57, 59, 72, 79, 82, 86, 95, 102, 105, 106, 109, 114, 115, 121, 141, 142, 168, 181, 198
Crux, 48, 59, 121, 156, 158, 159, 162, 165, 166, 206
Cuenca, 201
Cursa, 36, 105
Cybele, 207
Cycladic Islands, 107
cycle: of birth and death, 4, 10, 81; of the sky, 9, 18, 25, 26, 63
Cygnus, 48, 129, 152, 186

D

da Silva, C. Marciano, 124, 130
Danube, river, 106, 107, 108, 116
Dardanelles, Strait of, 111
Dark River, 2, 105, 108, 111
de Grazia, Alfred, 199
Decimator, Henricus, 204, 207
Decrux, 156
Delos, 100
demon, 171
Deneb, 48, 59, 130, 201
Deruelle, Jean, 199
Dias, Bartolomeu, 116
Diodorus Siculus, 65, 66, 67, 71, 72, 74, 100, 130, 158
ditch, 29, 32, 36, 41, 43, 46, 48, 178, 203
dolmen, 97, 98, 115, 121, 124, 133, 136, 150, 166, 205, 206, 208
Don, river, 116
Dover, river, 28, 115, 187
Dowth, 88, 205, 208
Draco, 48, 59, 139, 140, 143, 144, 152, 174, 185, 186
dragon, 48, 104, 127, 139, 141, 144, 154, 170, 176, 179, 181, 185, 186, 187, 205, 206
Durrington Walls, 55, 56

E

Earth, 4, 5, 10, 20, 26, 40, 63, 67, 70, 71, 74, 88, 93, 101, 106, 116, 138, 139, 140, 151, 153, 163, 165, 170, 175, 177, 181, 190, 197, 207, 208
East: Kennet Long Barrow, 32; Yorkshire, 96
Easter, 124, 204
Easter Aquhorthies, 204
Eastern Desert, 111, 113, 205
Ebro, river, 116, 134, 135, 151, 152, 161, 165, 206
Echeyde, 158
eclipse, 85
Ecliptic, 10, 20, 25, 48, 59, 74, 82, 134, 136, 137, 140, 141, 165,

175, 182, 192, 193; Pole, 48, 59, 140, 141, 192, 193
Egypt, 16, 23, 60, 108, 109, 111, 112, 116, 131, 152, 155, 188, 193, 195
El Djem, 204
El Hierro, island, 156
El Uted, 175, 176, 186
Elbrus, Mount, 128
Elephantine Island, 114, 158, 201
enclosure, 29, 47, 48, 121, 124
endogamic, 94
England, 7, 58, 75, 88, 167, 171, 187, 201, 206
English Channel, 29, 56, 167, 181, 186, 203
Equator: Celestial, 172, 184, 206; Galactic, 48, 156, 165, 205; Terrestrial, 114
equinox, 10, 20, 27, 28, 57, 59, 83, 86, 124, 126, 142, 186, 205
Eratosthenes, 106
Eridanus, 34, 35, 36, 51, 52, 54, 105, 106, 108, 112, 114, 131, 155, 195, 205
Erlingsson, Ulf, 199
Erytheia, 184, 185
Eurasian Steppes, 187
Europe, 3, 12, 13, 14, 16, 18, 19, 20, 21, 25, 27, 28, 31, 41, 59, 65, 73, 86, 96, 98, 99, 101, 106, 107, 108, 109, 112, 113, 114, 115, 116, 121, 128, 129, 130, 142, 152, 153, 155, 158, 187, 195, 197, 198, 199, 203, 205, 208, 222
Eurytion, 184
Euskera (see Basque), 158

F

Falkner's Circle, 31, 178
Faroe Islands, 130
Fengshui, 170
First Cataract, 101, 109
Fomalhaut, 82, 83, 137, 201, 205

France, 11, 18, 21, 97, 116, 129, 134, 141, 150, 167, 168, 186, 197, 199, 206
Frazer, James, 26, 28
Frozen Sea, 116
Fuerteventura, island, 156, 201

G

Gacrux, 156
Gadeira, 191
Gadeirus, 191
Gadir, 191
Gaia, 93
galaxy, 9, 165
Galicia, 18, 97, 137, 144, 151, 153, 181, 188, 196, 201, 205, 206, 207
Garajonay, Mount, 206, 208
Garonne, river, 134, 141, 142, 150, 167, 168
Gavrinis, island, 199
Gemini, 20, 144, 151, 153, 171
geodesy, 44, 63, 121, 171
Georgia, 128
Germanicus, 106
Germany, 116, 199, 204
Geryon, 184, 207, 208
Gibraltar, Strait of, 16, 97, 98, 109, 113, 116, 174, 191, 206
Giza Pyramids, 152
Glastonbury, 152
goat, 20, 94, 128, 130, 144, 151
Göbekli Tepe, 19
god, 9, 66, 67, 71, 74, 79, 80, 130, 194
God, 21, 74, 80, 115, 127, 190, 207
goddess, 79
Golden: Bough, The, 26, 28; Fleece, 2, 102, 107, 109, 126, 127, 139, 141, 179, 185, 205
Google Earth, 5, 207, 208
Gran Canaria, island, 156, 201, 206
granite, 21
Greece, 7, 14, 16, 18, 20, 59, 65, 74, 78, 79, 95, 96, 100, 101,

105, 106, 107, 108, 109, 129, 151, 152, 183, 188, 191, 195, 198, 207
Greenland, 101
Grooved Ware, 19
Guadalimar, river, 166
Guadalmena, river, 166
Guadalquivir, river, 161, 166
Guadarrama, range and river, 7, 199
Guanche, 2, 156, 157, 158, 206
Guernsey Island, 169
Guerrero Ayuso, Victor, 115
gyre, ocean, 115

H

hallucinogen (entheogenic), 94
Hammamata, wadi, 111, 205
Hancock, Graham, 152
Haqada, 111, 116
Harrison, Hank, 199
Hatysa, 179
Hawkins, Gerald, 11, 19, 85, 94
Heaven, 88, 158, 170, 177, 197
Hecataeus, 65
Heelstone, 43, 58, 83, 148, 149, 203, 206, 208
heliacal rising, 33, 34, 35, 36, 39, 41, 44, 73, 79, 118, 130, 203, 205
Helios, 74, 116, 127, 204, 207
Hell, 88, 91, 151, 158, 172, 177, 179, 187
Henares, river, 6, 134, 151
henge, 29, 30, 31, 36, 37, 39, 40, 41, 48, 54, 55, 58, 61, 75, 77, 83, 84, 90, 103, 172, 178, 179, 180, 181, 203, 204, 205
Hera, 102
Heracles or Hercules, 2, 51, 59, 181, 182, 183, 184, 185, 191, 201, 204, 207
hero, 59
Herodotus, 106, 116, 153, 204, 205, 208
Hesiod, 116

Hesperides, 185, 207
Hevelius, Johannes, 5, 204, 206, 207, 208
hierosgamos, 79, 83, 85, 86, 90, 92, 93, 94, 145, 181
Higinius, 106
Holland, 96
Holyhead Island, 187
Homer, 106, 144
Hoyle, Fred, 23, 85, 94
Humber, river, 96
Hydra, 34, 37, 149, 171, 172, 181, 184, 186, 206
Hyperborea, 1, 65, 66, 70, 73, 114, 204

I

Iberia, 2, 7, 16, 18, 28, 97, 98, 99, 100, 116, 117, 118, 120, 128, 129, 130, 131, 132, 133, 134, 135, 136, 137, 138, 139, 140, 141, 142, 143, 150, 151, 152, 153, 161, 162, 166, 171, 172, 174, 176, 177, 181, 182, 184, 185, 188, 191, 193, 195, 196, 197, 198, 199, 200, 206, 222
Iberians, 2, 153, 195, 222
Ice Age, 150, 222
Iceland, 101
Icon, 206
Ideler, Christian L., 177
Ierne, 116
India, 6, 26
Indian Ocean, 96
Iolcos, 101
Ireland, 18, 77, 88, 92, 116, 152, 161, 163, 166, 184, 187, 199, 200, 203, 205
Irish Sea, 166
Israel, 96
Istanbul, 111
Ister, river, 106
Italy, 193, 207

J

Jaén, 201

Jalón, river, 134, 151, 165
Japan, 6, 7
Jarama, river, 134, 151
Jarlshof, 70
Jason, 95, 101, 102, 103, 104, 105, 107, 114, 115, 117, 126, 127, 129, 139, 152, 159, 183, 185, 198, 205, 208
Jersey Island, 169
Jiloca, river, 165
Júcar, river, 161, 166
Julian date, 5
Jupiter, 10, 25, 26, 58, 71, 73, 76, 144, 153, 203
Juxta Crucem, 156

K

Kalb, Philine, 206, 208
Kaulins, Andis, 152
Keiller, Alexander, 37, 41
Kennet, river, 31, 32, 33, 35, 36, 38, 39, 40, 52, 56, 57, 111, 114, 178, 180, 204
kerbstone, 203
Kerlescan, 21, 24, 75, 142, 154
Kermario, 21, 22, 24, 75, 142, 143, 203
Khem, 108
Knowth, 88, 203, 205, 207, 208
Kura, river, 153

L

La Gomera, island, 156, 206
La Palma, island, 156
La Rochelle, 168
Laja Alta, 98
Languedoc, 150
Lanzarote, island, 156, 201
latitude, 15, 20, 44, 51, 63, 75, 101, 106, 118, 119, 120, 121, 129, 130, 158, 175, 204, 205
Le Ménec, 21, 24, 75, 142, 154
Leo, 20, 25, 27, 28, 33, 34, 35, 36, 37, 39, 40, 45, 48, 51, 57, 58, 73, 77, 78, 79, 82, 83, 103, 118, 124, 129, 143, 144, 146, 149, 151, 152, 153, 154, 171, 172, 178, 179, 181, 186, 190, 195, 203, 204, 205, 206, 207
León, 6, 153
Lernaean Hydra, 184
Leto, 66, 74
Levant, 133, 187
Lewis, Isle, 69, 204
Ley line, 169, 170
Libya, 107, 113, 193
lighthouse, 182, 188
lintel, 43, 58, 99, 144, 145, 146, 148, 154
lion, 20, 28, 51, 55, 59, 144, 149, 151, 153, 178, 179, 203, 204
Lisbon, 121, 150
Llobregat, river, 134, 141, 185
Lockyer, Norman, 23
longitude, 44, 74, 152
Longstones, The, 32, 38, 40, 90
luminary, 10, 25, 73, 74, 79, 126, 134, 141, 143, 146, 148, 153, 164, 165, 191, 199
lunar: abode, 82, 137; observatory, 69; principle, 81, 90; rite, 126; sign, 77; standstill, 68, 74
lunastice, 68, 69, 73, 74, 85, 92, 109, 146, 149
lunation, 75, 145, 193
Lundy, Isle, 187

M

MacKie, Euan, 19, 63
Madeira, 159, 191
Madrid, 5, 6, 7, 133, 150, 152, 153, 207
Maeshowe, 12, 19, 61, 138, 204, 207
Mainland Island, 61, 70
Málaga, 150
Malta, 205
Maltwood, Katherine, 152
Man, Isle, 60, 130
Marmara Sea, 111
Mars, 10, 144, 153, 191, 199, 200

mausoleum, 24, 63, 72, 86, 88, 91, 104, 105, 142, 172
Meath, County, 201
Medea, 127, 205
Mediterranean Sea, 12, 19, 97, 100, 101, 107, 109, 113, 114, 129, 133, 135, 136, 141, 153, 166, 188, 191, 193, 194, 196
megalithic: art, 16, 17, 18, 20, 74, 152, 203; culture, 65, 114, 199; epoch, 25, 48, 58, 66, 69, 74, 75, 83, 115, 120, 129, 151, 172, 186, 203, 205; monument, 7, 11, 12, 14, 19, 21, 22, 27, 29, 30, 33, 40, 43, 47, 60, 61, 70, 75, 77, 88, 92, 99, 100, 109, 111, 115, 118, 121, 126, 130, 132, 133, 136, 138, 150, 152, 163, 167, 169, 171, 186, 197, 200, 203, 205, 206, 222; phenomenon, 12, 13, 18, 21, 25, 27, 109, 111, 117, 193, 197, 198, 203
Megalithic Yard, 11, 19
Melas, 108
Menga, dolmen, 150, 208
menhir, 21, 24, 121, 175, 181, 187, 206
menstruation, 85, 86
Mercury, 10, 144, 153
Meseta, 140, 153
Mesolithic, 18, 19, 197, 222
Mesopotamia, 14, 16, 59, 112, 188
Meton of Athens, 67, 74, 154
Metonic Cycle, 68, 71, 72, 73, 75, 154, 193, 197, 204
Michell, John, 74, 138, 152
Middle Age, 187, 189, 196
Midi-Pyrénées, 201
midsummer or summer solstice, 10, 25, 27, 28, 33, 35, 39, 44, 58, 65, 68, 69, 74, 77, 86, 88, 90, 101, 109, 122, 133, 135, 141, 148, 151, 180, 181, 183, 188, 203, 205, 206
midwinter or winter solstice, 10, 44, 47, 58, 68, 70, 74, 83, 86, 90, 91, 109, 124, 133, 136, 137, 148, 163, 166, 181, 188, 203, 204, 206
Milesians, 200
Milky Way, 2, 34, 35, 36, 41, 48, 51, 103, 126, 130, 149, 154, 156, 158, 159, 161, 162, 163, 165, 166, 171, 175, 177, 178, 179, 184, 186, 191, 192, 193, 204, 205, 206, 207
Minoan, 2, 195, 200, 222
Mintaka, 167, 179
monarchical renewal, 25, 44, 55, 56, 58, 63, 71, 77, 88, 91, 121, 171, 172, 176, 178, 179, 186, 203
monarchy, 19, 27, 35, 39, 51, 56, 57, 71, 78, 86, 88, 92, 94, 101, 103, 120, 148, 181, 193, 204
Mondego, river, 98
Monoceros, 34, 36, 149, 177, 178, 179, 206, 208
Montacute, 138
Moon, 10, 67, 68, 69, 70, 71, 73, 74, 75, 78, 79, 82, 83, 85, 92, 93, 124, 126, 129, 130, 138, 143, 145, 146, 149, 151, 154, 195, 204, 205, 222
Moore, Richard, 152, 166
Morbihan, 199
Morocco, 162, 175, 206
mortise and tenon, 99, 154
Msoura Cromlech, 175, 176, 201, 206
mummy, 90, 91, 92, 157
Murphy, Anthony, 152, 164, 166
Mycenaean, 195, 198
myth, 4, 9, 65, 70, 71, 72, 73, 81, 95, 101, 102, 103, 104, 105, 107, 108, 109, 112, 113, 114, 116, 117, 126, 128, 129, 139, 151, 152, 183, 185, 190, 195, 198
mythology, 18, 74, 79, 80, 129, 144, 151, 176, 190, 191, 195, 198, 199

N

Nabta Playa, 152
Nazaré, 201
Nazca, Lines of, 152
Necao, Pharaoh, 116
necropolis, 22, 23, 88, 92, 105, 163, 206
Neolithic, 3, 11, 13, 14, 18, 19, 25, 61, 63, 70, 76, 79, 85, 94, 97, 98, 111, 130, 136, 150, 175, 197, 222
Nepal, 6
Neptune, 176, 207
Newgrange, 12, 61, 77, 88, 89, 90, 91, 92, 99, 105, 118, 163, 164, 166, 197, 201, 205, 206, 207, 208, 222
Nile, river, 101, 106, 108, 109, 111, 113, 114, 158, 205
Nordic, 96, 108
Normandy, 168, 186
North: Ferriby, 96; John, 60; Pole, 20, 192; Sea, 99, 108, 111, 116; Yorkshire, 75

O

Obelisk, The, 30, 83, 204
Ocean River, 106, 185
Olbers, Heinrich W. H., 177
Oléron Isle, 201
orichalcum, 192
Orion, 33, 34, 35, 36, 37, 38, 39, 48, 51, 54, 55, 57, 59, 71, 73, 79, 80, 81, 93, 95, 103, 105, 114, 118, 124, 129, 138, 149, 152, 165, 167, 168, 169, 171, 172, 174, 176, 177, 178, 179, 181, 184, 186, 203, 205, 206
Orkney Islands, 19, 61, 63, 67, 73, 75, 86, 88, 97, 99, 105, 118, 152, 204, 222
Orthus, 184
Oulst, river, 186
Overton Hill, 31

P

Paleolithic, 19, 96, 222
Palisaded Enclosures, 33, 39
Palma de Mallorca, 150
Parker Pearson, Mike, 56, 60
passage mound, 22, 32, 88, 169, 172
Pedornes, 97, 98, 205
Pelias, 101, 102, 127, 205
Persian Gulf, 96
Peru, 152
Petit-Ménec, 21, 24
petroglyph, 97, 98, 109, 111, 115
Phaeton, 114, 116
Phoenician, 97, 116, 153, 188, 191, 196, 222
Phrixus, 127
Pico, volcano, 159, 201
Pillars of Hercules, 116, 191
Pisces, 20, 132, 144, 151, 153
Piscis Austrinus, 82, 201
planet, 10, 25, 26, 143, 144, 145, 146, 153, 190
Plato, 190, 198
Pleiades, 130
Po, river, 107, 116
Pollux, 201
Pontevedra, 97
Portugal, 7, 18, 21, 98, 99, 116, 117, 121, 133, 138, 187, 197, 205, 206
Poseidon, 80, 127, 190, 207
precession of the equinoxes, 20, 27, 28, 57, 59, 186
Preseli Hills, 52, 204
priest, 18, 23, 38, 55, 63, 66, 67, 70, 73, 94, 101, 142, 197, 200
Procyon, 36, 37, 41, 149, 154, 172, 201
Puppis, 165
Putzger, Friedrich, 208
pyramid, 152, 204
Pyrenees Mountains, 2, 126, 129, 131, 132, 133, 134, 139, 141, 151, 152, 158, 185, 191, 198, 205, 208

Pytheas, 65
Pyxis, 165

Q

qi, 170
quartz, 163
Quiberon Bay, 203
Qusays, 111

R

Ra expedition, 207
radiocarbon, 12, 97, 98
Raphael, 206, 208
Ray, Tom, 166
recumbent stone, 69, 204
Red Sea, 111, 113
Regulus, 25, 27, 33, 34, 41, 44, 45, 47, 48, 54, 55, 58, 59, 71, 79, 82, 83, 118, 119, 122, 137, 148, 181, 183, 188, 201, 203, 204, 205, 206
Reiche, Maria, 152
Renfrew, Colin, 12, 19
Rex Nemorensis, 37
Rhine, river, 99, 107, 108, 111, 116
Rhone, river, 107, 116
Rif Mountains, 158
Rift, the Great, 177
Rigel, 34, 36, 38, 39, 41, 44, 59, 73, 79, 103, 105, 118, 119, 122, 131, 167, 179, 186, 201, 203, 205
Rigil Kent, 41, 156, 201
Ringstone, 37, 172, 179, 181, 203
rite of passage, 112, 114, 129, 142, 198
Roknia, 136, 206, 208
Roman, 21, 28, 59, 65, 74, 96, 135, 182, 188, 196, 200, 204, 222
roof-box, 163, 206
Roque Nublo, 206, 208
Rosarium philosophorum, 93, 204, 208
Round Table, 2, 139, 140, 153, 206, 208
Roussillon, 150
Ruggles, Clive, 13, 14, 19
Russia, 128

S

Sabbat, 94
Sado, river, 18
Sagittarius, 20, 144, 151, 153, 165
Saint-Malo, 168
Saint-Michel: Ilot, 168; Mont, 22, 168, 186, 203, 207, 208; tumulus, 22, 203
Saiph, 103, 167, 168, 179, 186
Salisbury-Avon, river, 53, 55, 56, 181
Sanches, Maria de Jesus, 166
Sanctuary, The, 31, 33, 36, 38, 39, 40, 103, 178
Santa Cruz de Tenerife, 165
Santander, 201
Santiago de Compostela, 151, 207
Santorini, island, 195, 207, 208
Saragossa, 135, 151, 166, 206
Sarsen Circle, 43, 48, 51, 52, 57, 85, 145, 146, 203, 206
Saturn, 10, 144, 153
Scaliger, Joseph J., 177
Schilling, Walter, 199
Scorpio (or Scorpius), 20, 51, 80, 83, 86, 138, 144, 151, 153, 162, 165, 175, 176, 177, 191, 206
scorpion, 20, 80, 93, 176, 179, 186, 191
Scotland, 61, 69, 70, 74, 138, 203, 204
seafaring, 97, 98, 134
Segre, river, 134, 151
Serpens Caput, 51, 204
Serra da Estrela, 138
Shannon, river, 166
Shee-Twohig, Elisabeth, 17, 20, 208
Shetland Islands, 70
Sicily, island, 65, 66

INDEX • 219

Silbury Hill, 31, 32, 36, 38, 39, 71, 111, 131, 142, 167, 186, 201, 203, 204
Sirius, 2, 36, 37, 41, 91, 122, 130, 149, 163, 166, 201, 205, 206
Sistema Central, 129
Skara Brae, 61, 67, 70, 204, 207
Slaughter Stone, 149, 154, 203, 206
snake, 21, 172
solar: abode, 82; carriage, 114, 116; culture, 14, 25, 26, 35, 88, 101, 151; pillar, 139, 185; principle, 81, 83, 90, 92, 137
Solon, 193
solstice, 10, 19, 28, 57, 58, 73, 91, 92, 109, 129, 133, 146, 166
soul, 90, 91, 92, 126, 146, 151, 165, 166, 177, 179, 191
South: America, 23, 114, 152; Pole, 115; Street Long Barrow, 32, 90
Spain, 6, 7, 18, 19, 116, 129, 134, 135, 150, 151, 153, 157, 187, 205, 206, 207, 208
sphere, 10, 105, 156, 171, 172, 177, 191
Spica, 201
spiral, 17, 165
spirit, 81, 83, 84, 86, 89, 90, 92, 126, 145, 146
spiritual technology, 83, 84
St Cornelius, 21
St George, 93, 181, 187, 206
St James, 187, 196
St Michael, 138, 168, 170, 181, 187, 206, 208; Hill, 138; Mount, 168, 171, 206, 208
standing stone (see menhir), 21, 31, 43, 58, 69, 99, 144, 145, 146, 148, 154, 204
star: brightness, 41, 59, 82, 179; circumpolar, 34, 37, 51, 55, 59, 69, 133, 140; culmination, 46, 48, 51, 58, 59, 203; -light extinction, 58; visual magnitude, 41

Stationed Stones, 43, 54, 60, 203
Stenness, Standing Stones of, 61, 74
Stone Age, 19
stone circle or ring, 29, 30, 31, 36, 37, 60, 67, 69, 74, 117, 121, 130, 146, 152, 176, 178
Stonehenge, 2, 5, 11, 12, 19, 27, 29, 44, 46, 47, 48, 51, 52, 53, 54, 55, 56, 57, 60, 61, 63, 67, 71, 72, 73, 75, 81, 83, 85, 86, 87, 88, 89, 91, 92, 94, 99, 105, 109, 114, 115, 120, 130, 144, 146, 154, 156, 178, 180, 181, 188, 197, 199, 203, 204, 205, 206, 207, 222
Stour, river, 115
Stukeley, William, 41, 205, 207
Styx River, 151
Sumer, 112
Summer Triangle, 130
Sun, 2, 10, 20, 25, 27, 28, 33, 35, 41, 44, 45, 48, 58, 59, 70, 71, 73, 74, 77, 78, 79, 83, 86, 90, 93, 101, 114, 115, 124, 126, 129, 130, 136, 138, 143, 145, 146, 151, 152, 153, 154, 163, 165, 166, 181, 182, 183, 193, 195, 199, 203, 204, 222
sunrise, 34, 41, 45, 48, 51, 57, 58, 90, 122, 124, 130, 133, 135, 136, 137, 141, 151, 163, 166, 183, 205, 206
sunset, 45, 54, 89, 133, 136, 151, 180, 204, 206
Swallowhead Spring, 32, 36
Sweden, 205
Swindon Stone, 41

T

Tagus, river, 18, 99, 118, 134, 151
Tanger-Tétouan, 201
Tanum, 205
Tartessos, 2, 195, 200, 207, 208
Tarxien, 205, 208

Taurus, 20, 83, 86, 130, 142, 144, 153, 167, 179, 198, 200
Teide, volcano, 158, 206
Temple, Robert, 199
Tenerife, island, 156, 157, 158, 165, 201
Thames, river, 52, 56, 57, 74, 108, 111, 204
Thera, volcano, 195, 207, 222
Thessaly, 101, 107, 109, 117
Thom, Alexander, 11, 14, 19, 21, 23, 152
Thornborough Henges, 75
Thuban, 48, 63, 74, 114, 174
Thule, 65
Thurston, Hugh, 15, 20
Timaeus, 189, 194
tin, 59, 192, 199
titan, 74, 191
Toubkal, Mount, 175
Toulouse, 142, 150, 153, 201
Tours, 168
Tower of Hercules, 2, 181, 182, 183, 188, 201, 207, 208
Tributsch, Helmut, 199
trilithon, 43, 51, 144, 145, 148, 154, 199, 203, 206
Tristan, Sylvain, 199
Tropic of Cancer, 101, 142, 156
tumulus (see passage mound), 22, 36, 175, 188, 203
Tunis, 136
Tunisia, 204
Turkey, 19
Twelve Labors of Hercules, 183
Tyrrhenian Sea, 107, 193

U

unicorn, 2, 149, 177, 178, 181, 187, 206
Universal Time, 58
Universe, 152
Uranometria, 5, 207, 208
Ursa Major, 48, 186

V

Valencia, 136
Valira, river, 134, 151
Vega, 41, 130, 201
Vela, 165
Venus, 10, 144, 153
vernal equinox, 86, 124, 130, 142, 153
Vilaine, river, 186
Virgen del Pilar, 135, 151, 166, 206, 208
Virgin, 135, 166
Virgo, 20, 27, 58, 144, 153
volcano, 158, 195, 200
Voyage Zero, 198

W

wadi, 111, 205
Wales, 52, 152, 187, 204
Watkins, Alfred, 169, 170
Way of St James, The, 196
West Kennet: Avenue, 31, 36, 38, 40, 178, 180; Long Barrow, 32, 33
Wilson, Alan, 152
Windmill Hill, 32, 39
Woodhenge, 55, 56

Y

Y & Z Holes, 43, 85, 86, 92, 93, 203, 205

Z

zenith, 47, 48, 51, 57, 59, 101, 115, 126, 130
Zeus, 79, 194
Zodiac, 10, 14, 20, 25, 82, 128, 131, 132, 133, 134, 136, 137, 140, 141, 142, 146, 151, 152, 153, 154, 155, 156, 161, 162, 165, 171, 177, 184, 191, 192, 203, 205, 206

TIMELINE

Age	Year (BC)	Main Events in Western Europe
Paleolithic	40000	Cave painting (cosmology development)
Mesolithic	8000	End of the Ice Age
	7000	Explorations
	6000	Iberian Confederation of ten kingdoms: Atlantis
		Long-distance navigation
Neolithic	5000	First megalithic monuments, in Brittany & Alentejo
		Almendres: The Sun defeats the Moon
	4000	Unified solar religion centered in Iberia
		Priests-Astronomers Headquarters in Orkney Isles
	3000	Royal Monuments: Carnac, Newgrange & Avebury
Copper	2300	Stonehenge substituted for Avebury
Bronze	2000	The capital is moved to Crete (Minoans)
	1630	Thera Volcano explodes (decline of Confederation)
Iron	1000	End of Megalithism
Classical		Celts, Iberians, Phoenicians, Carthaginians, Greeks
(AD)	0	Roman Empire & Christianity
Middle	1000	
Discovery	1492	Age of partial "Rediscovery"
Technology	2000	Reglobalization

222

Printed in Great Britain
by Amazon.co.uk, Ltd.,
Marston Gate.